Studies on
MYTHOLOGY

*THE DORSEY SERIES IN ANTHROPOLOGY
AND SOCIOLOGY*

Editor
ROBIN M. WILLIAMS, JR.
Cornell University

Hsu (ed.)   *Psychological Anthropology: Approaches to Culture and Personality*

Hagen   *On the Theory of Social Change: How Economic Growth Begins*

Bell   *Marriage and Family Interaction*   rev. ed.

Barnouw   *Culture and Personality*

Gottlieb & Ramsey   *The American Adolescent*

Jacobs   *Pattern in Cultural Anthropology*

Johnson   *Crime, Correction, and Society*   rev. ed.

Salisbury   *Religion in American Culture: A Sociological Interpretation*

Breer & Locke   *Task Experience as a Source of Attitudes*

Wilson   *Sociology: Rules, Roles, and Relationships*

Shostak   *Sociology in Action: Case Studies in Social Problems and Directed Social Change*

Goodman   *The Individual and Culture*

Gamson   *Power and Discontent*

Bell & Stub (eds.)   *The Sociology of Education: A Sourcebook*   rev. ed.

Georges (ed.)   *Studies on Mythology*

STUDIES ON

MYTHOLOGY

EDITED BY

ROBERT A. GEORGES

Assistant Professor of English and Folklore
University of California, Los Angeles

1968

THE DORSEY PRESS, Homewood, Illinois

IRWIN-DORSEY LIMITED, Nobleton, Ontario

First Printing, July, 1968

Library of Congress Catalog Card No. 68–30856

Printed in the United States of America

"For the mind, only that can be visible which has some definite form; but every form of existence has its source in some peculiar way of seeing, some intellectual formulation and intuition of meaning."
—*Ernst Cassirer,* Language and Myth

Acknowledgments

THE editor wishes to acknowledge the valuable assistance of Miss Alice Singer and Mr. Ralph Schuder, who served as research assistants for this project during 1966-67 and 1967-68 respectively. Frequent discussions and exchanges of views among Miss Singer, Mr. Schuder, and the editor contributed significantly to the establishment of criteria for selecting the essays and excerpts which are reprinted in this volume, and also resulted in the formulation and clarification of many of the concepts which are contained in the Prologue and Epilogue. The editor would also like to express his appreciation to Professor Wayland D. Hand, Director of the Center for the Study of Comparative Folklore and Mythology at UCLA, for having made research assistants available to work on the project; to Professors Hand and D. K. Wilgus, Chairman of the Folklore and Mythology Group at UCLA, for their support and encouragement; to the Academic Senate of the University of California, Los Angeles Division, for having made available to the editor a research grant during 1966-67 to help defray the cost of duplicating and preparing materials necessary for the project; and to those authors, editors, and publishing firms that granted the editor their kind permission to reprint the selections which appear in this volume. Finally, the editor wishes to acknowledge his great debt to his wife, Mary, whose patience, devotion, and understanding enabled him to bring the project to fruition.

June, 1968   Robert A. Georges

Table of Contents

Prologue

HISTORICALLY, the study of mythology has been a continuous search for and inquiry into the nature of an entity, on the one hand, and an attempt to formulate and communicate a concept, on the other. Anthropologists, folklorists, and linguists have recorded myth texts from peoples of diverse cultures and have scrutinized these texts in order to discern their intrinsic characteristics and social significance; and philosophers, theologians, and psychologists have examined mythological concepts for clues to the human values and universal truths presumed to be inherent in them. The study of mythology has thus been a quest for not one, but many different things at different times; and the concept of myth at any given point in time is shaped by the prevailing theories, objectives, and methods of the disciplines to which individual investigators who study mythology are committed. To study myth scholarship, then, necessitates studying the history of ideas of particular periods and specific disciplines.

The readings in this book exemplify this point with respect to anthropology, the study of man in society. The selections, written by nine distinguished anthropologists over a sixty-eight-year period, are examinations of the myths of preliterate peoples with whom the investigators have had firsthand contact through fieldwork. Each writer is concerned, on one level, with specific problems relating to the content and social functions of myths, and each discusses these problems within the context of the culture under consideration. Yet implicit in each discussion are certain theoretical assumptions which serve as the foundations for analysis. In his essay on "The Growth of Indian Mythologies" (pp. 15-26), for example, Franz Boas focuses on content similarities in the mythologies of several culturally contiguous North American Indian tribes; but underlying Boas' comments is a predilection for a cultural-historical approach to the study of man. In his selection on "The Mythology of the Kula" (pp. 72-

1

101), on the other hand, Bronislaw Malinowski eschews historical explanations and concentrates instead on the relationships between myths and other aspects of Trobriand social life, an approach which clearly indicates Malinowski's functionalist orientation and his preference for synchronic rather than diachronic studies of culture. Thus, what might appear in these selections to be mere differences in emphasis or disparate interpretations of mythology are actually exemplifications of major theoretical positions to which these nine writers have adhered, not merely in their studies of mythology, but in their analyses of cultural data in general. Their individual pronouncements on myth become most meaningful, therefore, when they are considered from an historical and disciplinary perspective.

Man's curiosity about stories concerning his existence arose early in the history of Western civilization. The ancient Greeks were apparently the first people to isolate and study a body of oral narratives, extant in their society, which explained the origins of natural and social phenomena and the interrelationships among man, his deities, and his universe. The veracity of these myths, as they were called, was the subject of vigorous debate among early Greek philosophers,[1] whose writings became well known to European scholars during the Renaissance. Subsequent translations of Greek and Roman literature added substantially to the available information on classical mythology and resulted in the intensification and diversification of scholarly inquiry into the nature and meaning of myth. The discovery during the eighteenth and nineteenth centuries of narratives with similar content among non-Western and preliterate peoples, however, further complicated the issues and raised additional questions for investigation.

To many early anthropologists, such similarities could be accounted for in terms of a theory of cultural evolution. These narratives had arisen, they argued, during an early stage of cultural development through which all societies had evolved. Primitive man, it was contended, had felt the need to draw analogies between natural forces and human behavior and had attributed personal actions to the inanimate objects around him. Yet the humanlike activities of

---

[1] Three brief surveys of myth scholarship which include considerable information about studies conducted by those other than anthropologists are the following: David Bidney, "The Concept of Myth and the Problem of Psychocultural Evolution," *American Anthropologist*, Vol. 52 (1950), 16-26; David Bidney, "Myth, Symbolism, and Truth," in *Myth: A Symposium*, ed. Thomas A. Sebeok (Bloomington, Ind., 1958), pp. 1-14; and Richard Chase, *Quest for Myth* (Baton Rouge, La., 1949).

sun, moon, stars, etc., were not considered to be metaphorical images of the type found in the written literatures of Western civilizations, as some philologists and literary scholars had indicated. Instead, they were regarded as realities which existed in the mythopoeic mind as a result of primitive man's widespread belief in animism.[2] Thus, Edward B. Tylor, an early proponent of cultural evolutionism, was able to write in his book *Primitive Culture* in 1871:

The general thesis maintained is that Myth arose in the savage condition prevalent in remote ages among the whole human race, that it remains comparatively unchanged among the modern rude tribes who have departed least from these primitive conditions, while higher and later grades of civilization, partly by retaining its actual principles, and partly by carrying on its inherited results in the form of ancestral traditions, continued it not merely in toleration but in honour (Tylor, 1871:I, 257).

This point of view, adopted widely by late nineteenth-century philologists, classicists, and folklorists as well as by anthropologists, provided satisfying answers to innumerable questions. It suggested that myth was a universal category, an entity common to all humanity, which had as its purpose to explain in fanciful and prescientific terms the origins of natural and social phenomena and the interrelationships among man, his gods, and his world. Furthermore, it accounted for recurrent narrative motifs and themes across cultures and justified the existence of so-called "savage" beliefs and practices among "civilized" peoples by designating them as survivals from a mythopoeic age.

By the turn of the century, however, as more ethnographic data were being gathered from remote parts of the world, monistic theories advanced by early students of man became increasingly untenable. Cultural evolution and alternative theories, which accounted for parallel culture traits exclusively on the basis of diffusion or in terms of the collective unconscious, provided convincing explanations for similarities in social phenomena; but they could not explain the significant differences which scientific field reports were bringing to light. Moreover, there was a growing uneasiness among anthropologists concerning the validity of generalizations drawn from cross-cultural studies of isolated social phenomena, a procedure commonly

---

[2] For an extensive early discussion of the concept of animism, see Edward B. Tylor, *Primitive Culture* (London, 1871), Vol. I, 377-453; Vol. II, 1-361. Most discussions of the subject consist of elaborations, modifications, or attempted clarifications of Tylor's early consideration of the concept.

employed by nineteenth-century scholars. Consequently, assumptions about culture which had been accepted a priori by pioneering generations of anthropologists were carefully examined and critically evaluated by their successors; and hypotheses about social processes which had been advanced on the basis of limited and often unreliable data were rigorously tested and significantly modified by experienced fieldworkers.

Among those who played a substantial role in evaluating the work of their predecessors and in raising new issues to be dealt with by subsequent generations of students of man were Franz Boas and W. H. R. Rivers. Born within six years of each other (Boas in 1858 and Rivers in 1864), Boas and Rivers became involved in anthropology more by accident than by design. Boas had been trained in physics and geography in Germany, and Rivers in experimental psychology in England. Early in their careers, however, both participated in field expeditions to alien cultures: Boas to East Greenland in 1883-84 for the purposes of mapping that region (Herskovits, 1953:10), and Rivers to the Torres Straits area of Australia and New Zealand in 1898-99 to conduct fieldwork in experimental psychology among the aborigines there (Smith, 1926: ix-xi). This initial confrontation with preliterate peoples was apparently sufficient to motivate both men to devote themselves to anthropological research, for each spent the remainder of his life gathering and interpreting data on cultural phenomena and social processes.

Considering the infrequency with which each man cites the writings of the other in his own publications, one can assume that Boas and Rivers had little direct influence on each other. But their pronouncements on many issues were remarkably similar. Both men recognized the importance of recording ethnographic data firsthand in the field; and, as a result of their own field expeditions (in North America for Boas and in Oceania and Asia for Rivers), both came to reject, early in their careers, the monistic theories proposed by their predecessors. For Boas, each culture had "its own unique history, dependent partly upon the peculiar inner development of the social group, and partly upon the foreign influences to which it was subjected," thus making it "quite impossible to understand, on the basis of a single evolutionary scheme, what happened to any particular people" (Boas, 1940: 286). To Rivers, it was apparent that "evolutionary speculations can have no firm basis unless there has been a preceding analysis of the cultures and civilizations now spread over the earth's surface" (Rivers, 1926:131-32). Both men also recognized the importance of the immediate and long-range effects of cultural contact; and both felt that psychology—in the sense of conscious and unconscious mental phenomena (a vague but typical concept of psychology at the turn of the century)—could provide important clues to understanding social processes. In general, then, both men espoused the doctrine of cultural relativism, insisting that the formulation of general laws of culture had to follow the intensive study of individual societies.

It was in their approach to the study of individual societies, however, that Boas and Rivers parted company. Boas regarded culture as an entity *sui generis,* and to him an understanding of a whole culture was dependent upon an understanding of its parts. He saw as the objectives of anthropology "to find the *processes* by which certain stages of culture had developed" and "to discover the history of their development" (Boas, 1940: 276; his italics). The method which he felt was best suited to this task was a "detailed study of customs in their relation to the total culture of the tribe practicing them, in connection with an investigation of their geographical distribution among neighboring tribes." This method, Boas insisted, "affords us almost always a means of determining with considerable accuracy the historical causes that led to the formation of the customs in question and to the psychological processes that were at work in their development" (Boas, 1940: 276). The effects of this cultural-historical bias on Boas' approach to the study of man in society have been effectively described by Margaret Mead, a student of Boas' at Columbia University from 1922 through 1929:

He saw the whole of the study of man . . . spread out in a great panorama, stretching back to the infrahuman world and forward as man gained greater control over those aspects of culture which he saw as cumulative—technological and scientific development. . . . Within this great panorama Boas saw the scientific task as one of progressive probing into a problem now of language, now of physical type, now of art style—each a deep, sudden, intensive stab at some strategic point into an enormous untapped and unknown mass of information which we would some day master. No probe must go too far lest it lead to premature generalization—a development which he feared like the plague and against which he continually warned us (Mead, 1959: 29).

Boas' theoretical position and his methodological approach are exemplified in his essay on "The Growth of Indian Mythologies," reprinted in this volume (pp. 15-26).

While Rivers was in essential agreement with Boas regarding the dangers of formulating general laws of culture prematurely, he did not regard working hypotheses as anathema. Quite the contrary, in fact, was true. In an address delivered to the Anthropological Section of the British Association for the Advancement of Science in 1911, Rivers asserted that "the only logical process which will in general be found possible [to analyze individual cultures] will be the formulation of hypothetical working schemes into which the facts can be fitted, and that the test of such schemes will be their capacity to fit in with themselves, or, as we generally express it, 'explain' new facts as they come to our knowledge" (Rivers, 1926:138). Furthermore, to Rivers, the social structure was "by far the firmest foundation on which to base the process of analysis of culture," for he had come to the conclusion, based on his studies of kinship among the Melanesians and the Todas of India, that "the social structure, the framework of society, is still more fundamentally important and still less easily changed except as the result of the intimate blending of peoples" (Rivers, 1926:134).

Rivers developed this thesis more fully in a series of essays delivered at Cambridge in 1921 and 1922 and published posthumously in book form in 1924 under the title *Social Organization.* In the opening essay of that volume, Rivers asserted that "the ultimate aim of all studies of mankind, whether historical or scientific, is to reach explanation in terms of psychology, in terms of the ideas, beliefs, sentiments, and instinctive tendencies by which the conduct of man, both individual and collective, is determined." "This conduct," Rivers continued, "whether individual or collective, but particularly the collective, is also determined by the social structure of which every person who comes into the world finds himself a member" (Rivers, 1924:3).

What Rivers was attempting to formulate, as his essay on "The Sociological Significance of Myth" reprinted in this volume (pp. 27-45) suggests, was a working hypothesis for the analysis of individual cultures based upon a sociological theory of kinship. But although he had been a pioneer in the study of primitive kinship systems, having earned his greatest acclaim (and his most severe criticisms) for his work on the subject, Rivers was unable to devise a dynamic model devoid of certain survivalist notions which had come to characterize much of his work. He had, however, in contrast to Boas, emphasized the need for, rather than the dangers of, a working hypothesis for the study of individual cultures; and while Boas felt that no single aspect of culture should take primacy over any other, Rivers had isolated social structure as the principal and most enduring indicator of the working of human society. It was in this way that Rivers was able to account for the existence of certain types of social myths in Australia, where human mobility had apparently brought peoples with contrasting forms of social organization into contact with each other and where some explanation was necessary to account for the element of "variety and inconstancy" to which he refers in "The Sociological Significance of Myth" (see p. 33 below).

Due in large part to the influence of Boas and Rivers, the study of social anthropology in the United States and Great Britain was transformed from the description of isolated cultural curiosities and speculative interpretations of their origin and significance to the objective analysis of ethnographic data collected firsthand in the field by trained investigators. Both men had considerable influence on their contemporaries, and many of their concepts relating to cultural phenomena and social processes were developed and modified by their students and successors. When Rivers died in 1922, Boas had just completed his twenty-third year as Professor of Anthropology at Columbia University. In the same year, two books were published in England which built upon but considerably modified many of the concepts which Rivers and his colleagues at Cambridge had been evolving. The appearance of these two works marked the beginning of a new era in social anthropology.

The Andaman Islanders by A. R. Radcliffe-Brown and *Argonauts of the Western Pacific* by Bronislaw Malinowski were studies of small-scale, insular societies based on data gathered by their respective authors in the Andaman Islands off the coast of Burma in 1906-8 and in the Trobriand Islands northeast of New Guinea in 1914-16 and 1917-18. In a strict sense, Radcliffe-Brown's work was concerned with the social organization and ritual actions of the Andamanese, while Malinowski's study concentrated on the *kula,* a system of primitive exchange of goods "rooted in myth, backed by traditional law, and surrounded with magical rites" (Malinowski, 1922:85). Underlying both studies, however, was the basic premise that each society is an organized, systematic, and integral whole, the parts of which are functionally interrelated. Every social custom and institution is regarded as meaningful within the social context; and the function of every custom and institution, it was contended, can only be determined in terms of these meanings (Radcliffe-Brown, 1922: viii-x). It is the task of the ethnographer, according to this point of view, to discover the meanings of, and the functional interrelationships among, the parts and between the parts and the whole. And since it was assumed that functions can change with time, it was clear that ethnographic studies needed to be synchronic—at least initially—rather than diachronic. There was no place in such an analytical scheme for conjectural history, which, Radcliffe-Brown noted, "cannot give us results of any importance for the understanding of human life and culture" (Radcliffe-Brown, 1922: vii). Neither did this approach admit into it any concept of survivals, for once a custom, belief, or institution had lost its function, it was presumed that it simply disappeared. This theoretical position, exemplified in the excerpts from the chapters on mythology from *The Andaman Islanders* (pp. 46-71) and *Argonauts of the Western Pacific* (pp. 72-101) reprinted in this book, came to be labeled "functionalism" by anthropologists and was to be developed somewhat differently by Malinowski and Radcliffe-Brown in their subsequent publications.

Malinowski's position is expressed succinctly in an essay on culture which he wrote for the *Encyclopaedia of the Social Sciences,* published in 1931:

> Culture consists of the body of commodities and instruments as well as customs and bodily or mental habits which work directly or indirectly for the satisfaction of human needs. All the elements of culture, if this conception be true, must be at work, functioning, active, efficient. The essentially dynamic character of cultural elements and of their relations suggests that it is in the study of cultural functions that the most important task of anthropology consists (Malinowski, 1931:625).

The component units of culture, Malinowski noted, are institutions, "organized systems of human activities," which have "a considerable degree of permanence, universality, and independence." Each institution "centers around a fundamental need, permanently unites a group of people in a cooperative task, and has its particular body of doctrine and its technique of craft." In essence, then, Malinowski conceived of culture as a complex whole, with individual social institutions contributing to its maintenance and with the whole functioning in turn to satisfy the basic needs of the people who constitute the culture.

In contrast, Radcliffe-Brown contended that "the concrete reality with which the social anthropologist is concerned . . . is not any sort of entity, but a process, the process of social life." This process, according to Radcliffe-Brown, "consists of an immense multitude of actions and interactions of human beings, acting as individuals or in combinations or groups" (Radcliffe-Brown, 1965: 4). People, then, are the components or units, and the network of relationships which exists among them constitutes the social structure. Social institutions—"standardized modes of behaviour"—contribute to the maintenance, stability, and continuity of this social structure (i.e., this "network of social relations"). Radcliffe-Brown thus evolved a theory of social relations in which each institution was regarded as a structured system (e.g., a kinship system, an economic system, a religious system) and in which, as one recent investigator has effectively expressed it, every structure "was part, or an aspect of, a total structure made up of all the social relations between people and called the *social structure*" (Jarvie, 1964: 190; his italics).

Radcliffe-Brown's theoretical model of social relations, frequently referred to today as "structural-functionalism" to differentiate it from the "functionalism" of Malinowski, represented a systematic formulation of a concept which had been suggested earlier by Rivers, under whom Radcliffe-Brown had studied at Cambridge and with whom both Malinowski and Radcliffe-Brown had discussed and debated theoretical and methodological points concerned with kinship. This structural-functional model, which began to exert considerable influence on anthropological thinking in the mid-1930's, made clear what other investigators were also beginning to discover at the time: that social anthropology should have as its principal objective to describe and analyze dynamic social processes rather than static states and arbitrarily designated entities.

This approach, with its requisite demands for intensive synchronic analysis, shifted the focus of myth studies from a preoccupation with definition and theories of origin and dissemination to the examination of the sociological significance of mythology. To Malinowski, Radcliffe-Brown, and their followers, the objective of studying myth was to determine its effects on the overall social structure and its interrelationships with other aspects of that total social structure. Malinowski's consideration of the role that mythology played in perpetuating certain rituals of the *kula* in the Trobriand Islands (see pp. 72-101 below) and Radcliffe-Brown's discussion of Andamanese myths as means of expressing and maintaining "certain ways of thinking and feeling about the society and its relation to the world of nature" (see pp. 46-71 below) make clear their conviction that mythology serves an integrative function and contributes to social cohesion.

Those anthropologists who studied under Malinowski from 1922 to 1939 at the London School of Economics and Political Science at the University of London or with Radcliffe-Brown at the University of Chicago between 1931 and 1937 and at Oxford from 1937 to 1946 concentrated on the description and analysis of the systems of social relationships inherent in specific institutions of primitive societies. Raymond Firth, one of Malinowski's first graduate students at London, wrote a series of studies on Tikopian social structure, beginning with an exemplary study of kinship—*We, the Tikopia* (1936)—and including *History and Traditions of Tikopia* (1961), a chapter of which is included in this volume (pp. 168-83). Edmund R. Leach, who studied with Malinowski and Firth at London, described with considerable acumen Burmese political organization in his book *Political Systems of Highland Burma* (1954), from which the chapter on mythology is reprinted below (pp. 184-98). Perusal of these two excerpts and comparison of them with the essays by Rivers, Malinowski, and Radcliffe-Brown indicate the development and testing of a theoretical position which has characterized British social anthropology during the twentieth century and which is clearly exemplified and substantiated in studies of primitive mythology published by British-trained scholars for more than three decades.

Those anthropologists who studied under Boas at Columbia University or who were influenced by his pronouncements adhered to no one theoretical model in preference to all others as did their British-trained colleagues. Instead, they ranged far and wide in their search for insights into the workings of human society, developing and modifying Boas' concepts of cultural relativism and acculturation, investigating the relationships among various aspects of social behavior, and exploring the effects of culture on the individual and of the individual on culture. In her "Introduction to Zuni Mythology," reprinted in this volume (pp. 102-36), Ruth Benedict, a student, colleague, and eventual successor of Boas' at Columbia, examined the correspondences and disparities between myths and other aspects of Zuni society and offered sociopsychological reasons for the uniqueness of Zuni traditional tales, an approach which she also utilized to differentiate among Zuni, Kwakiutl, and Dobu societies in her book

Patterns of Culture (1934). Similarly, Clyde Kluckhohn, who was greatly influenced by the work of Boas and Benedict even though he was a student of neither of them, sought psychological explanations for the kinds of symbolic systems present in specific societies and analyzed their effects on individual behavior, as his essay "Myths and Rituals: A General Theory," reprinted below (pp. 137-67), illustrates. The development from a somewhat vague notion of psychological phenomena and their possible effects upon culture growth in Boas' essay to a more specific discussion of the subject by Benedict and a sophisticated analysis in behavioral and psychoanalytical terms by Kluckhohn exemplifies one of the major research interests of American anthropologists, the relationships between culture and personality. One also finds in these three essays evidence of an eclecticism characteristic of much writing by American-trained anthropologists and an indication of the reluctance of American scholars to endorse a single theoretical model, to pursue one methodological approach, or to reject completely any single hypothesis in their study of man in society.

The contrasting emphases in the study of social anthropology in the United States and Great Britain are readily discernible in the first eight selections on mythology reprinted in this book. Yet it would be misleading to suggest that distinct "schools" developed independently of each other. While much has been written about the narrowness of the British approach (e.g., Murdock, 1951) and in criticism of the wide-ranging interests of American anthropologists (e.g., Meggers, 1946), the publications of the major figures in the history of the discipline dispel any notions of parochialism. The frequency with which many of the writers represented in this volume cite the works of each other indicates their knowledge of, and, in many cases, their debt to, the ideas and conclusions of their colleagues on both sides of the Atlantic. Kluckhohn admits, for instance, that he has little to add to Malinowski's discussions of the interdependence of myth and other forms of social behavior (see p. 145 below); and Firth refers to Kluckhohn's concept of myths as "symbolic representations of the dominant configurations of the particular culture" to account for the various kinds of myths found in Tikopia (see p. 174 below). Moreover, Boas and Rivers both attribute the existence of certain myths in given societies to culture contact rather than to independent invention; and Benedict's essay is, in its own way, a functional study in the Malinowskian sense of the term. Even Claude Lévi-Strauss, the

French anthropologist whose ideas do not fit readily into either of these mainstreams of anthropological thinking, is indebted to the concepts evolved by many of his predecessors. His "Overture to *Le Cru et le Cuit,*" which concludes the readings section of this volume, raises philosophical questions with which early anthropologists were concerned and outlines an approach to mythology in which he attempts to deal systematically with both the complex social aspects of myth and its elusive formal characteristics. Additional similarities, together with some significant differences, will become apparent as the nine selections are read and will be discussed further in the Epilogue.

As is true of any group of readings on a given subject, the selections in this book provide a mere sampling of what anthropologists have written about primitive mythology. If more space had been available, it would have been possible to have included a greater range of viewpoints, and, more importantly, to have eliminated many of the historical gaps which now exist. It can be argued, with some justification, that no collection of essays on primitive myth can be complete without a selection by Edward B. Tylor, the great pioneer in anthropological theory, or by Sigmund Freud, whose works are receiving renewed attention from anthropologists at the time of this writing. Yet while many of the ideas formulated by these men have stimulated research and fruitful debate, their theoretical assumptions cannot be said to have emerged as main currents of thought in twentieth-century anthropology. On the other hand, the omission of essays by such major figures in the history of the study of man as Émile Durkheim, A. L. Kroeber, E. E. Evans-Pritchard, Margaret Mead, Gregory Bateson, and A. I. Hallowell is not meant to suggest that the researches of these scholars have had an insignificant effect upon studies of primitive mythology or that these investigators themselves have necessarily had a lesser impact upon their discipline. Rather it indicates that their theoretical and methodological positions are not expressed as effectively in their writings on myth as are those of the anthropologists represented here.

No attempt has been made to include selections by anthropologists of specific nationalities or studies of the mythologies of primitive peoples from each of the continents. The inclusion of excerpts and essays by American, British, and French anthropologists alone and the discussion of myths only from the Americas, Oceania, and Southeast Asia results from chance rather than from design. The nine selections in this volume represent what the editor considers to be studies of primitive mythology which are significant precisely because they reflect major developments in the history of ideas of anthropology. For this reason, it is recommended that the selections be read in the order in which they appear.

A NOTE ON THE EDITING OF THE SELECTIONS

In preparing these excerpts and essays for republication, the editor has made every attempt to reproduce the originals with a minimal number of additions and deletions. Only in those cases in which confusion might have resulted from allusions or references to sections of larger studies from which some of the excerpts have been taken have any deletions been made at all. In such cases, the omissions have never consisted of more than a few words or phrases; and these are always indicated by the inclusion of ellipses (i.e., . . .). When it was felt that a clarification of or explanation for such omissions was necessary, one has been provided in an editor's footnote. Editor's footnotes have also been added to explain or clarify references to published works, names of individuals, or terms for which the authors of the excerpts and essays provided no such documentation or for which the editor felt additional clarification might be helpful. All footnotes added by the editor are so marked (i.e., Ed. note:).

Since footnote form varies considerably among publications, the editor has rewritten all footnotes so that they conform to one style. In doing so, he has found it necessary occasionally to add bibliographical data which were not included in the original notes. The editor's additions to footnotes are enclosed within brackets (i.e., [ ]).

REFERENCES

BOAS, FRANZ
   1940 Race, Language and Culture. New York, Macmillan Co.

HERSKOVITS, MELVILLE J.
   1953 Franz Boas: The Science of Man in the Making. New York, Charles Scribner's Sons.

JARVIE, I. C.
   1964 The Revolution in Anthropology. London, Routledge & Kegan Paul, Ltd.

MALINOWSKI, BRONISLAW

1922 Argonauts of the Western Pacific. London, George Routledge & Sons, Ltd.

1931 Culture. *In* Encyclopaedia of the Social Sciences, Edwin R. A. Seligman, ed. IV: 621-46.

MEAD, MARGARET

1959 Apprenticeship Under Boas. *In* The Anthropology of Franz Boas, Walter Goldschmidt, ed. Memoir No. 89, American Anthropological Association, pp. 29-45.

MEGGERS, BETTY J.

1946 Recent Trends in American Ethnology. American Anthropologist 48: 176-214.

MURDOCK, GEORGE P.

1951 British Social Anthropology. American Anthropologist 53:465-73.

RADCLIFFE-BROWN, A. R.

1922 The Andaman Islanders. Cambridge, Cambridge University Press.

1965 Structure and Function in Primitive Society. New York, Free Press.

RIVERS, W. H. R.

1924 Social Organization, W. J. Perry, ed. New York, Alfred A. Knopf, Inc.

1926 Psychology and Ethnology, G. Elliot Smith, ed. New York, Harcourt, Brace & Co., Inc.

SMITH, G. ELLIOT

1926 Introduction: Dr. Rivers and the New Vision in Ethnology. *In* W. H. R. Rivers, Psychology and Ethnology, pp. ix-xxviii.

TYLOR, EDWARD B.

1871 Primitive Culture. London, John Murray. 2 vols.

The Growth of Indian Mythologies*[1]

FRANZ BOAS

IN a collection of Indian traditions recently published,[2] I have discussed the development of the mythologies of the Indians of the
North Pacific coast. In the following I will briefly sum up the results
at which I arrived in my investigation, and try to formulate a number
of principles which, it seems to me, may be derived from it, and
which, I believe, ought to be observed in all work on mythologies
and customs of primitive people.

The region with which I deal, the North Pacific coast of our continent, is inhabited by people diverse in language but alike in culture.

The arts of the tribes of a large portion of the territory are so
uniform that it is almost impossible to discover the origin of even the
most specialized forms of their productions inside of a wide expanse
of territory. Acculturation of the various tribes has had the effect
that the plane and the character of the culture of most of them is
the same; in consequence of this we find also that myths have travelled from tribe to tribe, and that a large body of legends belongs to
many in common.

As we depart from the area where the peculiar culture of the North
Pacific coast has reached its highest development, a gradual change in
arts and customs takes place, and, together with it, we find a gradual

*Subtitled, "A Study Based upon the Growth of the Mythologies of the North Pacific
Coast." Reprinted with permission of the Macmillan Company from *Race, Language and
Culture* by Franz Boas. Copyright 1940 by Franz Boas, renewed 1968 by Franziska Boas
Michelson. The essay first appeared (with minor differences in style and spelling) in the *Jour-
nal of American Folklore,* Vol. 9 (1896), 1-11, published by the American Folklore Society.

[1] Paper read at the Seventh Annual Meeting of the American Folk-Lore Society, Phila-
delphia, December 27, 1895.

[2] *Indianische Sagen von der Nord-Pacifischen Küste Amerikas* (Berlin, 1895).

diminution in the number of myths which the distant tribe has in common with the people of the North Pacific coast. At the same time, a gradual change in the incidents and general character of the legends takes place.

We can in this manner trace what we might call a dwindling down of an elaborate cycle of myths to mere adventures, or even to incidents of adventures, and we can follow the process step by step. Wherever this distribution can be traced, we have a clear and undoubted example of the gradual dissemination of a myth over neighboring tribes. The phenomena of distribution can be explained only by the theory that the tales have been carried from one tribe to its neighbors, and by the tribe which has newly acquired them in turn to its own neighbors. It is not necessary that this dissemination should always follow one direction; it may have proceeded either way. In this manner a complex tale may dwindle down by gradual dissemination, but also new elements may be embodied in it.

It may be well to give an example of this phenomenon. The most popular tradition of the North Pacific coast is that of the raven. Its most characteristic form is found among the Tlingit, Tsimshian, and Haida. As we go southward, the connection between the adventurers becomes looser and their number less. It appears that the traditions are preserved quite fully as far south as the north end of Vancouver Island. Farther south the number of tales which are known to the Indians diminishes rapidly. At Nahwittee, near the north point of Vancouver Island, thirteen tales out of a whole of eighteen exist. The Comox have only eight, the Nootka six, and the Coast Salish only three. Furthermore, the traditions are found at Nahwittee in the same connection as farther north, while farther south they are very much modified. The tale of the origin of daylight, which was liberated by the raven, may serve as an instance. He had taken the shape of the spike of a cedar, was swallowed by the daughter of the owner of the daylight, and then born again; afterwards he broke the box in which the daylight was kept. Among the Nootka, only the transformation into the spike of a cedar, which is swallowed by a girl and then born again, remains. Among the Coast Salish the more important passages survive, telling how the raven by a ruse compelled the owner of the daylight to let it out of the box in which he kept it. The same story is found as far south as Grey's Harbor in Washington. The adventure of the pitch, which the raven kills by exposing it to the sunshine, intending to use it for calking his canoe, is found far south, but in an entirely new connection, embodied in the tradition of the origin of sun and moon.

But there are also certain adventures embodied in the raven myths of the north which probably had their origin in other parts of America. Among these I mention the story of the raven who was invited and reciprocated. The seal puts his hands near the fire, and grease drips out of them into a dish which he gives to the raven. Then the latter tries to imitate him, but burns his hands, etc. This tale is found, in one or the other form, all over North America, and there is no proof that it originally belonged to the raven myth of Alaska.

I believe the proposition that dissemination has taken place among neighboring tribes will not encounter any opposition. Starting from this point, we will make the following considerations:—

If we have a full collection of the tales and myths of all the tribes of a certain region, and then tabulate the number of incidents which all the collections from each tribe have in common with any selected tribe, the number of common incidents will be the larger the more intimate the relation of the two tribes and the nearer they live together. This is what we observe in a tabulation of the material collected on the North Pacific coast. On the whole, the nearer the people, the greater the number of common elements; the farther apart, the less the number.

But it is not the geographical location alone which influences the distribution of tales. In some cases, numerous tales which are common to a territory stop short at a certain point, and are found beyond it in slight fragments only. These limits do not by any means coincide with linguistic divisions. An example of this kind is the raven legend, to which I referred before. It is found in substantially the same form from Alaska to northern Vancouver Island; then it suddenly disappears almost entirely, and is not found among the southern tribes of Kwakiutl lineage, nor on the west coast of Vancouver Island, although the northern tribes, who speak the Kwakiutl language, have it. Only fragments of these legends have strayed farther south, and their number diminishes with increasing distance. There must be a cause for such a remarkable break. A statistical inquiry shows that the northern traditions are in close contact with the tales of the tribes as far south as the central part of Vancouver Island, where a tribe of Salish lineage is found; but farther they do not go. The closely allied tribes immediately south do not possess them. Only one explanation of this fact is possible, viz., lack of acculturation, which may be due to a difference of character, to long continued hostilities, or to recent changes in the location of the tribes, which has not allowed the slow process of acculturation to exert its deep-going influence. I consider the last the most probable cause. My reason for holding this opinion is that the Bella Coola, another Salish tribe, which has become separated from the people speaking related languages and live in the far north, still show in their mythologies the closest relations to the southern Salish tribes, with whom they have many more traits in common than their neighbors to the north and to the south. If their removal were a very ancient one, this similarity in mythologies would probably not have persisted, but they would have been quite amalgamated by their new neighbors.

We may also extend our comparisons beyond the immediate neighbors of the tribes under consideration by comparing the mythologies of the tribes of the plateaus in the interior, and even of those farther to the east with those of the coast. Unfortunately, the available material from these regions is very scanty. Fairly good collections exist from the Athapascan, from the tribes of Columbia River and east of the mountains, from the Omaha, and from some Algonquin tribes. When comparing the mythologies and traditions which belong to far-distant regions, we find that the number of incidents which they have in common is greater than might have been expected; but some of those incidents are so general that we may assume that they have no connection, and may have arisen independently. There is, however, one very characteristic feature which proves beyond cavil that this is not the sole cause of the similarity of tales and incidents. We know that in the region under discussion two important trade routes reached the Pacific coast, one along the Columbia River, which connected the region inhabited by Shoshonean tribes with the coast and indirectly led to territories occupied by Siouan and Algonquin tribes; another one which led from Athapascan territory to the country of the Bella Coola. A trail of minor importance led down Fraser River. A study of the traditions shows that along these routes the points of contact of mythologies are strongest, and rapidly diminish with increasing distances from these routes. On Columbia River, the points of contact are with the Algonquin and Sioux; among the Bella Coola with the Athapascan. I believe this phenomenon cannot be explained in any other way but that the myths followed the lines of travel, and that there has been dissemination of tales all over the continent. My tabulations include the Micmac of Nova Scotia, the Eskimo of Greenland, the Ponca of the Mississippi Basin, and the Athapascan of the Mackenzie River, and the results give the clearest evidence of extensive borrowing.

The identity of a great many tales in geographically contiguous areas has led me to the point of view of assuming that wherever considerable similarity between two tales is found in North America, it is more likely to be due to dissemination than to independent origin.

But without extending these theories beyond the clearly demonstrated truths of transmission of tales between neighboring tribes, we may reach some further conclusions. When we compare, for instance, the tales of the culture hero of the Chinook and that of the origin of the whole religious ceremonial of the Kwakiutl Indians, we find a far-reaching resemblance in certain parts of the legends which make it certain that these parts are derived from the same source. The grandmother of the divinity of the Chinook, when a child, was carried away by a monster. Their child became the mother of the culture hero, and by her help the monster was slain. In a legend from Vancouver Island, a monster, the cannibal spirit, carries away a girl, and is finally slain by her help. Their child becomes later on the new cannibal spirit. There are certain intermediate stages of these stories which prove their identity beyond doubt. The important point in this case is that the myths in question are perhaps the most fundamental ones in the mythologies of these two tribes. Nevertheless, they are not of native growth, but, partly at least, borrowed. A great many other important legends prove to be of foreign origin, being grafted upon more ancient mythologies. This being the case, I draw the conclusion that the mythologies as we find them now are not organic growths, but have gradually developed and obtained their present form by accretion of foreign material. Much of this material must have been adopted ready-made, and has been adapted and changed in form according to the genius of the people who borrowed it. The proofs of this process are so ample that there is no reason to doubt the fact. We are, therefore, led to the conclusion that from mythologies in their present form it is impossible to derive the conclusion that they are mythological explanations of phenomena of nature observed by the people to whom the myths belong, but that many of them, at the place where we find them now, never had such a meaning. If we acknowledge this conclusion as correct, we must give up the attempts at off-hand explanation of myths as fanciful,

and we must also admit that explanations given by the Indians themselves are often secondary, and do not reflect the true origin of the
myths.

I do not wish to be misunderstood in what I said. Certainly, the
phenomena of nature are at the bottom of numerous myths, else we
should not find sun, moon, clouds, thunder-storm, the sea and the
land playing so important a part in all mythologies. What I maintain
is only that the specific myth cannot be simply interpreted as the
result of observation of natural phenomena. Its growth is much too
complex. In most cases, the present form has undergone material
change by disintegration and by accretion of foreign material, so that
the original underlying idea is, at best, much obscured.

Perhaps the objection might be raised to my argument that the
similarities of mythologies are not only due to borrowing, but also
to the fact that, under similar conditions which prevail in a limited
area, the human mind creates similar products. While there is a certain truth in this argument so far as elementary forms of human
thought are concerned, it seems quite incredible that the same complex tale should originate twice in a limited territory. The very complexity of the tales and their gradual dwindling down to which I have
referred before, cannot possibly be explained by any other method
than by dissemination. Wherever geographical continuity of the area
of distribution of a complex ethnographical phenomenon is found,
the laws of probability exclude the theory that in this continuous
area the complex phenomenon has arisen independently in various
places, but compel us to assume that in its present complex form its
distribution is due to dissemination, while its composing elements
may have originated here and there.

It may be well to dwell on the difference between that comparative method which I have pursued in my inquiry and that applied by
many investigators of ethnographical phenomena. I have strictly confined my comparisons to contiguous areas in which we know intercourse to have taken place. I have shown that this area extends from
the Pacific coast to considerable distances. It is true that the mythologies of the far east and the extreme northeast are not as well connected with those of the Pacific coast by intermediate links as they
might be, and I consider it essential that a fuller amount of material
from intermediate points be collected in order that the investigation
which I have begun may be carried out in detail. But a comparison
of the fragmentary notes which we possess from intermediate points

proves that most of those tales which I have enumerated as common to the east, to the north, and to the west, will be found covering the whole area continuously. Starting from this fact, we may be allowed to argue that those complex tales which are now known only from isolated portions of our continent are actually continuous but have not been recorded from intermediate points; or that they have become extinct in intermediate territory; or, finally, that they were carried over certain areas accidentally, without touching the intermediate field. This last phenomenon may happen, although probably not to a very great extent. I observed one example of this kind on the Pacific coast, where a tale which has its home in Alaska is found only in one small group of tribes on northern Vancouver Island, where, as can be proved, it has been carried either by visitors or by slaves.

The fundamental condition, that all comparisons must be based on material collected in contiguous areas, differentiates our methods from that of investigators like Petitot and many others, who see a proof of dissemination or even of blood relationship in every similarity that is found between a certain tribe and any other tribe of the globe. It is clear that the greater the number of tribes which are brought forward for the purposes of such comparisons, the greater also the chance of finding similarities. It is impossible to derive from such comparisons sound conclusions, however extensive the knowledge of literature that the investigator may possess, for the very reason that the complex phenomenon found in one particular region is compared to fragmentary evidence from all over the world. By means of such comparisons, we can expect to find resemblances which are founded in the laws of the development of the human mind, but they can never be proofs of transmission of customs or ideas.

In the Old World, wherever investigations on mythologies of neighboring tribes have been made, the philological proof has been considered the weightiest, *i.e.,* when, together with the stories, the names of the actors have been borrowed, this has been considered the most satisfactory proof of borrowing. We cannot expect to find such borrowing of names to prevail to a great extent in America. Even in Asia, the borrowed names are often translated from one language into the other, so that their phonetic resemblance is entirely destroyed. The same phenomenon is observed in America. In many cases, the heroes of myths are animals, whose names are introduced in the myth. In other cases, names are translated, or so much changed according to the phonetic laws of various languages, that they can hardly be recognized. Cases of transmission of names are, however, by no means rare. I will give only a few examples from the North Pacific coast.

Almost all the names of Bella Coola mythology are borrowed from the Kwakiutl language. A portion of the great religious ceremony of the Kwakiutl has the name "dlo'gwala." This name, which is also closely connected with a certain series of myths, has spread northward and southward over a considerable distance. Southward we find it as far as Columbia River, while to the north it ceases with the Tsimshian; but still farther north another name of a part of the ceremonial of the Kwakiutl is substituted, viz., "nontlem." This name, as designating a ceremonial, is found far away, in Alaska. But these are exceptions; on the whole, the custom of translating names and of introducing names of animals excludes the application of the linguistic method of investigating the borrowing of myths and customs.

We will consider for a moment the method by which traditions spread over contiguous areas, and I believe this consideration will show that the standpoint which I am taking, viz., that similarity of traditions in a continuous area is always due to dissemination, not to independent origin, is correctly taken. I will exemplify this also by means of the traditions of the North Pacific coast, more particularly by those of the Kwakiutl Indians.

It seems that the Kwakiutl at one time consisted of a number of village communities. Numbers of these village communities combined and formed tribes; then each village community formed a division of the new tribe. Owing probably to the influence of the clan system of the northern tribes, crests were adopted, and with these came the necessity of acquiring a crest legend. The social customs of the tribe are based entirely upon the divisions of the tribe, and the ranking of each individual is the higher—at least to a certain extent—the more important the crest legend. This led to a tendency of building up such legends. Investigation shows that there are two classes of these legends: the first telling how the ancestor of the division came down from heaven, out of the earth, or out of the ocean; the second telling how he encountered certain spirits and by their help became powerful. The latter class particularly bear the clearest evidence of being of recent origin; they are based entirely on the custom of the Indians of acquiring a guardian spirit after long-continued fasting and bathing. The guardian spirit thus acquired by the ancestor became hereditary, and is to a certain extent the crest of the division,—and there is no doubt that these traditions, which rank now with the fundamental myths of the tribe, are based on the actual fastings and acquisitions of guardian spirits of ancestors of the present division. If that is so, we must conclude that the origin of the myth is identical with the origin of the hallucination of the fasting Indian, and this is due to suggestion, the material for which is furnished by the tales of other Indians, and traditions referring to the spiritual world which the fasting Indian has heard. There is, therefore, in this case a strong psychological reason for involuntary borrowing from legends which the individual may have heard, no matter from what source they may have been derived. The incorporation in the mythology of the tribe is due to the peculiar social organization which favors the introduction of any myth of this character if it promises to enhance the social position of the division concerned.

The same kind of suggestion to which I referred here has evidently moulded the beliefs in a future life. All myths describing the future life set forth how a certain individual died, how his soul went to the world of the ghosts, but returned for one reason or another. The experiences which the man told after his recovery are the basis of the belief in a future life. Evidently, the visions of the sick person are caused entirely by the tales which he had heard of the world of the ghosts, and the general similarity of the character of this tale along the Pacific coast proves that one vision was always suggested by another.

Furthermore, the customs of the tribe are such that by means of a marriage the young husband acquires the crest legends of his wife, and the warrior who slays an enemy those of the person whom he has slain. By this means a large number of traditions of the neighboring tribes have been incorporated in the mythology of the Kwakiutl.

The psychological reason for the borrowing of myths which do not refer to crest legends, but to the heavenly orbs and to the phenomena of nature, are not so easily found. There can be no doubt that the impression made by the grandeur of nature upon the mind of primitive man is the ultimate cause from which these myths spring, but, nevertheless, the form in which we find these traditions is largely influenced by borrowing. It is also due to its effects that in many cases the ideas regarding the heavenly orbs are entirely inconsistent. Thus the Nahwittee have the whole northern legend of the raven liberating the sun, but, at the same time, the sun is considered the father of the mink, and we find a tradition of the visit of the mink in heaven, where he carries the sun in his father's place. Other inconsistencies, as great as this one, are frequent. They are an additional proof that one or the other of such tales which are also found among neighboring tribes,—and there sometimes in a more consistent form,—have been borrowed.

These considerations lead me to the following conclusion, upon which I desire to lay stress. The analysis of one definite mythology of North America shows that in it are embodied elements from all over the continent, the greater number belonging to neighboring districts, while many others belong to distant areas, or, in other words, that dissemination of tales has taken place all over the continent. In most cases, we can discover the channels through which the tale flowed, and we recognize that in each and every mythology of North America we must expect to find numerous foreign elements. And this leads us to the conclusion that similarities of culture on our continent are always more likely to be due to diffusion than to independent development. When we turn to the Old World, we know that there also diffusion has taken place through the whole area from western Europe to the islands of Japan, and from Indonesia to Siberia, and to northern and eastern Africa. In the light of the similarities of inventions and of myths, we must even extend this area along the North Pacific coast of America as far south as Columbia River. These are facts that cannot be disputed.

If it is true that dissemination of cultural elements has taken place in these vast areas, we must pause before accepting the sweeping assertion that sameness of ethnical phenomena is *always* due to the sameness of the working of the human mind, and I take issue clearly and expressly with the view of those modern anthropologists who go so far as to say that he who looks for acculturation as a cause of similarity of culture has not grasped the true spirit of anthropology.

In making this statement, I wish to make my position perfectly clear. I am, of course, well aware that there are many phenomena of social life seemingly based on the most peculiar and most intricate reasoning, which we have good cause to believe have developed independently over and over again. There are others, particularly such as are more closely connected with the emotional life of man, which are undoubtedly due to the organization of the human mind. Their domain is large and of high importance. Furthermore, the similarities in cultures which may or may not be due to acculturation indicate that the same sort of distinct ideas will originate independently in different minds, modified to a greater or less extent by the character of environment. Proof of this are the ideas and inventions which even in our highly specialized civilization are "in the air" at certain periods, and are pronounced independently by more than one individual, until they combine in a flow which carries on the thought of man in a certain direction. All this I know and grant.

But I do take the position that this enticing idea is apt to carry us too far. Formerly, anthropologists saw acculturation or even common descent wherever two similar phenomena were observed. The discovery that this conclusion is erroneous, that many similarities are due to the psychical laws underlying human development, has carried us beyond its legitimate aim, and we start now with the presumption that all similarities are due to these causes, and that their investigation is the legitimate field of anthropological research. I believe this position is just as erroneous as the former one. We must not accuse the investigator who suspects a connection between American and Asiatic cultures as deficient in his understanding of the true principles of anthropology. Nobody has proven that the psychologic explanation holds good in all cases. On the contrary, we know many cases of diffusion of customs over enormous areas. The reaction against the uncritical use of similarities for the purpose of proving relationship and historical connections is overreaching its aim. Instead of demanding a critical examination of the causes of similarities, we say now *a priori,* they are due to psychical causes, and in this we err in method just as much as the old school did. If we want to make progress on the desired line, we must insist upon critical methods, based not on generalities but on each individual case. In many cases, the final decision will be in favor of independent origin; in others in favor of dissemination. But I insist that nobody has as yet proven where the limit between these two modes of origin lies, and not until this is done can a fruitful psychological analysis be made. We do not even know if the critical examination may not lead us to assume a persistence of cultural elements which were diffused at the time when man first spread over the globe.

It will be necessary to define clearly what Bastian terms the elementary ideas,[3] the existence of which we know to be universal, and

---

[3] Ed. note: Boas refers here to Adolf Bastian (1826-1905), German ethnologist, who coined the term *Elementargedanke* in 1860. The *Elementargedanken,* according to Bastian, are basic forms of thought which are shared by peoples of diverse cultures and which are presumed to have arisen independently as a result of the psychic unity of man. The forms that the *Elementargedanken* take in any particular culture are referred to by Bastian as *Völkergedanken.*

the origin of which is not accessible to ethnological methods. The forms which these ideas take among primitive people of different parts of the world, the "Völker-Gedanken," are due partly to the geographical environment and partly to the peculiar culture of the people, and to a large extent to their history. In order to understand the growth of psychical life, the historical growth of customs must be investigated most closely, and the only method by which the history can be investigated is by means of a detailed comparison of the tribe with its neighbors. This is the method which is necessary in order to make progress towards a better understanding of the development of mankind. This investigation will also lead us to inquire into the interesting psychological problems of acculturation, viz., what conditions govern the selection of foreign material embodied in the culture of the people, and the mutual transformation of the old culture and the newly acquired material.

To sum up, I maintain that the whole question is decided only in so far as we know that independent development as well as diffusion has made each culture what it is. It is still *sub judice* in how far these two causes contributed to its growth. The aspects from which we may look at the problem have been admirably set forth by Otis T. Mason in his address on similarities in culture.[4] In order to investigate the psychical laws of the human mind which we are seeing now indistinctly because our material is crude and unsifted, we must treat the culture of primitive people by strict historical methods. We must understand the process by which the individual culture grew before we can undertake to lay down the laws by which the culture of all mankind grew.

The end for which we are working is farther away than the methods which are now in greatest favor seem to indicate, but it is worth our struggles.

---

[4] ["Similarities in Culture,"] *American Anthropologist,* Vol. 8 (1895), 101-17.

The Sociological Significance of Myth[*][1]

W. H. R. RIVERS

TO those engaged in the attempt to trace out the history of social institutions among people of rude culture, the myths and traditions of the people themselves form a natural and attractive field of inquiry. At the present time, however, there is the widest divergence of opinion as to the value of this kind of knowledge. By some workers such narratives are used as evidence without hesitation, while by others they are put wholly on one side as the pure fruit of imagination, having no relevance where facts are concerned.

A striking example of this divergence of treatment is to be found in the utilisation of Arunta narratives by Messrs. Spencer and Gillen[2] and Dr. Frazer,[3] and their scant rejection by Mr. Andrew Lang[4] as traditions "dictated by the logic of fancy," and therefore, it is assumed, of no value as evidence. It does not seem to have occurred to these workers,[5] nor, so far as I am aware, has it occurred to others, to inquire whether it is possible to lay down any general principles which may enable us to assign its proper value to such evidence. It is the purpose of this paper to formulate one such principle and inquire to what conclusions it may lead us.

---

*Reprinted from *Folk-Lore*, Vol. 23 (1912), 307-31, by permission of the Folk-Lore Society.

[1] I am indebted to Miss C. S. Burne, Miss Jane Harrison, and Mr. H. M. Chadwick for suggestions which have led me to add to, or modify, this paper since it was read before the Folk-Lore Society [on June 19, 1912].

[2] [Baldwin Spencer and F. J. Gillen,] *The Native Tribes of Central Australia* [London, 1899], pp. 207, 209; and *The Northern Tribes of Central Australia* [London, 1904], p. 320.

[3] [James George Frazer,] *Totemism and Exogamy*, Vol. I [Edinburgh, 1887], 238.

[4] *Man*, Vol. 10 (1910), 119.

[5] Except insofar as Messrs. Spencer and Gillen lay stress on the divergence of tradition from present customs.

I must first say something about the sense in which I propose to use the term "myth." At the present time this word is used with many different meanings. By some it is limited to narratives which give an account of the doings of gods or of those who possess in some measure divine characters; to others a narrative is only a myth if it stands in a definite relation to ritual and serves to explain and justify this ritual; by others the term is used more widely, but is limited to narratives which give an account of or explain natural as opposed to social phenomena.

In the present state of our knowledge the chief justification of classifications and definitions lies in their usefulness, and a classification which may be useful from one point of view may not necessarily be so from another. I approach the subject of myth in this paper in its relation to the history of culture, and from this point of view, if from no other, the limitations implied by the usages I have mentioned are neither helpful nor necessary.

The general class of which myths form one group are narratives which give a concrete account of events. By thus laying stress on the concrete nature of "narratives" I intend to exclude the abstract accounts of events given by science.

From the point of view of the history of culture the first grouping of narratives depends on whether they are or are not historical, whether they are records of events which have actually happened or the work of the human imagination. We can be confident that even those narratives of peoples of rude culture which come nearest to history contain imaginative elements, but this only makes it the task of the student to distinguish the two elements from one another.

The first line of cleavage of narratives and of their elements, then, is into the historical and the imaginative. The latter class may be further broken up into two main sections, viz. those which purport to give an account of or explain any portion of the universe, and those which have no such purpose but are purely fictive, and I propose to distinguish these two sections as myth and fiction respectively. According to this mode of classification a myth is a narrative which gives an account of the coming into being of man himself or of any feature of his environment, natural or social.[6] Not only will it

---

[6] This definition limits the term "myth" to narratives which have an aetiological or explanatory motive. I have, however, expressly avoided the use of the word "explain" in the definition, because this term bears a rationalistic connotation which makes it a very inexact means of expressing the mental attitudes of those among whom myths arise. For want of a fully appropriate word, however, I shall speak of myths as explanatory in the general body of the paper.

include narratives which account for and justify man's religious practices, and thus extend to all which describe the doings of gods and serve to explain the general character as well as the details of ritual, but it will also include narratives which tell how there arose features and motions of any objects in sky, sea, or land. It will range in its connotation from the most elaborate doings of a god, in so far as these are not historical, to the origin of the elephant's trunk or the cause of a cleft in a rock.

I am not concerned in this paper with the group of narratives I include under fiction, and need only say that, though they often take the form of tales which give an account of events supposed to have happened, they differ from myths in having no explanatory motive. Their purpose is purely aesthetic, and, though such fictive tales undoubtedly exist among people of rude culture, they are probably less frequent and less important than among the civilised. Only one point need be noted here, viz. that a large proportion of the narratives of lowly culture are probably myths which have been transmitted from people to people, in which process their aetiological character has been lost or obscured.

The classification of narratives, then, which I propose is into historical traditions, myths, and tales. According to my use of the word, a myth is the pure product of the human imagination, an attempt to express the wonderful and the mysterious.

My definition of myth does not include a frequent feature of narratives in which actions or sayings are assigned to persons other than the real agent. Wonderful stories tend to cluster round the lives of exceptional men and round superhuman beings, and such stories are often called myths, but, except in so far as they help to show the divine or superhuman character of the being to whom they are attributed and thus assist in accounting for the mysteries of the universe, they would not come under my definition.

I may point out that my mode of defining myth corresponds closely with that of current English usage as indicated by the definition of Murray's dictionary, viz. "a purely fictitious narrative usually involving supernatural persons, actions, or events, and embodying some popular idea concerning natural or historical phenomena." My usage is more definite in its omission of the qualification beginning with the word "usually," and it has the advantage of avoiding the ambiguous word "supernatural," but the two agree in the important point that the term applies to all natural or historical, *i.e.* social, phenomena.

My definition also agrees in essence with current German usage as indicated by Bockh's *Encyclopaedie,* which is accepted by Ehrenreich,[7] viz. "der sinnliche in Personifikationen gegebene Ausdruck der gesammten ethischen und physischen Erkenntnis." Here again the word is made to cover the whole of human experience, and it also clearly implies the explanatory purpose of myth. The definition might be freely translated "the concrete expression of human knowledge, social and natural, by means of personification." A doubtful point is how far the term *Personifikation* necessarily implies anthropomorphic expression. If this term can be stretched to include the representation of ideas in animal or other non-human concrete forms, there would be little if any difference between the two definitions. R. M. Meyer[8] has expressed in brief but pregnant form the main idea of my definition. According to him a myth is any part of the universe seen from the point of view of primitive man, "ein Eckchen Welt, angeschaut durch das Temperament eines primitiven Menschen."[9]

Myths may deal with social topics in three distinct ways. First, it may be the primary motive of a myth, or of some part of a myth, to give an account of the coming into being of a social institution. Next, a myth may have a social setting. The whole myth may be coloured by some social atmosphere; thus, in the myths of a totemic people there will be a totemic colouring, shown by reference to persons in such a way as to leave it doubtful whether they are human beings or animals. Thirdly, a myth may include incidental references to specific social events, such as a special form of marriage.[10]

The significance of the social setting and of incidental references to social events is very great, but it is so obvious and, I think, so generally admitted, that I do not propose to deal with these aspects of myth in this paper. When a social condition is mentioned incidentally or is revealed by the general colouring of a myth, we can be confident that it is not the pure product of imagination, but has a definite historical value. Social incidents, still less the general colouring of a myth, could never appear unless they had their roots in the

---

7 [Paul M. A. Ehrenreich,] *Die allgemeine Mythologie* (Leipzig, 1910), p. 6.

8 *Altgermanische Religionsgeschichte* ([Leipzig,] 1910), p. 9.

9 Ed. note: Literally translated, this means "a little corner of the world, seen from the point of view of a primitive person."

10 A good example of such an incident is to be found in a narrative recorded by Dr. [R. H.] Codrington (*The Melanesians* [Oxford, 1891], p. 384), in which a man marries one of the wives of his maternal uncle.

social constitution either of the people who narrate the myth or of those from whom the myth has been derived.

I propose, then, to accept without question the value, as historical evidence, of incidental references to social conditions and of the social setting of mythical narratives. It is not with these aspects of myth that it is the special purpose of this paper to deal, but with that kind of myth the primary motive of which is to account for social phenomena. I may point out at once a feature of such myths which differentiates them from myths having natural phenomena as their subject. When people relate a story which provides an anthropomorphic or theriomorphic interpretation of the moon's periodical changes, or narrate the events which produced the features characteristic of some animal, it is clear that we have to do with myth. When, on the other hand, they give an account of events which led to the appearance of a form of social structure or of the mode of performing a rite, we have no such immediate certainty that we have to do with myth. It is possible that the people may be preserving the memory of an actual occurrence; that we may have to do, not with myth, but with historical tradition. A possibility, then, which must always be kept in mind in dealing with narratives which appear to be social myths is that they may not be myths at all but historical traditions, or combinations of both history and myth.

The first fact which meets us in our inquiry is that narratives of a mythical kind which serve to account for social conditions occur but seldom among the records of savage or barbarous peoples. Accounts dealing with features of the sun, moon, and stars, of land and sea, of winds and weather, of animals and plants, are abundant, but it is only exceptionally that we meet with narratives which serve primarily and especially to account for social conditions. This predominance of natural phenomena as the object of myth is so great that in many works on mythology the social myth is not mentioned. Thus, no reference is made to it in the three chapters devoted to Mythology in Tylor's *Primitive Culture,* nor does van Gennep refer to it in his recent work *La Formation des Légendes.*[11] Its existence is definitely recognised by Ehrenreich,[12] but, in so far as Wundt[13] deals with it at all, he includes it under the general heading of "Natur-Mythus."

---

[11] [Arnold van Gennep,] Paris, 1910.
[12] *Die allgemeine Mythologie.*
[13] [Wilhelm Wundt,] *Völkerpsychologie, Mythus und Religion,* Vol. II [Leipzig, 1911-12], 294, 341.

By some of these writers, as by van Gennep, the kind of narrative with which I propose to deal this evening is explicitly excluded by definition from the class "myth,"[14] and in view of its exclusion by some, and its neglect by other mythologists, it may be well to give an instance of a narrative, undoubtedly mythical, which has a definitely social subject. In one district of the Melanesian island of Santa Cruz, there are clans, one of which has as totem a bird called *taklai,* while most of the others take their names from fishes. It is narrated that once the *taklai* bird hatched out a brood of young by the side of a stream. The nestlings were carried out to sea by the stream and were taken in charge by various fishes, and it was the birds thus taken in charge who were the founders of the different clans. It is clear that we have here a narrative which gives an account of the origin of the totemic organisation, and explains why the *taklai* bird is the totem of one clan and fishes the totems of others. Taken apart from its social context this might be regarded as a purely fictive tale having the doings of animals as its subject, but the social setting in which it is found shows that it has an aetiological character. It is either a pure product of the constructive imagination seeking for an explanation of social conditions, or an instance of reversal of the more common anthropomorphic tendency of mankind in which the doings of men have, as befits a totemic people, been transmuted by the mythic fancy into the doings of birds and fishes.

It is rarely that one meets with a narrative concerning social origins of which the mythical character is so obvious. More generally the narratives of rude peoples which deal with social topics are of the kind often known as culture-myths or sagas.[15] Such myths or sagas give an account of the introduction of various elements of the culture of the people who narrate them, but, in general, it is the introduction of material objects and of magical or religious rites which are especially recorded in these narratives. It is only exceptionally that there is any explicit reference to the introduction of social institutions.

Having now defined my terms and the scope of the subject with which I propose to deal, I can turn to the special business of this paper, the attempt to discover a general principle which may guide

---

[14] See *Internationale Wochenschrift für Wissenschaft, Kunst und Technik,* Vol. IV ([Munich,] 1910), 1167.

[15] Sagas form a class of narrative dealing with heroes in which historical and mythical or fictive elements are blended.

us in the attempt to assign their proper value to myths as evidence of the history of social institutions. For this purpose it is necessary briefly to survey the whole field of mythology to see whether any definite proposition can be laid down concerning the objects which are especially prone to become the subject of the mythopoeic tendency.

The principle I venture to suggest is that it is not the especially familiar and uniform which becomes the subject of myth; that which is ever with us in the same form does not excite the mythic fancy, but for this purpose there is necessary such an element of variety and of apparent, if not real, inconstancy as will attract attention and arouse curiosity.

Let us now survey different fields of nature admittedly the subject of myth, and see how far this proposition can be justified. I will begin with myths having animals as their subject. Here, I think, there is definite evidence that it is not the especially familiar which becomes the subject of myth. Thus, in Melanesia, the animal which is ever present in the minds of the people, the subject of their daily, almost hourly, thought, is the pig, and yet I know of hardly a myth dealing either exclusively or mainly with this animal. It is about such features as the long tail of the rat, the red head of the rail, the thinness of one fish, and the grinning appearance of another, that myths have arisen and are still told by the people. Familiar animals may become the subject of myth when they are the object of religious ritual, as among the Todas, and myths may arise to explain exceptional features of a familiar animal, especially those which distinguish him from man, such as a wide mouth and the lack of speech, but with these exceptions I believe it to be a general rule that man has not mythologised about the domestic animals with which he is in daily contact, but rather about those he sees only occasionally, so that special features of their structure or behaviour have not a familiarity which has bred contempt and made them unfit subjects for the play of imagination.

Again, of features of land and sea, it is not the land which he clears and tills,[16] or the haunts he visits habitually to hunt or fish, which are the subject of myth, but rather strangely shaped rocks or dangerous reefs which he sees only occasionally, and then in such a way

---

[16] It is only when there is anything exceptional in the nature of this land that it will become the subject of myth. Thus, if an island has red earth only in one locality, it will naturally attract attention and be likely to form a subject for the play of imagination.

as especially to impress the imagination, and thus become the subject of the mythic fancy.

The same principle is even more striking in the case of meteorological conditions. Myths concerning the winds are well developed in parts of the world where their direction and strength are variable and uncertain, but in such a region as Melanesia, where the seasons are remarkably constant and regular, myths about the winds scarcely occur. The importance of these winds and their accompanying seasons in the life of the people is enormous; in one form or another ideas connected with them permeate the whole lives of the people, and yet it is not about them that one finds myths, but rather about the inconstant appearance of the rainbow or the meteor.

I turn now to the heavenly bodies, which probably at all times and in all places have been the most frequent subject of myth. In recent works on mythology, especially in Germany, the prominent place formerly occupied by the sun has been largely taken by the moon. It is in the moon that many modern mythologists see the subject of the early speculations they believe to underlie so many of the myths of the world, both civilised and uncivilised. Without in any way committing myself to accept the general views of the modern German school, I believe that it is right in the importance it attaches to the moon rather than to the sun, at any rate in tropical countries, and in the ruder stages of culture. If this be so, it is exactly what is to be expected on the principle I am now trying to establish. In tropical countries the daily course of the sun is almost exactly the same from day to day, year in, year out, while the variations of the moon are such as can hardly fail to arouse attention and wonder. Not only are there the changes of its times of appearance in relation to the distribution of night and day, not only is there its total disappearance for a time in every month, but there are such changes of form as cannot but arouse the speculative tendency, if it is to be aroused by anything. While the constancy of the sun's movements make it the daily means of orientation in time, its uniformity and familiarity is such as to make it a far less appropriate subject for the mythic fancy than the changeable and inconstant moon.[17]

---

[17] The greater apparent inconstancy of the moon's course has not been the only motive for its prominence in myth. The supposed connection of the moon with ideas of fertility (cf. E. J. Payne, *History of the New World Called America*, Vol. I [Oxford], 1892, 493), and with physiological conditions has certainly been an important motive working in the same direction. Further, it is probable that the visibility of the moon at night, when the emotions underlying the mythopoeic state are especially prone to arise, has been another very important factor.

You will have noticed that I have qualified this opinion by limiting its application especially to the tropics. In more temperate latitudes, where there are great variations in its yearly course, the sun may on my principle be expected to bulk more largely in mythology, and, though it is taking me from my proper subject, I cannot refrain from a passing suggestion that the principle I am trying to establish may serve as a guide to the home of myths, highly developed myths having the sun as their subject-matter being more likely to have arisen in high latitudes.[18]

There are certain frequent subjects of myth which are so constantly present and so familiar as to awaken doubts concerning the sufficiency of the generalisation I am trying to establish. Thus, fire is so familiar a feature of the surroundings of people at all known stages of culture that one would hardly expect it to be a frequent subject for the play of imagination. There are, however, certain features of fire and fire-making which serve to account for this apparent exception to our rule. Probably nowhere among people of low culture is the making of fire a frequent and familiar occurrence. Every one who has lived among rude people must be struck by the care taken to keep the fire alive on the hearth. Though fire is familiar, the act of making fire has just that occasional and recurrent character which affords the most suitable soil for the growth of myth. Further, fire is made by different methods, and it may well be that many of the myths dealing with fire have their basis, not in the origin of fire itself, but in the introduction of some new mode of making it.

Another frequent subject of myth is even more familiar than fire. If myths do not arise about the familiar, we should not expect to find the narratives of rude culture dealing with the origin of man himself or of the part of the earth on which he lives. The wide prevalence of creation-myths seems at first sight to form such an exception to my generalisation as to put it wholly out of court. At the present moment I am content thus to mention the problem raised by this exception, and shall return to it later when the general argument of my paper will have given us the clue to its solution.

The examination of nature-myths has now led us to the principle that people do not mythologise about the uniform and the familiar, and I proceed to inquire what aspects of social life we should expect to find the subject of myth if this principle also holds good of myths

---

[18] The bearing of this point on the problem of the original home of the Aryans is obvious.

having social conditions as their topic. The point on which I wish especially to lay stress as the foundation of my argument is that, if people do not make myths about the very familiar, social organisation is the very last aspect of social life which one would expect to be their subject. By social organisation I mean the fundamental setting in and around which social events take place,—such institutions as the family and clan and the relationships set up by membership of these social groupings. Of all aspects of social life this is the most constant and all-pervading. We often speak of it in general as social structure, because it forms the foundation and framework of the whole social life, and, if there is anything in the principle I have stated, I should no more expect to find its origin the subject of myth than I should expect to find myths about the origin of the floors and walls of our houses.

There is a very striking difference between phenomena belonging to the fundamental institutions of social organisation and those connected with other aspects of human life. A man who is carrying out a religious rite is doing something special, and, though religious practices pervade the lives of those of ruder culture far more thoroughly than among ourselves, there is, in every practice which can be called religious, an element of separateness from the ordinary life which excites the attention and makes the action one likely to excite curiosity and wonder. Indeed, the element of separateness from ordinary life is one of the essential features of religion. Similarly, one who goes out hunting, even though he does so every day, is doing something which he is not always doing. He is entering upon a mode of activity which brings into being a special set of ideas and emotions. The fundamental social relations, on the other hand, those of the family or clan, for instance, are in far more constant action, and are at the same time less obtrusive. They are present as an integral part of every activity upon which a man enters, and there is no intermission in their action. Not even during the partial unconsciousness of sleep do they cease to play a part, but here, as in the waking state, they form only the setting for other appearances far more calculated to excite the speculative tendency.

It may be urged that there are events such as marriage, in which the social interest is dominant, which might be expected to awaken curiosity, and thus excite speculation concerning origin in a preeminent degree. Here again, however, it is not the purely social elements which are the most obtrusive. In marriage, for instance, the features of the occasion which are of the most fundamental social significance pass almost without notice. The relationship of bride and bridegroom and other purely social factors which serve to regulate the marriage as a social institution are so obvious that, though they must have attracted attention during the arrangement of the marriage, they will have become part of the established order by the time the marriage ceremonies are performed, and will sink into insignificance beside the more purely ritual features of the occasion.

Further, in a rude state of culture, the fundamental social relations are even less obtrusive than in civilised communities. Among ourselves there has come to be a more or less sharp line of distinction between relatives and friends, and it is at important moments of life, such as birth, marriage, and death, that such distinctions are brought more obtrusively than usual to our notice. Even then, however, our imaginations are not excited by the fact, and, if we are led to indulge in speculation at all, these social relations are not their most probable subject. Still less are they likely to become the subject of speculation at ruder levels of culture, where the distinction between relative and friend can hardly be said to exist.

I shall have later to consider an important exception to the rule I am now formulating, but for the present I conclude that of all aspects of human life those of purely social character are the least likely to awaken speculative interest and become the subject of myth.

We should thus expect that myths having social organisation as their subject should be absent or very rare. It is only among people of advanced culture that we should expect to find a speculative interest in the origin and development of social institutions, and then we might expect that the speculations would be clothed, not in the form we know as myth, but in that different though allied form of expression we call science. It is therefore a remarkable and startling fact that there are few peoples of the earth whose myths deal more definitely and explicitly with social conditions than the Australians, who, while far more advanced than was once supposed, yet undoubtedly occupy a very lowly place in the scale of human culture. It is this paradox which will occupy our attention for the remainder of this paper.

The narratives with which I propose especially to deal are those of the Arunta, Dieri, and other tribes of central Australia. These people narrate long and complex accounts, full of circumstantial detail, concerning beings who introduced various rites, such as circumcision and subincision, and certain implements of material culture, such as the stone knife and the bull-roarer. In general, these narratives are good examples of the kind known as culture-myth, but the point in which they are exceptional is in the prominence they give to social institutions. Not only do they give an account of the introduction of totems, but they even account for the institution of so purely social an institution as exogamy. From two widely separated parts of the continent Howitt [19] records myths dealing with the formation of moieties or clans, while accounts of the institution of marriage regulations occur also in the narratives of the Arunta recorded by Spencer and Gillen and by Strehlow. These are elements of the social order so fundamental and so familiar to those who practise them that they seem the most unlikely subjects for myth. Widespread as is the institution of exogamy among those of rude culture, I know of few other examples [20] of native narratives, mythical or otherwise, dealing with its origin, and it is therefore most necessary to inquire why they should occur among the aborigines of Australia.

In the search for motives which will explain the prominence of social forms in the narratives of the Australians, a fact which will probably occur to every one is the great complexity of their social organisation. The social arrangements of these people are so complex that it is only by prolonged and severe effort that even the trained sociologist succeeds in understanding them fully, and probably there could be counted on the fingers of one hand the sociologists who possess even an approximate mastery of their complexities. One is therefore tempted to suggest that it is this complexity which makes the social organisation of the Australians so obtrusive that it comes into the focus of direct and fully conscious attention. If this argument from our own incapacity stood alone, I should attach little importance to it. It would be the utilisation of a line of argument which I believe to be thoroughly vicious, being based on the idea that because an institution is strange and unintelligible to us, it must therefore be so to those of whose life it forms an integral part. But this argument does not stand alone. The accounts of various writers

---

[19] [Alfred W. Howitt,] *The Native Tribes of South-East Australia* [London, 1904], pp. 480, 491.

[20] As examples from Melanesia, Joseph Meier, *Mythen und Erzählungen der Küstenbewohner der Gazelle-Halbinsel* (Neu-Pommern) ([Münster i. W.,] 1909), p. 23, gives a myth of the origin of the dual organisation in New Britain; and [P. J.] Suas (["Mythes et Legendes des Indigenes des Nouvelles-Hebrides (Oceanie),"] *Anthropos*, Vol. 7, 1912, 47) records a similar account from Lepers' Island in the New Hebrides.

make it probable that the social regulations of the Australians do not work smoothly; that doubtful cases frequently arise which have to be settled by the elders; and there seems also to be little doubt that these knotty points arise, not merely in personal and concrete matters, but may involve the interpretation and even in some cases the modification of customary social regulations. So far as I am aware, the Australians are again exceptional in this respect. In places with which I have myself had to deal, the chiefs or elders or other governing element of the community often have to decide matters of fact, such as the exact relationship of persons to one another, the paternity of a child, the right of persons to land, etc., but it is most exceptional that they have to interpret or modify social regulations. The only example of which I can think is when there arises the necessity for the interpretation of the extent of the classificatory principle of relationship, and I do not know of a single instance in which there has been such deliberate modification of social regulations as seems to occur in Australia.

There is reason to believe, then, that the complexities of Australian social structure are such as to bring it frequently into focal attention, and make it a matter with an obvious and vivid interest. It is at least remarkable that a people whose customary narratives deal so largely with social matters should at the same time be one whose social structure so frequently becomes the object of definite attention and interest.

My first suggestion, then, is that social relations are prominent in the myths of Australia because these relations are so complex that they are forced more frequently and obtrusively than elsewhere into the focus of social attention, and thus acquire such interest as to arouse wonder and speculation. I have now to point out certain facts which lead me to look elsewhere for the chief motive we are seeking, though it is not improbable that the element of complexity may be one factor tending to give persistence to the narratives, even if it played no part in their formation.

Before I proceed to point out the difficulties which lead me to look further afield in my search for an explanation of the exceptional character of Australian myth, I must consider one prominent feature of Australian social mechanism. I have elsewhere [21] briefly drawn

---

[21] Address, Section H, British Association, 1911. See *Report [of the Eighty-First Meeting of the British Association for the Advancement of Science]* (1911), pp. 490-99; or *Nature,* Vol. 87 (1911), 356-60. [Ed. note: The address to which Rivers refers – "The

attention to the fact that throughout Australia there are found in combination two forms of social structure which elsewhere, as in Melanesia, are wholly distinct and apparently belong to two quite different cultures. These forms of structure are the dual organisation and the organisation in totemic clans. The dual mechanism of Australia is much more complicated than any of which we know elsewhere, having added to it the system of matrimonial classes, but, whether there be four or eight of these matrimonial classes, they remain in essence modifications of the dual system, while the totemic system seems, in many cases at any rate, to be an additional mode of social grouping.

The fact to which I wish now to call attention is that it is the totemic aspect of social life which is especially prominent in the mythical narratives of the Australians. The names of matrimonial classes occur continually as part of the general setting of the myths, but the matter with which these narratives primarily deal is the appearance and conduct of beings who had the half human, half animal features which are so characteristic of the mythical personages of totemic peoples.

I know of only one definite case in which an Australian myth gives an account of the origin of the dual system, viz. the account given to Siebert by the Wurunjerri people which has been recorded by Howitt.[22] According to this account, the Kulin, of whom the Wurunjerri form only one tribe, were told by Bunjil to divide themselves into two parts. *"Bunjil* on this side and *Waang* on that side, and *Bunjil* should marry *Waang, and Waang* marry *Bunjil."* In his account of this narrative Howitt compares it with the well-known myth of the Dieri, ignoring the fact that in the latter it was the totemic groups which were instituted either by the order of a superior being or by the commands of the elders. It is noteworthy that, though the Wurunjerri have only two moieties, one is definitely connected with a totem. There is little doubt that we have to do with a much modified social system, and this isolated example of a myth concerning the origin of the dual organisation suggests that it may be a survival of a totemic myth, the subject of which has been transferred to the dual system.

In another case in which the matrimonial classes are concerned,

---

Ethnological Analysis of Culture" – was also reprinted in W. H. R. Rivers, *Psychology and Ethnology,* ed. G. Elliot Smith, New York, 1926, pp. 120-40.]

　[22] *Op. cit. [Report],* p. 491.

the evidence is conflicting. According to Spencer and Gillen,[23] the four class names of the Arunta were first conferred by certain Ulla-kupera or little hawk men, these Ullakupera men already belonging to these classes.[24] It is expressly stated that it was the names, Panun-ga, Bulthara, Purula, and Kumara, which were conferred by the visi-tors, and the narrative does not say that these people instituted the classes, much less the dual organisation which underlies them.

The narratives recorded by Strehlow[25] give a somewhat different account. In one place[26] it is said that, when the *rella manerinja* or *intarinja* (the *Inapertwa* of Spencer and Gillen) were first visited by the *altjirangamitjina* (the Alcheringa ancestors of Spencer and Gillen), they were already divided into eight classes. Later[27] it is stated that, when Mangarkunjerkunja, whose totem was a fly-catching lizard, came from the north, he instituted the rules of marriage between the classes, which, it is again stated, had been already distinguished from the beginning.

Taking the accounts of Strehlow and of Spencer and Gillen to-gether, it seems clear that the narratives do not give an account of the formation of the dual system or of the matrimonial classes, but of some change in the functions of this social grouping in the regu-lation of marriage.

The position to which we have now been led is that, when Aus-tralian myth deals with the origin of social institutions, it is usually the totemic system which forms the special topic of the narrative, and not the dual system and matrimonial classes which seem to form the essential basis of the social structure. This suggests that Austra-lian totemism has become the subject of myth, not through its social importance but for some other reason, and for this other reason we have not far to seek. I suggest that it is the magico-religious impor-tance of totemism, and not its social functions, which have made it so exceptionally and prominently the subject of Australian myth. If so, it will follow that the preoccupation of Australian narrative with social forms is largely apparent rather than real, an appearance due to the exceptional development of the magico-religious aspect of totemism in Australia.

---

[23] *The Native Tribes of Central Australia*, p. 396.
[24] *Op. cit.*, p. 394.
[25] [Carl Strehlow,] *Mythen, Sagen und Märchen des Aranda-Stammes in Zentral-Austra-lien* (Frankfurt-am-Main, 1907).
[26] *Op. cit.*, p. 3.
[27] *Op. cit.*, p. 6.

Even, however, if it be conceded that the prominence of social forms in Australia is a secondary result of the close connection of these social forms with magico-religious functions, we are still left with the fact that Australian myth does not deal solely with the magico-religious aspect of totemism, but that its purely social aspect occurs explicitly as the direct subject of myth. We cannot get over the fact that, even though the social side of totemism may be subsidiary, it yet has a social side which is the subject of myth. Further, we have the fact that Australian myth has not altogether passed over the dual organisation and matrimonial classes which have, so far as we know, a more purely social function. Though I have lightened my task by bringing in the magico-religious importance of totemism as the main motive for its prominence in myth, I have not disposed of the whole problem, but am still left with the necessity of explaining how the social aspect of totemism and the purely social dual system have come to be subjects of myth.

I have now to point out a condition which would make social forms such an object of attention, and even of mystery and wonder, that we may readily understand their becoming a fit subject for the mythic fancy. The statement on which I have hitherto relied, that social structure is too familiar to become the subject of myth, is only true so long as a people remains homogeneous and undisturbed by outside influence. If the social system of the Australians has been the result of a process of development working itself out within a homogeneous people, I cannot believe that there would ever have arisen myths so intimately associated with social institutions as those of the Arunta and other Central Australian tribes. If, on the other hand, the Australians are not a homogeneous people, but if their social institutions have arisen through a blend of widely different forms of culture belonging to different peoples, then there would be full opportunity for wonder and mystery such as are necessary to set in action the mythic fancy.

Imagine a society founded on the simple dual principle coming into contact with a people organised in totemic clans and having as a fundamental part of their psychology the belief in the identity of certain groups of men with certain kinds of beast or plant. Here we have every ground for curiosity amounting to wonder and for a sense of mystery amounting to awe. To the non-totemic people the social grouping founded on identity with animals must appear strange and wonderful; the totemic members of the united people would be plied

with questions concerning the motives and causes of the strange relation, and ample scope would be allowed for the play of imagination
out of which myths arise.

I have elsewhere suggested [28] that the various forms of social organisation found in Australia are the outcome of such a blend of peoples as I have just asked you to imagine, and this paper only takes
the suggestion a step further. If the narratives of the Australians are
myths, I can only see in them evidence of the blending of peoples; it
may be of peoples possessing widely different forms of totemism, or
it may be of a totemic people with one to whom relations with
totemic animals and plants were altogether new and strange.

At this point I must return to the creation-myths which seemed
to furnish so great an obstacle to the acceptance of the generalisation
that man does not make myths about the familiar. Here, again, I
believe that the explanation lies in the complexity of culture. So long
as mankind lives undisturbed, so long will his own existence and that
of the earth on which he lives form such a part of the established and
constant order of his life that his imagination will be untouched. If,
however, men come from elsewhere, and especially if these have
physical features and language different from his own, immediately
will mystery and wonder be aroused. Myths will arise, or, if the
strangers have a culture of which creation-myths form part, these will
be transferred and transmitted and become part of the permanent
heritage of the people.

It is noteworthy that creation-myths occur among the Australians,
and that they are intimately blended with the narratives in which the
description of social relations plays so prominent a part. In this combination of social myths with those accounting for the creation of
man himself I see only another indication of the complexity of Australian culture.

So far I have assumed without question that the narratives of the
Arunta and other tribes of central Australia are myths, the pure
product of the human imagination, serving to account for certain of
their social institutions and customs. From a study of myths having
natural phenomena as their subject I was led to formulate the principle that man does not make myths about the familiar and the
uniform, but rather about that which is exceptional and inconstant.
Then, applying this principle to myths having social conditions as

---

[28] *Loc. cit.*

their subject, I have tried to show that, in so far as such social conditions are the subject of myth in Australia, they can only be fully explained on the assumption that Australian society is complex and has arisen through the mixtures of peoples possessing different forms of social organisation. I suppose it to have been the sense of mystery aroused in one people by the social practices of another which acted as the seed and fertiliser of the mythic fancy.

It will follow that, if the Australian narratives are myths, they are not empty and meaningless fancies, but have a very definite sociological significance. If the principle which I have formulated is correct, Australian mythology provides clear evidence of a social condition of fundamental importance, the complex nature of Australian culture.

If, then, the Australian narratives are myths, they possess definite sociological significance. There remains to be considered the possibility that they are not myths. In an early part of this paper I pointed out an important feature which differentiates myths dealing with social conditions from those which have natural phenomena as their subject. In the case of narratives which give an account of social conditions, it is always possible that we have to deal, not with myths, but with historical traditions. I have now to consider this possibility.

All the narratives of central Australia with which I have been dealing have a remarkable similarity of content. All of them give an account of beings, coming from the north, who introduced certain elements of the material and magico-religious culture and modified the social institutions. It is a remarkable fact that the content of the narratives should thus point unmistakably to just such a mixture of cultures as I have been led to postulate on the assumption that the narratives are myths. I do not now propose to discuss how far the Australian narratives are historical or mythical, or to what extent they are compounded of both elements. I content myself with pointing out that, whether these narratives be historical traditions or myths, they lead to the same conclusion, the complexity of Australian culture. If the opponents of such complexity reject the view that these narratives are historical traditions, they still have to face the position it has been my purpose to establish this evening. These narratives are either historical or mythical, and, whichever alternative be chosen, we are led to the complexity of Australian culture. The opponents of this complexity can only escape from the dilemma by denying one or both of the two main principles on which my argument is based, viz. the fundamental character of social structure, and the failure of the familiar to arouse the mythic fancy.

There may be some who will accept this complexity and yet hold that it may have arisen through conditions present within Australia itself. It is possible that widely different forms of social organisation may have evolved in different parts of Australia, and that, when one of these was carried from one part of the continent to another by a movement of people, it seemed sufficiently strange to strike the imagination and become the subject of myth. It would be beyond the scope of this paper to consider this possibility, nor can I now attempt to develop the lessons to be learnt from the Australian narratives if their sociological significance be accepted. The object of this paper has been to formulate a principle to guide us in the study of social myth in general, and I have only chosen the Australians as my example because social myth seemed to be so well developed among them. I must leave for another occasion the inquiry into the exact nature of the social complexity which is indicated by the Australian narratives.

I cannot refrain, however, from concluding my paper with a suggestion that the main conclusion I have reached may furnish the solution of a problem which I used to introduce my subject. One of the grounds on which Mr. Lang rejects the historicity of Arunta myth[29] is that, as soon as the *Inapertwa,* or "undifferentiated animated bulks," became fully formed human beings with totems, they found themselves in possession of the distinction between elder and younger brother. The story runs that a number of newly made men and women were killed and eaten by certain evil beings called *Oruncha.* One man who had escaped the slaughter proceeded to search for his *okilia* or elder brother, and, when he had found his head, was able to bring him back to life. "How can we take as historical evidence," says Mr. Lang, "fables which transplant, into the first dawn of humanity, the terminology of the present classificatory system?" So long as we regard the narrative as an indigenous account of the origin or creation of mankind, so long will it be contradictory and not to be explained save as the uncontrolled and meaningless product of the rude imagination. If, on the other hand, the narrative records, though in mythical form, the settlement of one people among another who, though far inferior to the strangers in material culture and intelligence, yet possessed the classificatory system of relationship, it is no longer obscure or contradictory, but one which will, I hope, fit in with and confirm other results of the ethnological analysis of Australian culture.

---

[29] *Loc. cit.,* p. 119.

The Interpretation of Andamanese Customs
and Beliefs: Myths and Legends*[1]

A. R. RADCLIFFE-BROWN

I HAVE explained some of the more important of the legends as being expressions or statements of the social value of natural phenomena. The alternation of day and night, for example, affects the life of the society in a certain definite manner and this gives rise to a certain way of thinking and feeling about the phenomenon in question. These thoughts and feelings, however, remain vague and without fixity until they are formulated and expressed either in the form of some definite rule of behaviour, such as the prohibition against noise while the cicada is singing, or in some concrete statement, such as that afforded by the legend of the origin of night. Similarly the legends relating to the origin of fire or the saving of the fire during the flood serve to give definite and permanent form to the vague feelings that result from the way in which the possession of fire affects the social life. Finally, I have tried to show that the myths relating to *Biliku* and *Tarai* are nothing but the expression in concrete form of the ideas and feelings that result from the effects of the weather and the seasons on the life of the Andaman Islanders. From these examples I now propose to draw a general conclusion. All the legends, I wish to maintain, are simply the expression in concrete form of the feelings and ideas aroused by things of all kinds

*Reprinted from *The Andaman Islanders* (Cambridge, 1922), Chapter VI, pp. 376-405, by permission of the Cambridge University Press.

[1] Ed. note: The excerpt selected for reprinting in this volume consists of slightly less than one half of Chapter VI of *The Andaman Islanders*. The first 46 pages of the chapter have not been included.

as the result of the way in which these things affect the moral and social life of the Andaman Islanders. In other words the legends have for their function to express the social values of different objects,—to express in general the system of social values that is characteristic of the Andaman social organisation. To justify this general statement it will be necessary to show how it comes about that these representations are expressed in the form of myths and legends dealing with the ancestors and with such anthropomorphic beings as *Biliku* and *Tarai*.

Throughout the myths we meet with examples of what I have called the personification of natural phenomena. It is now necessary to give a more exact definition of this term. By it I mean the association of a natural phenomenon with the idea of a person in such a way that the characteristics of the phenomenon may be regarded as though they were actions or characteristics of the person. The simplest form is that in which the phenomenon itself is spoken of and thought of as if it were an actual person. Thus the sun and the moon are spoken of as Lady Sun and Sir Moon. Similarly, in the North Andaman, the night is personified and is called Lady Night *(Mimi Bat)*. In many cases of personification however, while the person may or may not possess the same name as the phenomenon, the latter is said to be produced by the former. Thus, in the North Andaman, *Ele* is the name of the lightning, and *Ele* is spoken of as a person; yet, if we enquire further, we are told that *Ele* (the person) produces the lightning by shaking his leg. A somewhat similar case is that of *Biliku* and *Tarai*. These two beings are said to produce the winds that blow from the different quarters of the compass. But when we enquire as to the names of the winds, we find that in the South Andaman *(A-Pučikwar* tribe) the S.W. wind is called *Teria,* and the other winds are all called *Bilik*. Thus the name of the person is also used as the name of the phenomenon of which he is (in the phraseology here used) the personification. In the North Andaman we find a difference, the winds being called "the *Biliku* wind" and "the *Tarai* wind." It is necessary to insist on this translation of the native *Biliku boto* and *Tarai boto*. We should expect, if *Biliku* were simply a person who produced the winds, that the latter would be called "the wind of *Biliku,"* possessive form *(Biliku ičo boto)* being used, but this is not so, and the phrase habitually used can only be properly translated "the *Biliku* wind" just as we might say "the north wind." Thus, even in the North Andaman *Biliku* and *Tarai* are used as the names of the two chief winds.

In all these cases, sun and moon, *Biliku* and *Tarai,* etc., I propose
to use the term personification, as being the most convenient and not
liable to be misunderstood after having been carefully defined. We
have now to seek an explanation of this process of personification.
A great deal has been written on the subject of personification in
mythology, and it is therefore not without diffidence that I venture
to put forward an explanation which can only be very briefly stated
in this place and would require for its full exhibition a lengthy psychological explanation.

An insight into the process of personification is afforded by considering our own use of figurative language. We talk of the angry
storm, the raging sea. In such cases we allow ourselves for a moment
to regard the natural phenomenon as if it were a person or the action
of a person, and we do not even trouble distinctly to express the "as
if." We use such phrases in order to attain a more forcible expression
of our thoughts and feelings. How is it that such expressions succeed
in the purpose for which they are used?

The reason would seem to be that our knowledge and understanding of persons is much more intimate than our knowledge of things.
The fact that we are able, by the action of sympathy, to know what
persons with whom we are in contact are feeling, gives us an understanding of them that we can never reach with inanimate objects.

In all human society the most important elements of the experience of the individual are due to his relations with other persons.
In the development of the emotional life of the child, persons inter-
vene at every turn, and there is thus built up a system of sentiments
and representations which forms the very foundation of the individual's affective life. In other words the first organised experience
that the individual attains is all connected with persons and their
relations to himself. This early experience provides a basis on which
we may and do organise later experiences. The perception of the
leaping waves and lashing spray of a sea in tempest arouses in us a
vague emotional reaction, but it is an experience that we have not
learned to formulate exactly. The feeling awakened in us is, so to
speak, unclassified, there is no exact word by which we can express
it. We therefore fall back upon that system of affective experiences
that have been classified, and for which we do have adequate words,
and we apply the word "angry" to the scene before us. At the utter-
ance of the word, with its appeal to infantile memories and to the
long series of experiences that have been associated with it, the emo-

tion becomes more definite, if not more intense. We are thus enabled
to classify our present experience, to associate it with past experiences that have been arranged in our minds in an organised system,
and to find a place for it in that system.

Applying this to the case of the myths we must first of all note
that the Andaman Islander has no interest in nature save in so far as
it directly affects the social life. Scientific and artistic interest in
nature are products of civilisation. The Andaman Islander has no
desire to understand the processes of nature as a scientist would wish
to do, nor has he any conception of nature as a subject of esthetic
contemplation. Natural phenomena affect him immediately by their
influence on his own life and on the life of his fellows, and are
thereby the source of a number of emotional experiences. In order
to express these he has to make use of that part of his own experience that is already thoroughly organised, namely, that relating to
the actions of one person as affecting another or as affecting the
society. Only in this way is he able to organise his experiences arising
from the processes of nature, to classify and render definite the vague
impressions that are aroused in him. He interprets nature in terms of
the world with which he is most familiar, the world of persons, being
enabled to do so by the presence within him of a regulated and
definite body of experience which he has derived from his relations
with persons from the time of his first awakening to the consciousness of the external world.

There is a parallelism here, as in many other matters, between the
psychological development of the individual and that of the race. The
fundamental need for the child is to learn to accommodate himself
to his environment. In this environment by far the most important
objects are persons—parents and other children—and the first business
of the growing child is to learn to adapt his actions to the requirements of this intercourse with persons. This is so overwhelmingly
important that the other need (of adapting himself to inanimate
objects) is quite overshadowed by it. The child has to make experi-
ments and observations upon persons, to learn how they will act. He
meets with such a phenomenon as anger, for example, the anger of a
parent, or of another child, and by means of a succession of experiences he comes to a satisfactory understanding of this particular
thing, and what it means with reference to himself and his actions.
This notion of the anger of a parent becomes the nucleus around
which is organised the experience of similar phenomena. In play or

sometimes in earnest, the child treats all sorts of inanimate objects and events connected with them as if they were persons or the actions of persons. By this means, and by this means alone, he is able to exercise himself in his newly acquired experience and to extend and organise it yet further.

In the history of the race the development of society depends upon the organisation of personal relations. The task of man in primitive society is therefore similar to the task of the child. The needs of his life compel him above everything else to devote himself to organising that part of his experience that relates to the actions of persons upon one another; all else is subordinated to this supreme need; and just as the child organises and develops his experience by treating inanimate objects as if they were persons in such a way that we can hardly tell if he is in play or in earnest, so primitive man, in exactly the same way, organises and develops his social experience by conceiving the whole universe as if it were the interaction of personal forces.

This explanation of the nature of personification helps us to understand some of the Andamanese beliefs. Natural phenomena such as the alternation of day and night, the changes of the moon, the procession of the seasons, and variations of the weather, have important effects on the welfare of the society. The latter, in so far as it is regulated from within, depends on the adaptation of persons to one another. Men must learn to live in harmony, to sacrifice their own desires at times to the needs of others, to avoid occasions of giving offence, and not readily to give way to anger when offence is given. The Andaman Islander represents this fundamental law of the society as though it were the fundamental law of the whole universe. When any evil befalls the society it is as though some personal power were in question, as though some one were angry at some offence. Thus the moon and *Biliku* are represented as persons who can be offended and whose anger has unpleasant results. Conversely when all goes well it is because there is harmony or solidarity between men and the nature beings which affect men's lives. In a word, the forces with which the Andaman Islander is most familiar as affecting his welfare are those of solidarity and opposition; it is solidarity that maintains the harmony of social life, opposition that destroys it. The forces of nature in so far as they affect the society are therefore represented as being of the same nature; there can be either solidarity or opposition between men and nature; the former leads to well-being, the latter to misfortune.

Thus the personification of natural phenomena is one of the methods by which the Andaman Islander projects into the world of nature the moral forces that he experiences in the society. . . . Perhaps, rather than speaking of it as a projection of moral forces into nature, we should regard it as a process of bringing within the circle of the social life those aspects of nature that are of importance to the well-being of the society, making the moon and the monsoons a part of the social order and therefore subject to the same moral forces that have sway therein.

The personification of natural phenomena is not, however, the only method by which their social value can be expressed. The *Akar-Bale* legend of the origin of day and night . . . expresses the social value of the alternation of light and darkness by means of a story of how it originated in the time of the ancestors. If we seek to understand all that this legend means we must ask why the Andaman Islanders believe in the existence of the ancestors, and why they attribute to them the characteristics that are exhibited in the stories they tell about them. The ground of the belief in the ancestors is to be found in the existence of a sentiment fundamental in all human society, which I shall call the feeling of tradition. When an Andaman Islander is asked the question "Why do you do so and so?" he very frequently replies "Because our fathers did so before us." This answer expresses in its simplest form the feeling of tradition. In all his actions, in the way he obtains and cooks his food, in the way in which he makes his various implements and weapons, in the moral and ritual customs that he is required to observe, the native acts in accordance with tradition. If he should ever feel inclined to deviate from it he finds himself in conflict with a powerful compulsive force. In tradition, therefore, the individual is aware of a force stronger than himself, to which he must submit whether he will or not. Further, he is aware that the power which he possesses, as a member of the society, whereby he is able to face the hostile or at best indifferent forces of nature and provide himself with food and maintain himself in security and happiness, is not simply a product of his own personality, but is derived by him from the past. Towards this past, therefore, on which his own life so obviously depends, he feels a grateful dependence. So long as he acts in conformity with tradition he can enjoy safety and happiness, because he is relying on something much greater than his own qualities of mind and body.

To put the matter in a few words, the individual finds himself in relation with an ordered system—the social order—to which he has to adapt himself. The two chief moments in his affective attitude towards that order are his sense of his own dependence upon it and of the need of conforming to its requirements in his actions. It is this,—his sense of his own relation to the social order,—that the Andaman Islander expresses in the legends about the ancestors, which recount how that order came into existence as the result of actions of anthropomorphic beings.

Some of the legends recount the invention of weapons or implements or the discovery of the uses of natural objects. In one of the North Andaman stories it is said that all the weapons and implements now used by men were invented by the first man, whose name, *Jutpu,* probably means "alone," i.e., the man who was at first by himself. This first man made himself a wife from the nest of the white ant. The regulated society of the ants, and the numerous population that a nest contains, give this story its symbolic meaning.

Besides what may be called general culture legends, of which the story of *Jutpu* is an example, there are several special culture legends relating to various discoveries and inventions, such as the tale of how the use of yams for food was first discovered, or that which tells how the monitor lizard discovered quartz and scarified himself with it. By means of these legends the Andaman Islander expresses his sense of his own dependence on the past. He pictures a time when the social order as it now is had not begun, or was just beginning; the knowledge he now possesses was then being acquired, the weapons he uses were being invented, the moral and ritual laws that he obeys were in process of being formulated.

It is obvious that the Andaman Islander cannot regard the ancestors as being persons exactly like himself, for they were responsible for the establishment of the social order to which he merely conforms and of which he has the advantage. He says, therefore, that they were bigger men than himself, meaning by this that they were bigger mentally or spiritually, rather than physically, that they were endowed with powers much greater than those even of the medicine-men of the present time. This explains the magical powers that are attributed to many, or indeed to all, of the ancestors; the belief in the existence in the past of men or beings endowed with what we may almost call supernatural powers is the inevitable result of the way in which the man of to-day feels towards the men of the past on whose inventions and discoveries he is dependent for his daily nourishment.[2]

Besides the social order there is another, the order of nature, which is constantly acting upon the social order. To this also the individual has to adapt himself, and his knowledge of how to do so is equally derived from the past. The order of nature only affects him through the social order, and the two therefore necessarily seem to him merely two parts of one whole,— the order of the universe. In the legends he tells how not only the social order but also the order of nature came into existence; an example is the story of the origin of night.

The Andaman Islander finds himself in an ordered world, a world subject to law, controlled by unseen forces. The laws are not to him what natural laws are to the scientist of to-day, they are rather of the nature of moral laws. He recognizes only one meaning of the word right and of the word wrong; right action is that which is in conformity with law, wrong action is that in opposition to the law; it is wrong to give way to anger, it is wrong to kill a cicada, or to have a bright light in camp when the moon is rising in the third quarter, and it is wrong also to try and use unsuitable material for an implement or weapon. Wrong actions always lead to harm; if you use unsuitable wood for your bow it will break and your labour be wasted; if you kill a cicada it will rain heavily; if you give way to anger readily you will earn the dislike of your fellows that may some day lead to your undoing. Right and wrong mean acting in accordance with the laws of the world or in opposition to them, and this means acting in accordance with or in opposition to custom. Custom and law are indeed here two words for the same thing.

The forces of the world, as the Andaman Islander conceives them, are not the blind mechanical forces of modern science: rather are they moral forces. Their action upon human beings is not only to be witnessed in external events, but is to be experienced in the man's own consciousness or conscience. He feels within himself their compulsion when he would run counter to them, and their support when he leans

---

[2] In the last chapter it was shown that the attribution of magical force to such things as foods and human bones is simply the means by which the social values of these things are represented and recognized. Similarly, here the magical powers of the ancestors are simply the representation of their social value, i.e., of the social value of tradition.

upon them. The law of the world, then, is a moral law, its forces are moral forces, its values moral values; its order is a moral order.

This view of the world is the immediate and inevitable result of the experience of man in society. It is a philosophy not reached by painful intellectual effort, by the searching out of meanings and reasons and causes; it is impressed upon him in all the happenings of his life, is assumed in all his actions; it needs only to be formulated. And the argument of this chapter has been that it is as the expression or formulation of this view of the world as an order regulated by law that the legends have their meaning, fulfil their function.

The legends of the Andamanese then, as I understand them, set out to give an account of how the order of the world came into existence. But the Andaman Islander has no interest in any part of it except in so far as it affects his own life. He is interested in the procession of the seasons or the alternation of day and night, or the phases of the moon, only in so far as these things have effects upon the community. In other words he is interested in natural phenomena only in so far as such phenomena are really parts of the social order. This I have expressed earlier in the chapter [3] by saying that the legends deal not with all aspects of natural phenomena but only with their social values.

A fundamental character of the natural order (as of the social order) is uniformity; the same processes are for ever repeated. This character of nature the legends take for granted; they assume that if a force is once set into action it will continue to act indefinitely. They assume also a period in which the present order did not exist. Anything that happened in that period has gone on happening ever since. One of the ancestors discovered how to cook yams, and men have been cooking yams in the same way down to the present day. A cicada was crushed and cried out and the night came, and since then the darkness has come every evening as soon as the cicada sings. In one of the legends the tree lizard was quarrelsome, and has remained so. Thus the legends represent the social order, including such natural phenomena as may be said to belong to it, as being due to the interaction of forces of a special character that came into existence in the beginning and have continued to act uniformly ever since. In this way they express two most important conceptions, that of uniformity (or law) and that of the dependence of the present on the past.

---

[3] Ed. note: The reference which Radcliffe-Brown makes here is to Chapter IV, "Myths and Legends," pp. 186-228, of *The Andaman Islanders*.

It is the need of expressing these two conceptions that gives the legends their function. They are not merely theoretical principles but are both intensely practical. The law of uniformity means that certain actions must be done and others not done if life is to run smoothly; any deviation from uniformity in conduct is dangerous as being contrary to the law that regulates the universe. What actions are to be done and what are to be left undone was determined once for all in the past when the present order came into existence. The knowledge of what to do and what to avoid doing is what constitutes the tradition of the society, to which every individual is required to conform.

The legends, then, set out to express and to justify these two fundamental conceptions. They do so by telling how the social order itself came into existence, and how, also, all those natural phenomena that have any bearing on the social well-being came to be as they are and came to have the relation to the society that they possess.

One group of facts that have an obvious relation to the society consists of the geographical features of the islands. The more notable features of the part of the country in which a man lives, and which he regards as his own, are intimately connected with his moral sentiments. His attachment to his group necessarily involves an attachment to the country of the group. The same sort of thing exists amongst ourselves. This attachment of the members of a group to their own country explains, I think, the part played by what may be called "local motives" in the legends of the Andamanese. Such motives are of considerable importance, of much more importance than would appear from the stories that I have transcribed.[4] The recent changes in their mode of life have had far more influence on the local organisation of the tribes than on any other part of their social organisation, and this has not been without its effect on the legends. We may say, briefly, that the local motives of the legends serve to express the social values of localities. In general each locality has its own versions of the legends, in which the events related are supposed to have taken place at some spot or other in the neighbourhood. Thus all the more prominent features of a locality are associated with the events of the legends. In some cases tales are told that explain these features as having come into existence when the ances-

---

[4] Ed. note: The transcribed stories to which Radcliffe-Brown refers are presented in Chapter IV, "Myths and Legends," pp. 186-228, of *The Andaman Islanders*. That entire chapter is largely a description of the content of the Andamanese tales.

tors were alive; a reef of rocks was formerly a canoe, for instance. A few such legends were recorded in an earlier chapter,[5] but it is probable that there were a vast number of similar tales that I did not hear. In some cases a locality has a special social value and therefore a special place in the legends. Thus *Wota-Emi* was the great meeting-place for the natives who lived on Baratang and on parts of the South Andaman and the Middle Andaman, and was also sometimes visited by the natives of the Archipelago. Consequently *Wota-Emi* is represented in the legends of the *A-Pučikwar* tribe as being the great meeting-place or dwelling-place of the ancestors. The effect of these associations between the places with which he is familiar and the events of the legendary epoch in the mind of the Andaman Islander probably is similar to the effect on ourselves of the historical associations of our own country; they serve to make him aware of his attachment to his country or to express his sense of that attachment.

There still remains a most important feature of the legends which has not yet been explained, namely the position of the animals as ancestors. Many of the actors in the legends bear the names of animals but at the same time are spoken of as though they were human beings. Many of the legends explain how some species of animal arose from some one of the ancestors who became an animal and the progenitor of the species. Thus, in the North Andaman, *Kolo* was one of the ancestors; he made wings for himself out of palm-leaves, and so was able to fly; he lived a solitary life in his home at the top of a tree, and was in the habit of stealing men's wives; in the end he became the sea-eagle, and this species still bears the name *kolo*. It is necessary to define as exactly as possible what meaning these stories have to the natives. It is not simply that the legendary person is a man with the name and some of the characteristics of an animal; nor is it simply that the legendary person is the ancestor of the species of which he bears the name. We can only adequately express the thought of the Andamanese by saying that he regards the whole species as if it were a human being. When, in the legends, he speaks of "Sea-eagle" he is thereby personifying the species in the sense in which the word personification has been used throughout this chapter; he is regarding the characteristics of the species as if they were characteristics or actions or results of actions of a person. Admittedly this is a vague description, but the vagueness is in the mental

<hr>

[5] Ed. note: The reference which Radcliffe-Brown makes here is to Chapter IV, "Myths and Legends," pp. 186-228, of *The Andaman Islanders*.

phenomenon described; the Andamanese do not, in this matter, think clearly and analyse their own thoughts. However, we can help ourselves to understand their thoughts by recalling the tales that amused us as children, in which the fox or the rabbit of the tale was an embodiment of the whole species.

The part played in the legends by any particular animal is determined either immediately or indirectly by its observable characteristics. Thus the connection of the kingfisher with fire is due to the fact that he is a fish-eating bird, and that he has a patch of bright red feathers, red being, in the Andamanese mind, always associated with fire. The other birds that are mentioned in the different versions of the fire legend either possess remarkable plumage (as the dove, and the parrot) or are fish-eating birds. The Andamanese regard fish as the fundamental human food, having only one word for "food" and "fish," and they never eat their fish raw as the kingfisher does. In the *Akar-Bale* story of the origin of the animals the tree lizard is characterised by his quarrelsomeness, and by the fact that he is very difficult to catch hold of; these are both actual characteristics of the animal itself. The crab appears in the same legend as a person with a very powerful grip, and with a hard shell to his body. The monitor lizard has his place in the legends determined by the fact that he can climb trees, run on the ground and swim in the water, and is thus equally at home at the top of the trees, on the ground, or in the creek. I have already given this as one of the reasons why he is chosen as the first ancestor of all the animals and of human beings.[6] The lizard also seems to be regarded by the Andamanese as a particularly libidinous animal, and is therefore regarded as the inventor of sexual intercourse and of procreation. Why he should have this sexual reputation I do not know.[7] The tale of how the lizard invented scarification depends on the fact that the marks on the lizard's skin bear a strong resemblance to the marks that the natives make on their own skins with sharp fragments of quartz. The position of the *Paradoxurus* or civet-cat in the stories in which she appears is due to the fact that while she can live in the trees or on the ground she cannot

---

[6] Ed. note: References are made to the monitor lizard as the first ancestor of the Andamanese on pp. 193, 196, 211, 213, and 225 of *The Andaman Islanders.*

[7] In Central Australia it is believed that if a boy who has not been initiated eats large lizards he will develop an abnormal and diseased craving for sexual intercourse ([Baldwin] Spencer and [F. J.] Gillen, *The Native Tribes of Central Australia* [London, 1899], p. 471). A friend who has observed the monitor lizard in Australia tells me that the animal fully deserves its reputation.

swim; hence, when the flood came, she fled from the water and climbed a steep hill and thus kept the fire alight. In the light of these examples we are justified, I think, in assuming that in all cases, even when the meaning is not clear, the part played by any animal in the legends is due to some actual characteristic of it.

There is thus a parallelism between the personification of natural phenomena and the personification of animal species. ...the characteristics of such beings as *Biliku* and *Tarai* are all to be explained by a consideration of the actual characteristics of the phenomena of which they are the personification (the winds) and of the phenomena immediately connected therewith. The same thing has now been shown to be true with regard to the personified animals. The process of personification is carried out in exactly the same way in the two different classes of cases. I gave as the reason for personifying natural phenomena the fact that in this way, and in this way only, the Andaman Islander is able to express the sentiments that are aroused in him by them. We must see if we can justify the personification of animals by a similar argument.

The habits of observation fostered in the mind of the Andaman Islander by his method of winning his sustenance lead him to take a lively interest in all the creatures of the jungle and the sea, about whose ways he therefore has a great store of knowledge. Every tree and plant of the forest, every bird and insect, every creature that lives in the sea or on the reef has its name. His interest, however, in the case of many of the animals has little or no relation to practical life, for he does not make use of them for food or in any other way. There is here therefore something that contradicts the fundamental assumption of the philosophy that is expressed in the legends, there is a lack of mental unity. These interests in the birds and insects are not correlated with the central mass of interests that control the Andamanese mind and give it its unity. Although his philosophy assumes that everything in which he takes an interest has some meaning in reference to his own life, yet here are things that at first sight have no such meaning. The correlation that is lacking in his experience is brought about by means of the legends; a meaning is provided for the apparently meaningless. The fundamental interest of the Andaman Islander, as of all men in primitive societies, is his interest in persons and personal relations. By regarding the animals as persons and relating stories about them he is able to correlate his interest in them with the fundamental basis of his mental life.

This explanation does not perhaps sound very satisfactory. We do not at present understand the forces that compel the normal mind to strive after unity in its experience. Let us examine the matter a little more closely. All the thoughts and feelings of the Andaman Islander (or at any rate all those that are expressed in the legends) centre in the society; for him the world is merely a stage on which the social drama is perpetually enacted. He coordinates all his thoughts, emotions, and interests around the society, and in the legends he builds up a picture showing the connection between the society and those phenomena of nature that affect it. The majority of the animals (the birds, the insects, and innumerable kinds of fish), not being used for food, or in any other way, bear no apparent relation to the social life. Yet by reason of the woodcraft developed by the necessities of his life he is compelled to take notice of these creatures and to become interested in their ways. Here, therefore, are two conflicting elements in his consciousness, (1) his belief that the whole of nature derives its meaning and interest from its relation to the society, and (2) his consciousness of an alien world (of the birds, etc.) which seems to have no direct relation to the society, and which nevertheless he cannot help being constantly aware of. The Andaman Islander, as I have stated more than once, does not possess any scientific or abstract interest in nature. He never asks himself "What is the meaning of this?" in the same way that a scientist of our own civilisation might do. He asks "What is the meaning of this thing in relation to me and my interests and feelings, and to the social life of which my life is a fragment?" It is because he does feel the need of answers to questions of this kind that the conflict we have noticed arises. This conflict has to be resolved, and there are apparently three alternatives: (1) to admit that there is a meaning in nature apart from its relation to the society, (2) to refuse to take any interest in birds and insects, (3) to explain away the apparent lack of relation. It is this third alternative that is chosen by the Andaman Islander, and there are obvious reasons why it should be so. The explanation is accomplished in a direct and simple manner. In the beginning men and animals were one; then came an event or series of events (the discovery of fire, the great flood, or a great quarrel amongst the ancestors) whereby the men and the animals became cut off from one another, to live henceforward in the same world, but separated by an unseen barrier.

The argument may be put in another way that may perhaps be

more convincing. The actual sentiment that is aroused in the mind of the native by the animals is that here is an important and interesting part of the universe that is alien to him, from which he is cut off in some strange way. It is this real sentiment, itself the inevitable result of his life and his surroundings, that is expressed in the belief in the animals as ancestors.

If this explanation be correct we should expect to find that the animals that figure in the legends are those that have no immediate social value either as food or in any other way, while on the other hand the animals that are used for food will not appear in the legends, or will occupy therein a very different place from the others. The only land animal that is regularly used for food is the pig. It is therefore a confirmation of the explanation that we find that the pig is never under any circumstances regarded as one of the ancestors, that is to say, is never personified in the same way that other animals are. One legend about the pig explains, not how the animal came into existence (that seems to be assumed), but how it acquired its senses. Another legend tells how the civet-cat persuaded some of the ancestors to play a game in which they pretended to be pigs, and they were turned into these animals. Here we are clearly dealing with something different from the ordinary process of personification, for we have not one ancestor in whom the species is personified, but a number of persons who were suddenly changed from men and women into pigs by the magical performance of the civet-cat. In the sea there are several animals that are regularly used for food. The dugong is spoken of as an ancestor in an *Akar-Bale* legend, but in the North Andaman there is a story of how the dugong originated from a pig that *Perjido* tried to roast without first disembowelling it and cutting the joints of its legs. There is also in the North Andaman a story of how turtles originated. The existence of these legends shows that the pig, the turtle and the dugong occupy a different position in the minds of the Andamanese from that of the other animals. This serves, in some measure, to confirm the explanation given above.

We may briefly consider what may be regarded as a kind of negative instance by which to test the argument. The world of the stars constitutes a part of the universe just as alien, just as devoid of apparent meaning, as that of the birds. We may ask therefore how it is that the Andaman Islanders have no star myths of the kind that are common in other primitive societies. The answer is, I think, that the Andamanese do not have their attention called to the stars. As their camps are in the dense forest there are very few occasions on which they see the sky at night. When fishing at night on the reefs or in canoes they are too busy to pay much attention to the stars. They have not learnt to relate the procession of the stars and the change of the seasons, nor have they learnt to tell the time at night from their declination. Their navigation is only along the coast and they have therefore no use for the stars as guides of direction. On the contrary, wherever we find a developed star-mythology we find that the stars are studied either as guides to navigation or journeying over-land, or as giving indications of the changes of the seasons.

We have considered all the more important aspects of the subject matter of the legends; it remains for us to turn to the form and enquire how it comes about that the representations which analysis reveals are expressed in just the way they are, in a word, why the expression takes the form of a story. It is obvious that in this place no attempt can be made to deal with the general problems of the psychology of story-telling. All that I wish to do is to point out one or two reasons why the legend is an appropriate form (perhaps we might say, the only possible form) for the expression of the view of the world that is revealed in the Andaman mythology.

The Andamanese, like other savages, have not acquired the power of thinking abstractly. All their thought necessarily deals with concrete things. Now the story form provides a means of expressing concretely what could otherwise only be put in an abstract statement. (A large part of the interpretation of the legends, as here undertaken, consists in restating the content of the legends in abstract terms.) Moreover, even if the Andaman Islanders were capable of thinking abstractly, yet, since what they need to express are not thoughts so much as feelings (not intellectual so much as affective processes), they would still need a concrete form of expression. For it is a familiar fact that the concrete has a much greater power of awakening or appealing to our feelings than has the abstract. In particular the story has ever been a popular medium by which to appeal to sentiments of all kinds.

The chief ground for the interest in stories shown by children and by savages is, I believe, that they afford the means of exercising the imagination in certain specific directions and thereby play an important part in enabling the individual to organise his experience. The course of the development of the human mind (from childhood to adolescence, and from the earliest human ancestor to ourselves) depends upon or involves the existence at certain stages of growth (and to a certain extent throughout the whole process) of a conscious egoistic interest. Mankind, to develop what we call character and conscience, must learn to take a conscious interest in himself, in his own actions, and their motives. The development of this self-consciousness in children is a process of great interest to the psychologist and has already been studied in an imperfect fashion. You have only to watch a child playing a game in which he or she enacts some imaginary part to see how such games afford a means by which the child develops and widens his interest in himself. Children, and many grown-up people (particularly during conditions of lessened mental activity), indulge in what are called daydreams, which take the form of an imaginary succession of adventures of which the dreamer is always the hero. The character of daydreams is that they are always frankly egoistic and boastful. Now this sort of interest in stories is found in the Andamanese, though not in the legends. At the end of a day a group of Andamanese may often be seen seated round a fire listening while one of them recounts adventures. The narration may be merely an exaggerated account of real happenings, but is more often purely fictitious. The narrator will tell, with few words, but with many expressive gestures, how he harpooned a turtle or shot a pig. He may, if his hearers are content to remain and listen, as they sometimes are, go on killing pig after pig for an hour or two together. The point to be noted is that these tales are always frankly egoistic and boastful, and it is for this reason that they may well be compared with the daydreams of the more civilised.

Besides this egoistic interest in stories there is another that is closely connected with it in origin and function. The necessities of social life, particularly in childhood and in primitive societies where a small number of people are constantly reacting upon one another, involve an intense degree of interest in persons and personal qualities. This interest is aroused and fostered by the constant play of personal forces in the social life. Its strength accounts, I believe, for the power of appeal to sentiments that is possessed by stories.

It is a commonplace that in many forms of play the child or the adult (and it is also true of animals) exercises faculties that are important parts of the system of habits or dispositions by which the individual adapts himself to his surroundings. We may regard the interest in stories as similar to play-interests in general. Life in society requires the individual to develop a faculty of what may be called character-estimation, whereby he may judge the motives that are likely to influence the conduct of another person. I have myself noticed that savages such as the Andaman Islanders and the Australian aborigines are as a rule good judges of character. They can quickly estimate how to adapt their conduct and conversation to the character of a person they meet for the first time. They are often excellent mimics, being able to imitate exactly the tone of voice or manner of walking or any other idiosyncrasy of a person whom they have only seen for a short time. I believe, then, that the legends of the Andamanese may be regarded as a means whereby they give exercise to their interest in human character, just as in other kinds of play they exercise other interests and faculties that are integral parts of their adaptation to their environment. By means of the personification of natural phenomena and of species of animals, and through the assumption of the existence of the ancestors and their times, they are able to develop a special kind of unwritten literature, which has for them just the same sort of appeal that much of our own literature has for us. Doubtless it is not a very polished form of art; the characterisation that it exhibits is simple and even crude; the story is not told very skilfully, and indeed the story-teller relies much on his use of expressive gesture to convey his meaning; nevertheless it does fulfil amongst the Andamanese the same sort of function that more developed literary art does in civilised society.

There remains one other matter to be dealt with briefly. I have pointed out on several occasions that the legends contain inconsistencies. Some of these only appear when the real meaning of the legend is discovered, but others are on the surface. It is clear that the Andamanese do not always apply to their legends the laws of logical consistency. It must not, however, be supposed that they are equally illogical in other matters, for this is not so. In matters of everyday practical life the Andamanese show just as much sound commonsense as the inhabitants of a civilised country. They are excellent observers of natural phenomena and are capable of putting their observations to practical use. In any attempt to explain their mythology, therefore, it is necessary to show why in this sphere they do not apply their powers of reasoning. We can understand this when we recall the purpose of the legends as here described, which is, not to give rational explanations, but to express sentiments. When there are two alternative rational explanations of a phenomenon between which we cannot definitely choose we say that either one or other is probably true. In those mental processes in which the purpose is to find a symbolic expression for sentiments or desires, the *either-or* relation is inadmissible owing to the very nature of the thought-process itself. If two expressions of the same sentiment are present, both equally adequate, we must either reject one of them or by making use of both on different occasions admit the possibility of inconsistency. Where the inconsistency becomes more or less obvious we expect the reason to step in and insist that a choice shall be made. But a mind intent on expressing certain feelings, faced with two alternative and equally satisfactory but inconsistent symbols, will hesitate to choose between them even at the command of the desire for logical consistency. It will cling as long as possible to both of them. This is just what the Andaman Islander seems to do in his mythology. The view of lightning as a person who shakes his leg seems to express in some way certain notions of the natives about the lightning. The alternative explanation of lightning as a fire-brand thrown by *Biliku* also satisfies in some way his need of expressing the impressions that the phenomena make upon him. In spite of the inconsistency he clings to both symbols as best he can.

The very existence of inconsistencies of this kind proves without any doubt that the mental processes underlying the legends of the Andamanese are not similar to those that we ourselves follow when we attempt to understand intelligently the facts of nature and of life, but rather are to be compared to those that are to be found in dreams and in art,—processes of what might conveniently be called symbolic thought. It would perhaps hardly be necessary to point this out were it not that many ethnologists still try to interpret the beliefs of savages as being the result of attempts to *understand* natural facts, such as dreams, death, birth, etc. Such writers assume that the savage is impelled by the same motive that so strongly dominates themselves, the desire to understand,—scientific curiosity—and that such beliefs as animism or totemism are of the nature of scientific hypotheses invented to explain the facts of dreaming and of death on the one hand and of conception and birth on the other. If this view of the nature of primitive thought were correct it would be impossible to conceive how such inconsistencies as those that we meet with among the Andamanese could be permitted. On the view that the myths of primitive societies are merely the result of an endeavour to express certain ways of thinking and feeling about the facts of life which are brought into existence by the manner in which life is regulated in society, the presence of such inconsistencies need not in the least surprise us, for the myths satisfactorily fulfil their function not by any appeal to the reasoning powers of the intellect but by appealing, through the imagination, to the mind's affective dispositions.

The thesis of this chapter has been that the legends are the expression of social values of objects of different kinds. By the social value of an object is meant the way in which it affects the life of the society, and therefore, since every one is interested in the welfare of the society to which he belongs, the way in which it affects the social sentiments of the individual. The system of social values of a society obviously depends upon the manner in which the society is constituted, and therefore the legends can only be understood by constant reference to the mode of life of the Andamanese.

The legends give us in the first place a simple and crude valuation of human actions. Anger, quarrelsomeness, carelessness in observing ritual requirements are exhibited as resulting in harm. This is the moral element of the stories strictly so called, and is to be observed in many of them. The young men who failed to observe the rules laid down for those who have recently been through one of the initiation ceremonies were turned to stone. The quarrelsomeness of the lizard led to the ancestors being turned into animals. The bad temper of one of the ancestors resulted in darkness covering the earth, or in a great cyclone in which many were destroyed.

Secondly, the legends as a whole give expression to the social value of the past, of all that is derived from tradition, whether it be the knowledge by which men win their sustenance, or the customs that they observe. In the wonderful times of the ancestors all things were ordered, all necessary knowledge was acquired, and the rules that must guide conduct were discovered. It remains for the individual of the present only to observe the customs with which his elders are familiar.

The legends of a man's own tribe serve also to give a social value to the places with which he is familiar. The creeks and hills that he knows, the camping sites at which he lives, the reefs and rocks that act as landmarks by reason of any striking feature they may present, are all for him possessed of a historic interest that makes them dear to him. The very names, in many cases, recall events of the far-off legendary epoch.

Again, many of the legends express the social value of natural phenomena. By reference to *Biliku* and *Tarai,* for instance, the native can express what he feels with respect to the weather and the seasonal changes that so profoundly affect the common life. Finally, in the legends he is able to express what he feels about the bright plumaged birds and the other creatures with which he is constantly meeting in the jungles, which are a source of perennial interest, and are yet so clearly a part of the world cut off from himself and his life, having no immediately discernible influence upon his welfare.

This system of social values, or rather this system of sentiments, that we find expressed in the legends is an essential part of the life of the Andamanese; without it they could not have organised their social life in the way they have. Moreover the sentiments in question need to be regularly expressed in some way or another if they are to be kept alive and passed on from one generation to another. The legends, which are related by the elders to the young folk, are one of the means (the various ceremonial customs analysed in the last chapter being another) by which they are so expressed, and by which their existence is maintained.

Although the term "social value" has been used as a convenient expression, yet the meaning of the legends might be expressed in other ways. We may say, for instance, that they give a representation of the world as regulated by law. The conception of law which they reveal is not, however, that to which we are accustomed when we think of natural law. We may perhaps adequately state the Andaman notion by saying that moral law and natural law are not distinguished from one another. The welfare of the society depends upon right actions; wrong actions inevitably lead to evil results. Giving way to anger is a wrong action, as being a cause of social disturbance. In the legends the catastrophes that overwhelmed the ancestors are in many instances represented as being caused by some one giving way to anger. There is a right way and a wrong way to set about making such a thing as a bow. We should explain this by saying that the right way will give a good serviceable weapon, whereas the wrong way will give an inferior or useless one. The Andaman Islander tends to look at the matter from a different angle; the right way is right because it is the one that has been followed from time immemorial, and any other way is wrong, is contrary to custom, to law. Law, for the Andaman Islander, means that there is an order of the universe, characterised by absolute uniformity; this order was established once for all in the time of the ancestors, and is not to be interfered with, the results of any such interference being evil, ranging from merely minor ills such as disappointment or discomfort to great calamities. The law of compensation is absolute. Any deviation from law or custom will inevitably bring its results, and inversely any evil that befalls must be the result of some lack of observance. The legends reveal to our analysis a conception of the universe as a moral order.

Here I must conclude my attempt to interpret the customs and beliefs of the Andaman Islanders, but in doing so I wish to point out, though indeed it must already be fairly obvious, that if my interpretation be correct, then the meaning of the customs of other primitive peoples is to be discovered by similar methods and in accordance with the same psychological principles. It is because I have satisfied myself of the soundness of these methods and principles, by applying them to the interpretation of other cultures, that I put forward the hypotheses of these two chapters with an assurance that would not perhaps be justified if I relied solely on a study of the Andamanese. To put the matter in another way, I have assumed a certain working hypothesis, and I have shown that on the basis of this hypothesis there can be built up a satisfactory explanation of the customs and beliefs of the Andamanese. But the hypothesis is of such a nature, stating or involving as it does certain sociological or psychological laws and principles, that if it be true for one primitive people it must be true for others, and indeed, with necessary modifications, must be true of all human society. Such a hypothesis, it is obvious, cannot be adequately tested by reference only to one limited set of facts, and it will therefore be necessary, if it is to become something more than a hypothesis, to test its application over a wider range of ethnological facts.

The matter is so important that it is necessary, even at the risk of wearisome repetition, to give a final statement of the hypothesis that, in this chapter and the last, has been applied to and tested by the facts known to us concerning the Andaman Islanders.

In an enquiry such as this, we are studying, I take it, not isolated facts, but a "culture," understanding by that word the whole mass of institutions, customs and beliefs of a given people. For a culture to exist at all, and to continue to exist, it must conform to certain conditions. It must provide a mode of subsistence adequate to the environment and the existing density of population; it must provide for the continuance of the society by the proper care of children; it must provide means for maintaining the cohesion of the society. All these things involve the regulation of individual conduct in certain definite ways; they involve, that is, a certain system of moral customs.

Each type of social organisation has its own system of moral customs, and these could be explained by showing how they serve to maintain the society in existence. Such an explanation would be of the psychological, not of the historical type; it would give not the cause of origin of any custom, but its social function. For example it is easy to see the function of the very strong feelings of the Andamanese as to the value of generosity in the distribution of food and of energy in obtaining it, and as to the highly reprehensible nature of laziness and greediness (meaning by the latter word, eating much when others have little). It has only been by the cultivation of these virtues, or by the eradication of the opposite vices, that the Andaman society has maintained itself in existence in an environment where food is only obtainable by individual effort, where it cannot be preserved from day to day, and where there are occasional times of scarcity. It could be shown, to take a further example, how the manner in which the life of the family is organised is closely related to certain fundamental social needs. If we were attempting an explanation of the Andamanese culture as a whole and in all its details it would be necessary to examine all the moral customs of the people and show their relations one to another and to the fundamental basis on which the society is organised.

The necessary regulation of conduct in a given society depends upon the existence in each individual of an organised system of sentiments. That system of sentiments or motives will clearly be different in different cultures, just as the system of moral rules is different in societies of different types. Yet there is, so to speak, a general substratum that is the same in all human societies. No matter how the society may be organised there must be in the individual a strong feeling of attachment to his own group, to the social division (nation, village, clan, tribe, caste, or what not) to which he belongs. The particular way in which that sentiment is revealed in thought and action will depend upon the nature of the group to which it refers. Similarly, no society can exist without the presence in the minds of its members of some form or other of the sentiment of moral obligation—the sentiment that certain things must be done, certain other things must not be done, because those are right, good, virtuous, these are wrong, bad, vicious or sinful. Further, though perhaps less important, yet not less necessary, there is the sentiment of dependence in its various forms—dependence on others, on the society, on tradition or custom.

For a culture to exist, then, these sentiments (and others connected with them, that need not be enumerated) must exist in the minds of individuals in certain definite forms, capable of influencing action in the direction required to maintain the cohesion of the society on its actual basis of organisation. This, we may say, is the social function of these sentiments.

Leaving aside altogether the question of how sentiments of these kinds come into existence, we may note that they involve the existence of an experience of a particular type. The individual experiences the action upon himself of a power or force—constraining him to act in certain ways not always pleasant, supporting him in his weakness, binding him to his fellows, to his group. This force is clearly something not himself—something outside of him therefore, and yet equally clearly it makes itself felt not as mere external compulsion or support, but as something within his own consciousness—within himself, therefore. If we would give a name to this force we can only call it the moral force of society. The very existence of a human society, the argument has run, necessarily involves the existence of this actual experience of a moral force, acting through the society upon the individual, and yet acting within his own consciousness. The experience, then, is there, but it does not follow that the primitive man can analyse his own experience; it is obvious enough that such analysis is beyond him. Still the experience does lead him to form certain notions or representations, and it is possible to show how these notions are psychologically related to the experience of a moral force.

The experience of this moral force comes to the individual in definite concrete experiences only. We first learn to experience our own dependence in our dealings with our parents, and thus we derive the concrete form in which we clothe our later adult feeling of our dependence upon our God. Or, to take an example from the vast number provided by the customs of the Andamanese, the Andaman Islander, like other savages, the main concern of whose lives is the getting and eating of food, inevitably finds his experience of a moral force most intimately associated with the things he uses for food. Inevitably, therefore, he regards food as a substance in which, in some way, the moral force is inherent, since it is often through food that the force actually affects him and his actions. . . . From the analysis . . . of different customs and beliefs it should be obvious that the way in which the Andaman Islander regards all the things that influence the social life is due to the way in which they are associated with his experience of the moral force of the society.

In this way there arises in the mind of primitive man, as the result of his social life and the play of feeling that it involves, the more or less crude and undefined notion of a power in society and in nature having certain attributes. It is this power that is responsible for all conditions of social euphoria or dysphoria because in all such conditions the power itself is actually experienced. It is the same power that compels the individual to conform to custom in his conduct, acting upon him both within as the force of conscience and without as the force of opinion. It is the same force on which the individual feels himself to be dependent, as a source of inner strength to him in times of need. It is this force also that carries him away during periods of social excitement such as dances, ceremonies or fights, and which gives him the feeling of a sudden great addition to his own personal force.

The Andamanese have not reached the point of recognizing by a special name this power of which they are thus aware. I have shown that in some of its manifestations they regard it, symbolically, as being a sort of heat, or a force similar to that which they know in fire and heat.[8] In more developed societies, however, we find a nearer approach to a definite recognition of this power or force in its different manifestations by means of a single name. The power denoted by the word *mana* in Melanesia, and by the words *orenda, wakan, nauala,* etc., amongst different tribes of North America, is this same power of which I have tried to show that the notion arises from the actual experience of the moral force of the society.

These sentiments and the representations connected with them, upon the existence of which, as we have seen, the very existence of the society depends, need to be kept alive, to be maintained at a given degree of intensity. Apart from the necessity that exists of keeping them alive in the mind of the individual, there is the necessity of impressing them upon each new individual added to the society, upon each child as he or she develops into an adult. Even individual sentiments do not remain in existence in the mind unless they are exercised by being expressed. Much more is this the case with collec-

---

[8] Ed. note: The discussion of this pervasive "force" is discussed by Radcliffe-Brown in greater detail on pp. 307-15 of *The Andaman Islanders.*

tive sentiments, those shared by a number of persons. The only possible way by which such collective sentiments can be maintained is by giving them regular and adequate expression.

Here then, . . . we find the function of the ceremonial customs of primitive peoples such as the Andamanese. All these customs are simply means by which certain ways of feeling about the different aspects of social life are regularly expressed, and, through expression, kept alive and passed on from one generation to another. Thus the customs connected with foods serve to maintain in existence certain ways of feeling about foods and the moral duties connected with them, and similarly with other customs.

Affective modes of experience (sentiments, feelings or emotions) can be expressed not only in bodily movements but also by means of language. I have tried to show that the function of the myths and legends of the Andamanese is exactly parallel to that of the ritual and ceremonial. They serve to express certain ways of thinking and feeling about the society and its relation to the world of nature, and thereby to maintain these ways of thought and feeling and pass them on to succeeding generations. In the case of both ritual and myth the sentiments expressed are those that are essential to the existence of the society.

In Tewara and Sanaroa–Mythology of the Kula*[1]

BRONISLAW MALINOWSKI

II

O NCE more we must pause, this time in an attempt to grasp the natives' mental attitude towards the mythological aspect of the Kula.[2] Right through this account it has been our constant endeavour to realise the vision of the world, as it is reflected in the minds of the natives. The frequent references to the scenery have not been given only to enliven the narrative, or even to enable the reader to visualise the setting of the native customs. I have attempted to show how the scene of his actions appears actually to the native, to describe his impressions and feelings with regard to it, as I was able to read them in his folk-lore, in his conversations at home, and in his behaviour when passing through this scenery itself.

Here we must try to reconstruct the influence of myth upon this vast landscape, as it colours it, gives it meaning, and transforms it into something live and familiar. What was a mere rock, now becomes

---

*From the book *Argonauts of the Western Pacific* by Bronislaw Malinowski, pp. 298-330. Dutton Paperback Edition (1961). Reprinted by permission of E. P. Dutton & Co., Inc., and Routledge & Kegan Paul, Ltd.

[1] Ed. note: The excerpt selected for reprinting in this volume consists of parts II through VII of Chapter XII of *Argonauts of the Western Pacific*. Parts I and VIII, which constitute slightly more than one fourth of the original chapter, have been omitted.

[2] Ed. note: The kula, as Malinowski describes it, is an economic institution which involves intertribal exchanges of two kinds of articles—long necklaces of red shell *(soulava)* and bracelets of white shell *(mwali)*. These items are exchanged in a clockwise and counterclockwise direction respectively among inhabitants of a wide ring of islands which constitutes a closed circuit for purposes of the exchanges. Associated with the kula are what Malinowski calls "subsidiary and associated activities," such as canoe building and bartering of items which are plentiful in one island and difficult to procure in another. All activities of the kula are prescribed by traditional custom and controlled by social codes.

a personality; what was a speck on the horizon becomes a beacon, hallowed by romantic associations with heroes; a meaningless configuration of landscape acquires a significance, obscure no doubt, but full of intense emotion. Sailing with natives, especially with novices to the Kula, I often observed how deep was their interest in sections of landscape impregnated with legendary meaning, how the elder ones would point and explain, the younger would gaze and wonder, while the talk was full of mythological names. It is the addition of the human interest to the natural features, possessing in themselves less power of appealing to a native man than to us, which makes the difference for him in looking at the scenery. A stone hurled by one of the heroes into the sea after an escaping canoe; a sea passage broken between two islands by a magical canoe; here two people turned into rock; there a petrified *waga*—all this makes the landscape represent a continuous story or else the culminating dramatic incident of a familiar legend. This power of transforming the landscape, the visible environment, is one only of the many influences which myth exercises upon the general outlook of the natives. Although here we are studying myth only in its connection with the Kula, even within these narrow limits some of its broader connections will be apparent, notably its influence upon sociology, magic and ceremonial.

The question which presents itself first, in trying to grasp the native outlook on the subject is: what is myth to the natives? How do they conceive and define it? Have they any line of demarcation between the mythical and the actual reality, and if so, how do they draw this line?

Their folk-lore, that is, the verbal tradition, the store of tales, legends, and texts handed on by previous generations, is composed of the following classes: first of all, there is what the natives call *libogwo,* "old talk," but which we would call tradition; secondly, *kukwanebu,* fairy tales, recited for amusement, at definite seasons, and relating avowedly untrue events; thirdly, *wosi,* the various songs, and *vinavina,* ditties, chanted at play or under other special circumstances; and last, not least, *megwa* or *yopa,* the magical spells. All these classes are strictly distinguished from one another by name, function, social setting, and by certain formal characteristics. This brief outline of the Boyowan folk-lore in general must suffice here, as we cannot enter into more details, and the only class which interests us in the present connection is the first one, that called *libogwo.*

This, the "old talk," the body of ancient tradition, believed to be true, consists on the one hand of historical tales, such as the deeds of past chiefs, exploits in the Koya, stories of shipwreck, etc. On the other hand, the *libogwo* class also contains what the natives call *lili'u*—myths, narratives, deeply believed by them, held by them in reverence, and exercising an active influence on their conduct and tribal life. Now the natives distinguish definitely between myth and historic account, but this distinction is difficult to formulate, and cannot be stated but in a somewhat deliberate manner.

First of all, it must be borne in mind, that a native would not trouble spontaneously to analyse such distinctions and to put them into words. If an Ethnographer succeeded in making the problem clear to an intelligent informant (and I have tried and succeeded in doing this) the native would simply state:

"We all know that the stories about Tudava, about Kudayuri, about Tokosikuna, are *lili'u;* our fathers, our *kadada* (our maternal uncles) told us so; and we always hear these tales; we know them well; we know that there are no other tales besides them, which are *lili'u*. Thus, whenever we hear a story, we know whether it is a *lili'u* or not."

Indeed, whenever a story is told, any native, even a boy, would be able to say whether this is one of his tribal *lili'u* or not. For the other tales, that is the historical ones, they have no special word, but they would describe the events as happening among "humans like ourselves." Thus tradition, from which the store of tales is received, hands them on labelled as *lili'u,* and the definition of a *lili'u,* is that it is a story transmitted with such a label. And even this definition is contained by the facts themselves, and not explicitly stated by the natives in their current stock of expressions.

For us, however, even this is not sufficient, and we have to search further, in order to see whether we cannot find other indices, other characteristic features which differentiate the world of mythical events from that of real ones. A reflection which would naturally present itself would be this: "Surely the natives place their myths in ancient, pre-historic times, while they put historical events into recent ages?" There is some truth in this, in so far as most of the historical events related by the natives are quite recent, have occurred within the community where they are told and can be directly connected with people and conditions existing at present, by memory of living man, by genealogies or other records. On the other hand, when historical events are told from other districts, and cannot be directly linked with the present, it would be erroneous to imagine that the natives place them into a definite compartment of time different from that of the myth. For it must be realised that these natives do not conceive of a past as of a lengthy duration, unrolling itself in successive stages of time. They have no idea of a long vista of historical occurrences, narrowing down and dimming as they recede towards a distant background of legend and myth, which stands out as something entirely different from the nearer planes. This view, so characteristic of the naive, historical thinking among ourselves, is entirely foreign to the natives. Whenever they speak of some event of the past, they distinguish whether it happened within their own memory or that of their fathers' or not. But, once beyond this line of demarcation, all the past events are placed by them on one plane, and there are no gradations of "long ago" and "very long ago." Any idea of epochs in time is absent from their mind; the past is one vast storehouse of events, and the line of demarcation between myth and history does not coincide with any division into definite and distinct periods of time. Indeed, I have found very often that when they told me some story of the past, for me obviously mythological, they would deem it necessary to emphasise that this did not happen in their fathers' time or in their grand-fathers' time, but long ago, and that it is a *lili'u*.

Again, they have no idea of what could be called the evolution of the world or the evolution of society; that is, they do not look back towards a series of successive changes, which happened in nature or in humanity, as we do. We, in our religious and scientific outlook alike, know that earth ages and that humanity ages, and we think of both in these terms; for them, both are eternally the same, eternally youthful. Thus, in judging the remoteness of traditional events, they cannot use the co-ordinates of a social setting constantly in change and divided into epochs. To give a concrete example, in the myths of Torosipupu and Tolikalaki, we saw them having the same interest and concerns, engaged in the same type of fishing, using the same means of locomotion as the present natives do. The mythical personages of the natives' legends, as we shall presently see, live in the same houses, eat the same food, handle the same weapons and implements as those in use at present. Whereas in any of our historical stories, legends or myths, we have a whole set of changed cultural conditions, which allow us to co-ordinate any event with a certain epoch, and which make us feel that a distant historical event, and still more, a mythological one, is happening in a setting of cultural conditions entirely different from those in which we are living now. In the very telling of the stories of, let us say, Joan of Arc, Solomon, Achilles, King Arthur, we have to mention all sorts of things and conditions long since disappeared from among us, which make even a superficial and an uneducated listener realise that it is a story of a remote and different past.

I have said just now that the mythical personages in the Trobriand tradition are living the same type of life, under the same social and cultural conditions as the present natives. This needs one qualification, and in this we shall find a very remarkable criterion for a distinction between what is legendary and what is historical: in the mythical world, although surrounding conditions were similar, all sorts of events happened which do not happen nowadays, and people were endowed with powers such as present men and their historical ancestors do not possess. In mythical times, human beings come out of the ground, they change into animals, and these become people again; men and women rejuvenate and slough their skins; flying canoes speed through the air, and things are transformed into stone.

Now this line of demarcation between the world of myth and that of actual reality—the simple difference that in the former things happen which never occur nowadays—is undoubtedly felt and realised by the natives, though they themselves could not put it into words. They know quite well that to-day no one emerges from underground; that people do not change into animals, and *vice versa;* nor do they give birth to them; that present-day canoes do not fly. I had the opportunity of grasping their mental attitude towards such things by the following occurrence. The Fijian missionary teacher in Omarakana was telling them about white man's flying machines. They inquired from me, whether this was true, and when I corroborated the Fijian's report and showed them pictures of aeroplanes in an illustrated paper, they asked me whether this happened nowadays or whether it were a *lili'u*. This circumstance made it clear to me then, that the natives would have a tendency, when meeting with an extraordinary and to them supernatural event, either to discard it as untrue, or relegate it into the regions of the *lili'u*. This does not mean, however, that the untrue and the mythical are the same or even similar to them. Certain stories told to them, they insist on treating as *sasopa* (lies), and maintain that they are not *lili'u*. For instance, those opposed to missionary teaching will not accept the view that

Biblical stories told to them are a *lili'u,* but they reject them as *sasopa.* Many a time did I hear such a conservative native arguing thus:—

"Our stories about Tudava are true; this is a *lili'u.* If you go to Laba'i you can see the cave in which Tudava was born, you can see the beach where he played as a boy. You can see his footmark in a stone at a place in the Raybwag. But where are the traces of Yesu Keriso? Who ever saw any signs of the tales told by the misinari? Indeed they are not *lili'u.*"

To sum up, the distinction between the *lili'u* and actual or historical reality is drawn firmly, and there is a definite cleavage between the two. *Prima facie,* this distinction is based on the fact that all myth is labelled as such and known to be such to all natives. A further distinctive mark of the world of *lili'u* lies in the super-normal, supernatural character of certain events which happen in it. The supernatural is believed to be true, and this truth is sanctioned by tradition, and by the various signs and traces left behind by mythical events, more especially by the magical powers handed on by the ancestors who lived in times of *lili'u.* This magical inheritance is no doubt the most palpable link between the present and the mythical past. But this past must not be imagined to form a pre-historic, very distant background, something which preceded a long evolution of mankind. It is rather the past, but extremely near reality, very much alive and true to the natives.

As I have just said, there is one point on which the cleavage between myth and present reality, however deep, is bridged over in native ideas. The extraordinary powers which men possess in myths are mostly due to their knowledge of magic. This knowledge is, in many cases, lost, and therefore the powers of doing these marvellous things are either completely gone, or else considerably reduced. If the magic could be recovered, men would fly again in their canoes, they could rejuvenate, defy ogres, and perform the many heroic deeds which they did in ancient times. Thus, magic, and the powers conferred by it, are really the link between mythical tradition and the present day. Myth has crystallised into magical formulae, and magic in its turn bears testimony to the authenticity of myth. Often the main function of myth is to serve as a foundation for a system of magic, and, wherever magic forms the backbone of an institution, a myth is also to be found at the base of it. In this perhaps, lies the greatest sociological importance of myth, that is, in its action upon institutions through the associated magic. The sociological point of view and the idea of the natives coincide here in a remarkable manner. In this book we see this exemplified in one concrete case, in that of the relation between the mythology, the magic, and the social institution of the Kula.

Thus we can define myth as a narrative of events which are to the native supernatural, in this sense, that he knows well that to-day they do not happen. At the same time he believes deeply that they did happen then. The socially sanctioned narratives of these events; the traces which they left on the surface of the earth; the magic in which they left behind part of their supernatural powers, the social institutions which are associated with the practice of this magic—all this brings about the fact that a myth is for the native a living actuality, though it has happened long ago and in an order of things when people were endowed with supernatural powers.

I have said before that the natives do not possess any historical perspective, that they do not range events—except of course, those of the most recent decades — into any successive stages. They also do not classify their myths into any divisions with regard to their antiquity. But in looking at their myths, it becomes at once obvious that they represent events, some of which must have happened prior to others. For there is a group of stories describing the origin of humanity, the emerging of the various social units from underground. Another group of mythical tales gives accounts of how certain important institutions were introduced and how certain customs crystallised. Again, there are myths referring to small changes in culture, or to the introduction of new details and minor customs. Broadly speaking, the mythical folk-lore of the Trobrianders can be divided into three groups referring to three different strata of events. In order to give a general idea of Trobriand mythology, it will be good to give a short characterisation of each of these groups.

1. *The oldest myths,* referring to the origin of human beings; to the sociology of the sub-clans and villages; to the establishment of permanent relations between this world and the next. These myths describe events which took place just at the moment when the earth began to be peopled from underneath. Humanity existed, somewhere underground, since people emerged from there on the surface of Boyowa, in full decoration, equipped with magic, belonging to social divisions, and obeying definite laws and customs. But beyond this we know nothing about what they did underground. There is, however,

a series of myths, of which one is attached to every one of the more important sub-clans, about various ancestors coming out of the ground, and almost at once, doing some important deed, which gives a definite character to the sub-clan. Certain mythological versions about the nether world belong also to this series.

2. *Kultur myths.* – Here belong stories about ogres and their conquerors; about human beings who established definite customs and cultural features; about the origin of certain institutions. These myths are different from the foregoing ones, in so far as they refer to a time when humanity was already established on the surface of the earth, and when all the social divisions had already assumed a definite character. The main cycle of myths which belong here, are those of a culture hero, Tudava, who slays an ogre and thus allows people to live in Boyowa again, whence they all had fled in fear of being eaten. A story about the origins of cannibalism belongs here also, and about the origin of garden making.

3. *Myths in which figure only ordinary human beings,* though endowed with extraordinary magical powers. These myths are distinguished from the foregoing ones, by the fact that no ogres or non-human persons figure in them, and that they refer to the origin, not of whole aspects of culture, such as cannibalism or garden-making, but to definite institutions or definite forms of magic. Here comes the myth about the origins of sorcery, the myth about the origins of love magic, the myth of the flying canoe, and finally the several Kula myths. The line of division between these three categories is, of course, not a rigid one, and many a myth could be placed in two or even three of these classes, according to its several features or episodes. But each myth contains as a rule one main subject, and if we take only this, there is hardly ever the slightest doubt as to where it should be placed.

A point which might appear contradictory in superficial reading is that before, we stressed the fact that the natives had no idea of change, yet here we spoke of myths about "origins" of institutions. It is important to realise that, though natives do speak about times when humanity was not upon the earth, of times when there were no gardens, etc., yet all these things arrive ready-made; they do not change or evolve. The first people, who came from underground, came up adorned with the same trinkets, carrying their lime-pot and chewing their betel-nut. The event, the emergence from the earth was

mythical, that is, such as does not happen now; but the human beings
and the country which received them were such as exist to-day.

III

The myths of the Kula are scattered along a section of the present
Kula circuit. Beginning with a place in Eastern Woodlark Island, the
village of Wamwara, the mythological centres are spread round almost
in a semi-circle, right down to the island of Tewara, where we have
left for the present our party from Sinaketa.

In Wamwara there lived an individual called Gere'u, who, according to one myth, was the originator of the Kula. In the island of
Digumenu, West of Woodlark Island, Tokosikuna, another hero of the
Kula, had his early home, though he finished his career in Gumasila,
in the Amphletts. Kitava, the westernmost of the Marshall Bennetts,
is the centre of canoe magic associated with the Kula. It is also the
home of Monikiniki, whose name figures in many formulae of the
Kula magic, though there is no explicit myth about him, except that
he was the first man to practice an important system of *mwasila*
(Kula magic), probably the most widespread system of the present
day. Further West, in Wawela, we are at the other end of the Kasabwaybwayreta myth, which starts in Tewara, and goes over to
Wawela in its narrative of events, to return to Tewara again. This
mythological narrative touches the island of Boyowa at its southern-
most point, the passage Giribwa, which divides it from Vakuta. Almost all myths have one of their incidents laid in a small island
between Vakuta and the Amphletts, called Gabuwana. One of the
myths leads us to the Amphletts, that of Tokosikuna; another has
its beginning and end in Tewara. Such is the geography of the Kula
myths on the big sector between Murua and Dobu.

Although I do not know the other half through investigations
made on the spot, I have spoken with natives from those districts,
and I think that there are no myths localised anywhere on the sector
Murua (Woodlark Island), Tubetube, and Dobu. What I am quite
certain of, however, is that the whole of the Trobriands, except the
two points mentioned before, lie outside the mythological area of
the Kula. No Kula stories, associated with any village in the Northern
half of Boyowa exist, nor does any of the mythical heroes of the
other stories ever come to the Northern or Western provinces of
the Trobriands. Such extremely important centres as Sinaketa and

Omarakana are never mentioned. This would point, on the surface of it, to the fact that in olden days, the island of Boyowa, except its Southern end and the Eastern settlement of Wawela, either did not enter at all or did not play an important part in the Kula.

I shall give a somewhat abbreviated account of the various stories, and then adduce in extenso the one last mentioned, perhaps the most noteworthy of all the Kula myths, that of Kasabwaybwayreta, as well as the very important canoe myth, that of the flying *waga* of Kudayuri.

The Muruan myth, which I obtained only in a very bald outline, is localised in the village of Wamwara, at the Eastern end of the island. A man called Gere'u, of the Lukuba clan, knew very well the *mwasila* magic, and wherever he went, all the valuables were given to him, so that all the others returned empty-handed. He went to Gawa and Iwa, and as soon as he appeared, *pu-pu* went the conch shells, and everybody gave him the *bagi* necklaces. He returned to his village, full of glory and of Kula spoils. Then he went to Du'a'u, and obtained again an enormous amount of armshells. He settled the direction in which the Kula valuables have to move. *Bagi* necklaces have "to go," and the armshells "to come." As this was spoken on Boyowa, "go" meant to travel from Boyowa to Woodlark, "come" to travel from Gere'u's village to Sinaketa. The culture hero Gere'u was finally killed, through envy of his success in the Kula.

I obtained two versions about the mythological hero, Tokosikuna of Digumenu. In the first of them, he is represented as a complete cripple, without hands and feet, who has to be carried by his two daughters into the canoe. They sail on a Kula expedition through Iwa, Gawa, through the Straits of Giribwa to Gumasila. Then they put him on a platform, where he takes a meal and goes to sleep. They leave him there and go into a garden which they see on a hill above, in order to gather some food. On coming back, they find him dead. On hearing their wailing, an ogre comes out, marries one of them and adopts the other. As he was very ugly, however, the girls killed him in an obscene manner, and then settled in the island. This obviously mutilated and superficial version does not give us many clues to the native ideas about the Kula.

The other version is much more interesting. Tokosikuna, according to it, is also slightly crippled, lame, very ugly, and with a pitted skin; so ugly indeed that he could not marry. Far North, in the mythical land of Kokopawa, they play a flute so beautifully that the

chief of Digumenu, the village of Tokosikuna, hears it. He wishes to
obtain the flute. Many men set out, but all fail, and they have to
return half way, because it is so far. Tokosikuna goes, and, through
a mixture of cunning and daring, he succeeds in getting possession
of the flute, and in returning safely to Digumenu. There, through
magic which one is led to infer he has acquired on his journey, he
changes his appearance, becomes young, smooth-skinned and beautiful. The *guya'u* (chief) who is away in his garden, hears the flute
played in his village, and returning there, he sees Tokosikuna sitting
on a high platform, playing the flute and looking beautiful. "Well,"
he says, "all my daughters, all my granddaughters, my nieces and my
sisters, you all marry Tokosikuna! Your husbands, you leave behind!
You marry Tokosikuna, for he has brought the flute from the distant
land!" So Tokosikuna married all the women.

   The other men did not take it very well, of course. They decided
to get rid of Tokosikuna by stratagem. They said: "The chief would
like to eat giant clam-shell, let us go and fish it." "And how shall I
catch it?" asks Tokosikuna. "You put your head, where the clam-
shell gapes open." (This of course would mean death, as the clam-
shell would close, and if a really big one, would easily cut off his
head.) Tokosikuna, however, dived and with his two hands, broke a
clam-shell open, a deed of super-human strength. The others were
angry, and planned another form of revenge. They arranged a shark-
fishing, advising Tokosikuna to catch the fish with his hands. But he
simply strangled the big shark, and put it into the canoe. Then, he
tears asunder a boar's mouth, bringing them thus to despair. Finally
they decide to get rid of him at sea. They try to kill him first by
letting the heavy tree, felled for the *waga,* fall on him. But he supports it with his outstretched arms, and does no harm to himself. At
the time of lashing, his companions wrap some *wayugo* (lashing
creeper) into a soft pandanus leaf; then they persuade him to use
pandanus only for the lashing of his canoe, which he does indeed,
deceived by seeing them use what apparently is the same. Then they
sail, the other men in good, seaworthy canoes, he in an entirely
unseaworthy one, lashed only with the soft, brittle pandanus leaf.

   And here begins the real Kula part of the myth. The expedition
arrives at Gawa, where Tokosikuna remains with his canoe on the
beach, while the other men go to the village to *kula.* They collect all
the smaller armshells of the *soulava* type, but the big ones, the *bagi,*
remain in the village, for the local men are unwilling to give them.

Then Tokosikuna starts for the village after all the others have returned. After a short while, he arrives from the village, carrying all the *bagido'u bagidudu,* and *bagiriku*—that is, all the most valuable types of spondylus necklaces. The same happens in Iwa and Kitava. His companions from the other canoes go first and succeed only in collecting the inferior kinds of valuables. He afterwards enters the village, and easily obtains the high grades of necklace, which had been refused to the others. These become very angry; in Kitava, they inspect the lashings of his canoe, and see that they are rotten. "Oh well, to-morrow, Vakuta! The day after, Gumasila,—he will drown in Pilolu." In Vakuta the same happens as before, and the wrath of his unsuccessful companions increases.

They sail and passing the sandbank of Gabula (this is the Trobriand name for Gabuwana, as the Amphlettans pronounce it) Tokosikuna eases his helm; then, as he tries to bring the canoe up to the wind again, his lashings snap, and the canoe sinks. He swims in the waves, carrying the basket-full of valuables in one arm. He calls out to the other canoes: "Come and take your *bagi!* I shall get into your *waga!*" "You married all our women," they answer, "now, sharks will eat you! We shall go to make Kula in Dobu!" Tokosikuna, however, swims safely to the point called Kamsareta, in the island of Domdom. From there he beholds the rock of Selawaya standing out of the jungle on the eastern slope of Gumasila. "This is a big rock, I shall go and live there," and turning towards the Digumenu canoes, he utters a curse.

"You will get nothing in Dobu but poor necklaces, *soulava* of the type of *tutumuyuwa* and *tutuyanabwa.* The big *bagido'u* will stop with me." He remains in the Amphletts and does not return to Digumenu. And here ends the myth.

I have given an extensive summary of this myth, including its first part, which has nothing to do with the Kula, because it gives a full character sketch of the hero as a daring sailor and adventurer. It shows, how Tokosikuna, after his Northern trip, acquired magic which allowed him to change his ugly and weak frame into a powerful body with a beautiful appearance. The first part also contains the reference to his great success with women, an association between Kula magic and love magic, which as we shall see, is not without importance. In this first part, that is, up to the moment when they start on the Kula, Tokosikuna appears as a hero, endowed with extraordinary powers, due to his knowledge of magic.

In this myth, as we see, no events are related through which the natural appearance of the landscape is changed. Therefore this myth is typical of what I have called the most recent stratum of mythology. This is further confirmed by the circumstance that no allusion is made in it to any origins, not even to the origins of the *mwasila* magic. For, as the myth is at present told and commented upon, all the men who go on the Kula expedition with our hero, know a system of Kula magic, the *mwasila* of Monikiniki. Tokosikuna's superiority rests with his special beauty magic; with his capacity to display enormous strength, and to face with impunity great dangers; with his ability to escape from drowning, finally, with his knowledge of the evil magic, *bulubwalata,* with which he prevents his companions from doing successful Kula. This last point was contained in a commentary upon this myth, given to me by the man who narrated it. When I speak about the Kula magic more explicitly further on, the reader will see that the four points of superiority just mentioned correspond to the categories into which we have to group the Kula magic, when it is classified according to its leading ideas, according to the goal towards which it aims.

One magic Tokosikuna does not know. We see from the myth that he is ignorant of the nature of the *wayugo,* the lashing creeper. He is therefore obviously not a canoe-builder, nor acquainted with canoe-building magic. This is the point on which his companions are able to catch him.

Geographically, this myth links Digumenu with the Amphletts, as also did the previous version of the Tokosikuna story. The hero, here as there, settles finally in Gumasila, and the element of migration is contained in both versions. Again, in the last story, Tokosikuna decides to settle in the Amphletts, on seeing the Selawaya rock. If we remember the Gumasilan legend about the origin of Kula magic, it also refers to the same rock. I did not obtain the name of the individual who is believed to have lived on the Selawaya rock, but it obviously is the same myth, only very mutilated in the Gumasilan version.

IV

Moving Westwards from Digumenu, to which the Tokosikuna myth belongs, the next important centre of Kula magic is the island of Kitava. With this place, the magical system of Monikiniki is associated by tradition, though no special story is told about this individual. A very important myth, on the other hand, localised in Kitava, is the one which serves as foundation for canoe magic. I have obtained three independent versions of this myth, and they agree substantially. I shall adduce at length the story as it was told to me by the best informant, and written down in Kiriwinian, and after that, I shall show on what points the other versions vary. I shall not omit from the full account certain tedious repetitions and obviously inessential details, for they are indispensable for imparting to the narrative the characteristic flavour of native folk-lore.

To understand the following account, it is necessary to realise that Kitava is a raised coral island. Its inland part is elevated to a height of about three hundred feet. Behind the flat beach, a steep coral wall rises, and from its summit the land gently falls towards the central declivity. It is in this central part that the villages are situated, and it would be quite impossible to transport a canoe from any village to the beach. Thus, in Kitava, unlike what happens with some of the Lagoon villages of Boyowa, the canoes have to be always dug out and lashed on the beach.

THE MYTH OF THE FLYING CANOE OF KUDAYURI

"Mokatuboda of the Lukuba clan and his younger brother Toweyre'i lived in the village of Kudayuri. With them lived their three sisters Kayguremwo, Na'ukuwakula and Murumweyri'a. They had all come out from underground in the spot called Labikewo, in Kitava. These people were the *u'ula* (foundation, basis, here: first possessors) of the *ligogu* and *wayugo* magic."

"All the men of Kitava decided on a great Kula expedition to the Koya. The men of Kumwageya, Kaybutu, Kabululo and Lalela made their canoes. They scooped out the inside of the *waga*, they carved the *tabuyo* and *lagim* (decorated prow boards), they made the *budaka* (lateral gunwale planks). They brought the component parts to the beach, in order to make the *yowaga* (to put and lash them together)."

"The Kudayuri people made their canoe in the village. Mokatuboda, the head man of the Kudayuri village, ordered them to do so. They were angry: 'Very heavy canoe. Who will carry it to the beach?' He said: 'No, not so; it will be well. I shall just lash my *waga* in the village.' He refused to move the canoe; it remained in the village. The other people pieced their canoe on the beach; he pieced it together in the village. They lashed it with the *wayugo* creeper on the beach; he lashed his in the village. They caulked their canoes on the sea-shore; he caulked his in the village. They painted their canoes on the beach with black; he blackened his in the village. They made the *youlala* (painted red and white) on the beach; he made the *youlala* in the village. They sewed their sail on the beach; he did it in the village. They rigged up the mast and rigging on the beach; he in the village. After that, the men of Kitava made *tasasoria* (trial run) and *kabi-gidoya* (visit of ceremonial presentation), but the Kudayuri canoe did not make either."

"By and by, all the men of Kitava ordered their women to prepare the food. The women one day put all the food, the *gugu'a* (personal belongings), the *pari* (presents and trade goods) into the canoe. The people of Kudayuri had all these things put into their canoe in the village. The headman of the Kudayuri, Mokatuboda, asked all his younger brothers, all the members of his crew, to bring some of their *pari,* and he performed magic over it, and made a *lilava* (magical bundle) of it."

"The people of other villages went to the beach; each canoe was manned by its *usagelu* (members of the crew). The man of Kudayuri ordered his crew to man his canoe in the village. They of the other villages stepped the mast on the shore; he stepped the mast in the village. They prepared the rigging on the shore; he prepared the rigging in the village. They hoisted the sail on the sea; he spoke 'May our sail be hoisted,' and his companions hoisted the sail. He spoke: 'Sit in your places, every man!' He went into the house, he took his *ligogu* (adze), he took some coco-nut oil, he took a staff. He spoke magic over the adze, over the coco-nut oil. He came out of the house, he approached the canoe. A small dog of his called Tokulubweydoga jumped into the canoe. He spoke to his crew: 'Pull up the sail higher.' They pulled at the halyard. He rubbed the staff with the coco-nut oil. He knocked the canoe's skids with the staff. Then he struck with his *ligogu* the *u'ula* of his canoe and the *dobwana* (that is, both ends of the canoe). He jumped into the canoe, sat down, and the canoe flew!"

"A rock stood before it. It pierced the rock in two, and flew through it. He bent down, he looked; his companions (that is, the other canoes of Kitava) sailed on the sea. He spoke to his younger brothers, (that is to his relatives in the canoe): 'Bail out the water, pour it out!' Those who sailed on the earth thought it was rain, this water which they poured out from above."

"They (the other canoes) sailed to Giribwa, they saw a canoe anchored there. They said: 'Is that the canoe from Dobu?' They thought so, they wanted to *lebu* (take by force, but not necessarily as a hostile act) the *buna* (big cowrie) shells of the Dobu people. Then they saw the dog walking on the beach. They said: 'Wi-i-i! This is Tokulubweydoga, the dog of the Lukuba! This canoe they lashed in the village, in the village of Kudayuri. Which way did it come? It was anchored in the jungle!' They approached the people of Kudayuri, they spoke: 'Which way did you come?' 'Oh, I came together with you (the same way).' 'It rained. Did it rain over you?' 'Oh yes, it has rained over me.'"

"Next day, they (the men of the other villages of Kitava), sailed to Vakuta and went ashore. They made their Kula. The next day they sailed, and he (Mokatuboda) remained in Vakuta. When they disappeared on the sea, his canoe flew. He flew from Vakuta. When they (the other crews) arrived in Gumasila, he was there on the promontory of Lububuyama. They said: 'This canoe is like the canoe of our companions,' and the dog came out. 'This is the dog of the Lukuba clan of Kudayuri.' They asked him again which way he came; he said he came the same way as they. They made the Kula in Gumasila. He said: 'You sail first, I shall sail later on.' They were astonished. 'Which way does he sail?' They slept in Gumasila."

"Next day they sailed to Tewara, they arrived at the beach of Kadimwatu. They saw his canoe anchored there, the dog came out and ran along the beach. They spoke to the Kudayuri men, 'How did you come here?' 'We came with you, the same way we came.' They made Kula in Tewara. Next day, they sailed to Bwayowa (village in Dobu district). He flew, and anchored at the beach Sarubwoyna. They arrived there, they saw: 'Oh, look at the canoe, are these fishermen from Dobu?' The dog came out. They recognised the dog. They asked him (Mokatuboda) which way he came: 'I came with you, I anchored here.' They went to the village of Bwayowa, they made Kula in the village, they loaded their canoes. They received presents from the Dobu people at parting, and the Kitava men sailed on the return journey. They sailed first, and he flew through the air.' "

On the return journey, at every stage, they see him first, they ask him which way he went, and he gives them some sort of answer as the above ones.

"From Giribwa they sailed to Kitava; he remained in Giribwa; he flew from Giribwa; he went to Kitava, to the beach. His *gugu'a* (personal belongings) were being carried to the village when his companions came paddling along, and saw his canoe anchored and the dog running on the beach. All the other men were very angry, because his canoe flew."

"They remained in Kitava. Next year, they made their gardens, all the men of Kitava. The sun was very strong, there was no rain at all. The sun burned their gardens. This man (the head man of Kudayuri, Mokatuboda) went into the garden. He remained there, he made a *bulubwalata* (evil magic) of the rain. A small cloud came and rained on his garden only, and their gardens the sun burned. They (the other men of Kitava) went and saw their gardens. They arrived there, they saw all was dead, already the sun had burned them. They went to his garden and it was all wet: yams, *taitu,* taro, all was fine. They spoke: 'Let us kill him so that he might die. We shall then speak magic over the clouds, and it will rain over our gardens.' "

"The real, keen magic, the Kudayuri man (i.e. Mokatuboda) did not give to them; he gave them not the magic of the *ligogu* (adze); he gave them not the magic of *kunisalili* (rain magic); he gave them not the magic of the *wayugo* (lashing creeper), of the coco-nut oil and staff. Toweyre'i, his younger brother, thought that he had already received the magic, but he was mistaken. His elder brother gave him only part of the magic, the real one he kept back."

"They came (to Mokatuboda, the head man of Kudayuri), he sat in his village. His brothers and maternal nephews sharpened the spear, they hit him, he died."

"Next year, they decided to make a big Kula expedition, to Dobu. The old *waga,* cut and lashed by Mokatuboda, was no more good, the lashings had perished. Then Toweyre'i, the younger brother, cut a new one to replace the old. The people of Kumwageya and Lalela (the other villages in Kitava) heard that Toweyre'i cuts his *waga,* and they also cut theirs. They pieced and lashed their canoes on the beach. Toweyre'i did it in the village."

Here the native narrative enumerates every detail of canoe making, drawing the contrast between the proceedings on the beach of the other Kitavans, and of Toweyre'i building the canoe in the village of Kudayuri. It is an exact repetition of what was said at the beginning, when Mokatuboda was building his canoe, and I shall not adduce it here. The narrative arrives at the critical moment when all the members of the crew are seated in the canoe ready for the flight.

"Toweyre'i went into the house and made magic over the adze and the coconut oil. He came out, smeared a staff with the oil, knocked the skids of the canoe. He then did as his elder brother did. He struck both ends of the canoe with the adze. He jumped into the canoe and sat down; but the *waga* did not fly. Toweyre'i went into the house and cried for his elder brother, whom he had slain; he had killed him without knowing his magic. The people of Kumwageya and Lalela went to Dobu and made their Kula. The people of Kudayuri remained in the village."

"The three sisters were very angry with Toweyre'i, for he killed the elder brother and did not learn his magic. They themselves had learnt the *ligogu,* the *wayugo* magic; they had it already in their *lopoula* (belly). They could fly through the air, they were *yoyova.* In Kitava they lived on the top of Botigale'a hill. They said: 'Let us leave Kitava and fly away.' They flew through the air. One of them, Na'ukuwakula, flew to the West, pierced through the sea-passage Dikuwa'i (somewhere in the Western Trobriands); she arrived at Simsim (one of the Lousançay). There she turned into a stone, she stands in the sea."

"The two others flew first (due West) to the beach of Yalumugwa (on the Eastern shore of Boyowa). There they tried to pierce the coral rock named Yakayba—it was too hard. They went (further South on the Eastern shore) through the sea passage of Vilasasa and tried to pierce the rock Kuyaluya—they couldn't. They went (further South) and tried to pierce the rock of Kawakari—it was too hard. They went (further South). They tried to pierce the rocks at Giribwa. They succeeded. That is why there is now a sea passage at Giribwa (the straits dividing the main island of Boyowa from the island of Vakuta)."

"They flew (further South) towards Dobu. They came to the island of Tewara. They came to the beach of Kadimwatu and pierced it. This is where the straits of Kadimwatu are now between the islands of Tewara and Uwama. They went to Dobu; they travelled further South, to the promontory of Saramwa (near Dobu island). They spoke: 'Shall we go round the point or pierce right through?' They went round the point. They met another obstacle and pierced it through, making the Straits of Loma (at the Western end of Dawson Straits). They came back, they returned and settled near Tewara. They turned into stones; they stand in the sea. One of them cast her eyes on Dobu, this is Murumweyri'a; she eats men, and the Dobuans are cannibals. The other one, Kayguremwo, does not eat men, and her face is turned towards Boyowa. The people of Boyowa do not eat man."

This story is extremely clear in its general outline, and very dramatic, and all its incidents and developments have a high degree of consistency and psychological motivation. It is perhaps the most telling of all myths from this part of the world which came under my notice. It is also a good example of what has been said before in Division II. Namely that the identical conditions, sociological and cultural, which obtain at the present time, are also reflected in mythical narratives. The only exception to this is the much higher efficiency of magic found in the world of myth. The tale of Kudayuri, on the one hand, describes minutely the sociological conditions of the heroes, their occupations and concerns, and all these do not differ at all from the present ones. On the other hand, it shows the hero endowed with a truly super-normal power through his magic of canoe building and of rain making. Nor could it be more convincingly stated than is done in this narrative that the full knowledge of the right magic was solely responsible for these supernatural powers.

In its enumeration of the various details of tribal life, this myth is truly a fount of ethnographic information. Its statements, when made complete and explicit by native comment, contain a good deal of what is to be known about the sociology, technology and organisation of canoe-making, sailing, and of the Kula. If followed up into detail, the incidents of this narrative make us acquainted for instance, with the division into clans; with the origin and local character of these latter; with ownership of magic and its association with the totemic group. In almost all mythological narratives of the Trobriands, the clan, the sub-clan and the locality of the heroes are stated. In the above version, we see that the heroes have emerged at a certain spot, and that they themselves came from underground; that is, that they are the first representatives of their totemic sub-clan on the surface of the earth. In the two other versions, this last point was not explicitly stated, though I think it is implied in the incidents of this myth, for obviously the flying canoe is built for the first time, as it is for the last. In other versions, I was told that the hole from which this sub-clan emerged is also called Kudayuri, and that the name of their magical system is Viluvayaba.

Passing to the following part of the tale, we find in it a description of canoe-building, and this was given to me in the same detailed manner in all three versions. Here again, if we would substitute for the short sentences a fuller account of what happens, such as could be elicited from any intelligent native informant; if for each word describing the stages of canoe-building we insert a full description of the processes for which these words stand—we would have in this myth an almost complete, ethnographic account of canoe-building. We would see the canoe pieced together, lashed, caulked, painted, rigged out, provided with a sail till it lies ready to be launched. Besides the successive enumeration of technical stages, we have in this myth a clear picture of the rôle played by the headman, who is the nominal owner of the canoe, and who speaks of it as his canoe and at the same time directs its building; overrides the wishes of others, and is responsible for the magic. We have even the mention of the *tasasoria* and *kabigidoya,* and several allusions to the Kula expedition of which the canoe-building in this myth is represented as a preliminary stage. The frequent, tedious repetitions and enumerations of customary sequences of events, interesting as data of folklore, are not less valuable as ethnographic documents, and as illustrations of the natives' attitude towards custom. Incidentally, this feature of native mythology shows that the task of serving as ethnographic informant is not so foreign and difficult to a native as might at first appear. He is quite used to recite one after the other the various stages of customary proceedings in his own narratives, and he does it with an almost pedantic accuracy and completeness, and it is an easy task for him to transfer these qualities to the accounts, which he is called upon to make in the service of ethnography.

The dramatic effect of the climax of the story, of the unexpected flight of the canoe is clearly brought out in the narrative, and it was given to me in all its three versions. In all three, the members of the crew are made to pass through the numerous preparatory stages of sailing. And the parallel drawn between the reasonable proceedings of their fellows on the beach, and the absurd manner in which they are made to get ready in the middle of the village, some few hundred feet above the sea, makes the tension more palpable and the sudden *denouement* more effective. In all accounts of this myth, the magic is also performed just before the flight, and its performance is explicitly mentioned and included as an important episode in the story.

The incident of bailing some water out of a canoe which never touched the sea, seems to show some inconsistency. If we remember, however, that water is poured into a canoe, while it is built, in order to prevent its drying and consequently its shrinking, cracking and warping, the inconsistency and flaw in the narrative disappear. I may add that the bailing and rain incident is contained in one of my three versions only.

The episode of the dog is more significant and more important to the natives, and is mentioned in all three versions. The dog is the animal associated with the Lukuba clan; that is, the natives will say that the dog is a Lukuba, as the pig is a Malasi, and the igwana a Lukulabuta. In several stories about the origin and relative rank of the clans, each of them is represented by its totemic animal. Thus the igwana is the first to emerge from underground. Hence the Lukulabuta are the oldest clan. The dog and the pig dispute with one another the priority of rank, the dog basing his claims on his earlier appearance on the earth, for he followed immediately the igwana; the pig, asserting himself in virtue of not eating unclean things. The pig won the day, and therefore the Malasi clan are considered to be the clan of the highest rank, though this is really reached only in one of its subclans, that of the Tabalu of Omarakana. The incident of the *lebu* (taking by force) of some ornaments from the Dobuans refers to the custom of using friendly violence in certain Kula transactions (see Chapter XIV, Division II).

In the second part of the story, we find the hero endowed again with magical powers far superior to those of the present-day wizards. They can make rain, or stay the clouds, it is true, but he is able to create a small cloud which pours copious rain over his own gardens, and leaves the others to be shrivelled up by the sun. This part of the narrative does not touch the canoe problem, and it is of interest to us only in so far as it again shows what appears to the natives the real source of their hero's supernatural powers.

The motives which lead to the killing of Mokatuboda are not stated explicitly in the narrative. No myth as a rule enters very much into the subjective side of its events. But, from the lengthy, indeed wearisome repetition of how the other Kitava men constantly find the Kudayuri canoe outrunning them, how they are astonished and angry, it is clear that his success must have made many enemies to Mokatuboda. What is not so easily explained, is the fact that he is killed, not by the other Kitava men, but by his own kinsmen. One of the versions mentions his brothers and his sister's sons as the slayers.

One of them states that the people of Kitava ask Toweyre'i, the younger brother, whether he has already acquired the flying magic and the rain magic, and only after an affirmative is received, is Moka-tuboda killed by his younger brother, in connivance with the other people. An interesting variant is added to this version, according to which Toweyre'i kills his elder brother in the garden. He then comes back to the village and instructs and admonishes Mokatuboda's children to take the body, to give it the mortuary attentions, to prepare for the burial. Then he himself arranges the *sagali,* the big mortuary distribution of food. In this we find an interesting document of native custom and ideas. Toweyre'i, in spite of having killed his brother, is still the man who has to arrange the mortuary proceedings, act as master of ceremonies, and pay for the functions performed in them by others. He personally may neither touch the corpse, nor do any act of mourning or burial; nevertheless he, as the nearest of kin of the dead man, is the bereaved one, is the one from whom a limb has been severed, so to speak. A man whose brother has died cannot mourn any more than he could mourn for himself.[3] To return to the motives of killing, as this was done according to all accounts by Mokatuboda's own kinsmen, with the approval of the other men, envy, ambition, the desire to succeed the headman in his dignity, must have been mixed with spite against him. In fact, we see that Toweyre'i proceeds confidently to perform the magic, and bursts out into wailing only after he has discovered he has been duped.

Now we come to one of the most remarkable incidents of the whole myth, that namely which brings into connection the *yoyova,* or the flying witches, with the flying canoe, and with such speed of a canoe, as is imparted to it by magic. In the spells of swiftness there are frequent allusions to the *yoyova* or *mulukwausi.* This can be clearly seen in the spell of the *wayugo,* already adduced (Chapter V, Division III), and which is still to be analysed linguistically (Chapter XVIII, Divisions II to IV). The *kariyala* (magical portent, cf. Chapter XVII, Division VII) of the *wayugo* spell consists in shooting stars, that is, when a *wayugo* rite is performed at night over the creeper coils, there will be stars falling in the sky. And again, when a magician, knowing this system of magic, dies, shooting stars will be

---

[3] Cf. Professor C. G. Seligman, *The Melanesians [of British New Guinea* (Cambridge, 1910)], Chapter LIV, "Burial and Mourning Ceremonies" (among the natives of the Trobriand Islands, of Woodlark and the Marshall Bennetts).

seen. Now, as we have seen (Chapter X, Division I), falling stars are *mulukwausi* in their flight.

In this story of the Kudayuri we see the mythological ground for this association. The same magic which allowed the canoe to sail through the air gives the three sisters of Kudayuri their power of being *mulukwausi,* and of flying. In this myth they are also endowed with the power of cleaving the rocks, a power which they share with the canoe, which cleft a rock immediately after leaving the village. The three sisters cleave rocks and pierce the land in several places. My native commentators assured me that when the canoe first visited Giribwa and Kadimwatu at the beginning of this myth, the land was still joined at these places and there was a beach at each of them. The *mulukwausi* tried to pierce Boyowa at several spots along the Eastern coast, but succeeded only at Giribwa. The myth thus has the archaic stamp of referring to deep changes in natural-features. The two sisters, who fly to the South return from the furthest point and settle near Tewara, in which there is some analogy to several other myths in which heroes from the Marshall Bennett Islands settle down somewhere between the Amphletts and Dobu. One of them turns her eyes northwards towards the non-cannibal people of Boyowa and she is said to be averse to cannibalism. Probably this is a sort of mythological explanation of why the Boyowan people do not eat men and the Dobuans do, an explanation to which there is an analogy in another myth shortly to be adduced, that of Atu'a'ine and Aturamo'a, and a better one still in a myth about the origins of cannibalism, which I cannot quote here.

In all these traditions, so far, the heroes belonged to the clan of Lukuba. To it belong Gere'u, Tokosikuna, the Kudayuri family and their dog, and also the dog, Tokulubwaydoga of the myth told in Chapter X, Division V. I may add that, in some legends told about the origin of humanity, this clan emerges first from underground and in some it emerges second in time, but as the clan of highest rank, though in this it has to yield afterwards to the Malasi. The main Kultur-hero of Kiriwina, the ogre-slayer Tudava, belongs, also to the clan of Lukuba. There is even a historic fact, which agrees with this mythological primacy, and subsequent eclipse. The Lukuba were, some six or seven generations ago, the leading clan in Vakuta, and then they had to surrender the chieftainship of this place to the Malasi clan, when the sub-clan of the Tabalu, the Malasi chiefs of

the highest rank in Kiriwina, migrated South, and settled down in
Vakuta. In the myths quoted here, the Lukuba are leading canoe-
builders, sailors, and adventurers, that is with one exception, that of
Tokosikuna, who, though excelling in all other respects, knows nothing of canoe construction.

V

Let us now proceed to the last named mythological centre, and
taking a very big step from the Marshall Bennetts, return to Tewara,
and to its myth of the origin of the Kula. I shall tell this myth in a
translation, closely following the original account, obtained in Kiriwinian from an informant at Oburaku. I had an opportunity of
checking and amending his narrative, by the information obtained
from a native of Sanaro'a in pidgin English.

THE STORY OF KASABWAYBWAYRETA
AND GUMAKARAKEDAKEDA

"Kasabwaybwayreta lived in Tewara. He heard the renown of a *soulava*
(spondylus necklace) which was lying (kept) in Wawela. Its name was Gumakarakedakeda. He said to his children: 'Let us go to Wawela, make Kula to get
this *soulava*.' He put into his canoe unripe coco-nut, undeveloped betel-nut,
green bananas."

"They went to Wawela; they anchored in Wawela. His sons went ashore, they
went to obtain Gumakarakedakeda. He remained in the canoe. His son made
offering of food, they (the Wawela people) refused. Kasabwaybwayreta spoke a
charm over the betel-nut: it yellowed (became ripe); he spoke the charm over
the coco-nut: its soft kernel swelled; he charmed the bananas: they ripened. He
took off his hair, his gray hair; his wrinkled skin, it remained in the canoe. He
rose, he went, he gave a *pokala* offering of food, he received the valuable necklace as Kula gift, for he was already a beautiful man. He went, he put it down, he
thrust it into his hair. He came to the canoe, he took his covering (the sloughed
skin); he donned the wrinkles, the gray hairs, he remained."

"His sons arrived, they took their places in the canoe, they sailed to Giribwa.
They cooked their food. He called his grandson; 'Oh, my grandson, come here,
look for my lice.' The grandson came there, stepped near him. Kasabwaybwayreta spoke, telling him: 'My grandson, catch my lice in the middle (of my hair).'
His grandson parted his hair; he saw the valuable necklace, Gumakarakedakeda
remaining there in the hair of Kasabwaybwayreta. 'Ee. . .' he spoke to his father,
telling him, 'My father, Kasabwaybwayreta already obtained Gumakarakedakeda.' 'O, no, he did not obtain it! I am a chief, I am beautiful, I have not
obtained that valuable. Indeed, would this wrinkled old man have obtained the

necklace? No, indeed!' 'Truly, my father, he has obtained it already. I have seen it; already it remains in his hair!'"

"All the water-vessels are empty already; the son went into the canoe, spilled the water so that it ran out, and only the empty vessels (made of coco-nut shell) remained. Later on they sailed, they went to an island, Gabula (Gabuwana in Amphlettan and in Dobuan). This man, Kasabwaybwayreta wanted water, and spoke to his son. This man picked up the water vessels—no, they were all empty. They went on the beach of Gabula, the *usagelu* (members of the crew) dug out their water-holes (in the beach). This man remained in the canoe and called out: 'O my grandson, bring me here my water, go there and dip out my water!' The grandson said: 'No, come here and dip out (yourself)!' Later on, they dipped out water, they finished, and Kasabwaybwayreta came. They muddied the water, it was muddy. He sat down, he waited."

"They went, they sailed in the canoe. Kasabwaybwayreta called out, 'O, my son, why do you cast me off?' Spoke the son: 'I think you have obtained Gumakarakedakeda!' 'O, by and by, my son, when we arrive in the village, I shall give it to you!' 'O, no! Well, you remain, I shall go!' He takes a stone, a *binabina* one, this man Kasabwaybwayreta, he throws so that he might make a hole in the canoe, and the men might go into the sea. No! they sped away, they went, this stone stands up, it has made an island in the sea. They went, they anchored in Tewara. They (the villagers) asked: 'And where is Kasabwaybwayreta?' 'O, his son got angry with him, already he had obtained Gumakarakedakeda!'"

"Well, then, this man Kasabwaybwayreta remained in the island Gabula. He saw Tokom'mwawa (evening star) approach. He spoke: 'My friend, come here, let me just enter into your canoe!' 'O no, I shall go to another place.' There came Kaylateku (Sirius). He asked him: 'Let me go with you.' He refused. There came Kayyousi (Southern Cross). Kasabwaybwayreta wanted to go with him. He refused. There came Umnakayva'u (Alpha and Beta Centauri). He wanted a place in his canoe. He refused. There came Kibi (three stars widely distant, forming no constellation in our sky-chart). He also refused to take Kasabwaybwayreta. There came Uluwa (the Pleiades). Kasabwaybwayreta asked him to take him. Uluwa said: 'You wait, you look out, there will come Kaykiyadiga, he will take you.' There came Kaykiyadiga (the three central stars in Orion's belt). Kasabwaybwayreta asked him: 'My friend, which way will you go?' 'I shall come down on top of Taryebutu mountain. I shall go down, I shall go away.' 'Oh, my friend, come here, let me just sit down (on you).' 'Oh come,— see on one side there is a *va'i* (stingaree) on the other side, there is the *lo'u* (a fish with poisonous spikes); you sit in the middle, it will be well! Where is your village?' 'My village is Tewara.' 'What stands in the site of your village?' 'In the site of my village, there stands a *busa* tree!'"

"They went there. Already the village of Kasabwaybwayreta is straight below them. He charmed this *busa* tree, it arose, it went straight up into the skies. Kasabwaybwayreta changed place (from Orion's belt on to the tree), he sat on the *busa* tree. He spoke: 'Oh, my friend, break asunder this necklace. Part of it, I shall give you; part of it, I shall carry to Tewara.' He gave part of it to his companion. This *busa* tree came down to the ground. He was angry because his son left him behind. He went underground inside. He there remained for a long time. The dogs came there, and they dug and dug. They dug him out. He came out on top, he became a *tauva'u* (evil spirit, see Chapter II, Division VII). He hits human beings. That is why in Tewara the village is that of sorcerers and witches, because of Kasabwaybwayreta."

To make this somewhat obscure narrative clearer, a short commentary is necessary. The first part tells of a Kula expedition in which the hero, his son, his grandson, and some other members of the crew take part. His son takes with him good, fresh food, to give as solicitory offering and thus tempt his partners to present him with the famous necklace. The son is a young man and also a chief of renown. The later stages are clearer; by means of magic, the hero changes himself into a young, attractive man, and makes his own unripe, bad fruit into splendid gifts to be offered to his partner. He obtains the prize without difficulty, and hides it in his hair. Then, in a moment of weakness, and for motives which it is impossible to find out from native commentators, he on purpose reveals the necklace to his grandson. Most likely, the motive was vanity. His son, and probably also the other companions, become very angry and set a trap for him. They arrange things so that he has to go for his own water on the beach of Gabula. When they have already got theirs and while he is dipping it out, they sail away, leaving him marooned on the sandbank. Like Polyphemus after the escaping party of Odysseus, he throws a stone at the treacherous canoe, but it misses its mark, and becomes an outstanding rock in the sea.

The episode of his release by the stars is quite clear. Arrived at the village, he makes a tree rise by his magic, and after he has given the bigger part of his necklace to his rescuer, he descends, with the smaller part. His going underground and subsequent turning into a *tauva'u* shows how bitter he feels towards humanity. As usual, the presence of such a powerful, evil personality in the village, gives its stamp to the whole community, and this latter produces sorcerers and witches. All these additions and comments I obtained in cross-questioning my original informant.

The Dobuan informant from Sanaro'a introduced one or two variants into the second part of the narrative. According to him,

Kasabwaybwayreta marries while in the sky, and remains there long enough to beget three male and two female children. After he has made up his mind to descend to earth again, he makes a hole in the heavens, looks down and sees a betel-nut tree in his village. Then he speaks to his child, "When I go down, you pull at one end of the necklace." He climbs down by means of the necklace on to the betel palm and pulls at one end of Gumakarakedakeda. It breaks, a big piece remains in the skies, the small one goes with him below. Arrived in the village, he arranges a feast, and invites all the villagers to it. He speaks some magic over the food and after they have eaten it, the villagers are turned into birds. This last act is quite in harmony with his profession of *tauva'u,* which he assumed in the previous version of the myth. My Dobuan informant also added, by way of commentary, that the companions of Kasabwaybwayreta were angry with him, because he obtained the necklace in Boyowa, which was not the right direction for a necklace to travel in the Kula. This, however, is obviously a rationalisation of the events of the myth.

Comparing the previously related story of Tokosikuna with this one, we see at once a clear resemblance between them in several features. In both, the heroes start as old, decrepit, and very ugly men. By their magical powers, they rejuvenate in the course of the story, the one permanently, the other just sloughing off his skin for the purpose of a Kula transaction. In both cases, the hero is definitely superior in the Kula, and by this arouses the envy and hatred of his companions. Again, in both stories, the companions decide to punish the hero, and the island or sandbank of Gabuwana is the scene of the punishment. In both, the hero finally settles in the South, only in one case it is his original home, while in the other he has migrated there from one of the Marshall Bennett Islands. An anomaly in the Kasabwaybwayreta myth, namely, that he fetches his necklace from the North, whereas the normal direction for necklaces to travel is from South to North in this region, makes us suspect that perhaps this story is a transformation of a legend about a man who made the Kula from the North. Ill-treated by his companions, he settled in Tewara, and becoming a local Kultur-hero, was afterwards described as belonging to the place. However this might be, and the hypothetical interpretation is mine, and not obtained from the natives, the two stories are so similar that they must be regarded obviously as variants of the same myth, and not as independent traditions.

VI

So much about the ethnographic analysis of these myths. Let us now return to the general, sociological considerations with which we opened this digression into mythology. We are now better able to realise to what extent and in what manner Kula myths influence the native outlook.

The main social force governing all tribal life could be described as the inertia of custom, the love of uniformity of behaviour. The great moral philosopher was wrong when he formulated his *categorical imperative,* which was to serve human beings as a fundamental guiding principle of behaviour. In advising us to act so that our behaviour might be taken as a norm of universal law, he reversed the natural state of things. The real rule guiding human behaviour is this: "what everyone else does, what appears as norm of general conduct, this is right, moral and proper. Let me look over the fence and see what my neighbour does, and take it as a rule for my behaviour." So acts every "man-in-the-street" in our own society, so has acted the average member of any society through the past ages, and so acts the present-day savage; and the lower his level of cultural development, the greater stickler he will be for good manners, propriety and form, and the more incomprehensive and odious to him will be the non-conforming point of view. Systems of social philosophy have been built to explain and interpret or misinterpret this general principle. Tarde's "Imitation," Giddings' "Consciousness of Kind," Durkheim's "Collective Ideas,"[4] and many such conceptions as "social consciousness," "the soul of a nation," "group mind" or nowadays prevalent and highly fashionable ideas about "suggestibility of the crowd," "the instinct of herd," etc., etc., try to cover this simple empirical truth. Most of these systems, especially those evoking the Phantom of Collective Soul are futile, to my mind, in so far as they try to explain in the terms of a hypothesis that which is most fundamental in sociology, and can therefore be reduced to nothing else, but must be simply recognised and accepted as the basis of our science. To frame verbal definitions and quibble over terms does not seem to bring us much more forward in a new branch of learning, where a knowledge of facts is above all needed.

---

[4] Ed. note: Malinowski refers here to Jean Gabriel de Tarde, French sociologist-philosopher (1843-1904); Franklin H. Giddings, American sociologist (1855-1931); and Émile Durkheim, French sociologist (1858-1917).

Whatever might be the case with any theoretical interpretations of this principle, in this place, we must simply emphasise that a strict adherence to custom, to that which is done by everyone else, is the main rule of conduct among our natives in the Trobriands. An important corollary to this rule declares that the past is more important than the present. What has been done by the father — or, as the Trobriander would say, by the maternal uncle—is even more important as norm of behaviour than what is done by the brother. It is to the behaviour of the past generations that the Trobriander instinctively looks for his guidance. Thus the mythical events which relate what has been done, not by the immediate ancestors but by mythical, illustrious forbears, must evidently carry an enormous social weight. The stories of important past events are hallowed because they belong to the great mythical generations and because they are generally accepted as truth, for everybody knows and tells them. They bear the sanction of righteousness and propriety in virtue of these two qualities of preterity and universality.

Thus, through the operation of what might be called the elementary law of sociology, myth possesses the normative power of fixing custom, of sanctioning modes of behaviour, of giving dignity and importance to an institution. The Kula receives from these ancient stories its stamp of extreme importance and value. The rules of commercial honour, of generosity and punctiliousness in all its operations, acquire through this their binding force. This is what we could call the normative influence of myth on custom.

The Kula myth, however, exercises another kind of appeal. In the Kula, we have a type of enterprise where the vast possibilities of success are very much influenced by chance. A man, whether he be rich or poor in partners, may, according to his luck, return with a relatively big or a small haul from an expedition. Thus the imagination of the adventurers, as in all forms of gambling, must be bent towards lucky hits and turns of extraordinarily good chance. The Kula myths feed this imagination on stories of extreme good luck, and at the same time show that it lies in the hands of man to bring this luck on himself, provided he acquires the necessary magical lore.

I have said before that the mythological events are distinct from those happening nowadays, in so far as they are extraordinary and super-normal. This adds both to their authoritative character and to their desirability. It sets them before the native as a specially valuable

standard of conduct, and as an ideal towards which their desires must
go out.

VII

But I also said before that, distinct as it is, the mythical world is
not separated by an unbridgable gulf from the present order of
events. Indeed, though an ideal must be always beyond what actually
exists, yet it must appear just within reach of realisation if it is to be
effective at all. Now, after we have become acquainted with their
stories, we can see clearly what was meant when it was said, that
magic acts as a link between the mythical and the actual realities. In
the canoe myth, for instance, the flying, the super-normal achievement of the Kudayuri canoe, is conceived only as the highest degree
of the virtue of speed, which is still being imparted nowadays to
canoes by magic. The magical heritage of the Kudayuri clan is still
there, making the canoes sail fast. Had it been transmitted in its
complete form, any present canoe, like the mythical one, could be
seen flying. In the Kula myths also, magic is found to give super-
normal powers of beauty, strength and immunity from danger. The
mythological events demonstrate the truth of the claims of magic.
Their validity is established by a sort of retrospective, mythical em-
piry. But magic, as it is practised nowadays, accomplishes the same
effects, only in a smaller degree. Natives believe deeply that the
formulae and rites of *mwasila* magic make those who carry them out
attractive, irresistible and safe from dangers (compare next chapter).

Another feature which brings the mythical events into direct connection with the present state of affairs, is the sociology of mythical
personages. They all are associated with certain localities, as are the
present local groups. They belong to the same system of totemic
division into clans and sub-clans as obtains nowadays. Thus, members
of a sub-clan, or a local unit, can claim a mythical hero as their direct
ancestor, and members of a clan can boast of him as of a clansman.
Indeed, myths, like songs and fairy stories, are "owned" by certain
sub-clans. This does not mean that other people would abstain from
telling them, but members of the sub-clan are supposed to possess
the most intimate knowledge of the mythical events, and to be an
authority in interpreting them. And indeed, it is a rule that a myth
will be best known in its own locality, that is, known with all the
details and free from any adulterations or not quite genuine additions and fusions.

This better knowledge can be easily understood, if we remember that myth is very often connected with magic in the Trobriands, and that this latter is a possession, kept by some members of the local group. Now, to know the magic, and to understand it properly, it is necessary to be well acquainted with the myth. This is the reason why the myth must be better known in the local group with which it is connected. In some cases, the local group has not only to practise the magic associated with the myth, but it has to look after the observance of certain rites, ceremonies and taboos connected with it. In this case, the sociology of the mythical events is intimately bound up with the social divisions as they exist now. But even in such myths as those of the Kula, which have become the property of all clans and local groups within the district, the explicit statement of the hero's clan, sub-clan and of his village gives the whole myth a stamp of actuality and reality. Side by side with magic, the sociological continuity bridges over the gap between the mythical and the actual. And indeed the magical and the sociological bridges run side by side.

I spoke above (beginning of Division II) of the enlivening influence of myth upon landscape. Here it must be noted also that the mythically changed features of the landscape bear testimony in the native's mind to the truth of the myth. The mythical word receives its substance in rock and hill, in the changes in land and sea. The pierced sea-passages, the cleft boulders, the petrified human beings, all these bring the mythological world close to the natives, make it tangible and permanent. On the other hand, the story thus powerfully illustrated, re-acts on the landscape, fills it with dramatic happenings, which, fixed there for ever, give it a definite meaning. With this I shall close these general remarks on mythology though with myth and mythical events we shall constantly meet in further inquiries.

Introduction to Zuni Mythology[*][1]

RUTH BENEDICT

FOLKLORISTIC studies, since the days of Cosquin[2] and the students stimulated by the collections of the Grimm brothers,[3] have been extensive rather than intensive. Whether the proposed problem was historical reconstruction, or a study of creative processes in mythology, the method that has been followed is that of far-flung comparative studies. This method has been used by Ehrenreich[4] and the psychoanalytic students of myth, both of whom are interested in the role of symbolism in folklore, as well as by the modern school of Aarne,[5] which is interested in reconstructing archetypal forms of

---

* Reprinted from *Zuni Mythology*, Columbia University Contributions to Anthropology, Vol. 21 (2 vols., New York, 1935), Vol. I, xi-xliii, by permission of the Columbia University Press.

[1] Ed. note: Within the body of this essay as it appeared originally, Benedict included numerous references to texts of Zuni folktales published by other investigators and/or contained within the two volumes of her own study. Those internal text references which Benedict included to *exemplify* points made in her discussion have been omitted from this reprinted version of the essay. Those internal text references which either *elaborate upon* or *offer alternative explanations for* the points which Benedict makes have been included in footnotes.

[2] Ed. note: Emmanuel G. Cosquin (1841-1919), French folklorist and proponent of the thesis that the vast majority of folktales extant in Eurasia had either originated in India or had been disseminated to Eurasian cultures by way of Indian sources.

[3] Ed. note: Jakob L. and Wilhelm K. Grimm (1785-1863 and 1786-1859 respectively), German collectors and editors of folktale texts, whose *Kinder-und Hausmärchen* (1st ed., 1812) is a seminal work in folk narrative research.

[4] Ed. note: Paul M. A. Ehrenreich (1855-1914), German scholar whose works include *Die allgemeine Mythologie und ihre ethnologischen Grundlagen* (Leipzig, 1910), an important discussion of the theoretical positions of early comparative mythologists.

[5] Ed. note: Antti A. Aarne (1867-1925), Finnish folklorist and major contributor to the formulation and development of the historic-geographic methodological approach to the comparative study of folkloristic texts.

folktales, and by students like Bolte and Polívka[6] who are committed simply to documenting distribution.

The intensive study of one body of folklore has been scanted throughout the history of folkloristic studies, and little stress has been laid upon its possible rewards. The most valuable studies of this kind have tabled and analyzed the cultural behavior embodied in the tales, and these have been made only in American Indian material.[7] Such studies show the great amount of cultural material in myth, and stress the value of folklore for an understanding of the culture. This is not the only kind of intensive study of folklore. Boas has defined, and contrasted with other regions, the themes of Eskimo folklore.[8] He has indicated the relation of these themes to the cultural behavior and ideals among that people. In addition, there is also the possibility of the study of the native narrator, that is, the literary materials which he has at his disposal and his handling of them.[9]

These problems have seldom been attacked, and several circumstances have contributed to this neglect on the part of folklore students. In the first place, the most striking and obvious result of research in the early days of folkloristic study was always the fantastically wide distribution of episodes and plots, and everyone therefore joined in diffusion studies. In the second place, there are certain conditions which must be fulfilled before intensive study of one body of folklore can yield any considerable fruits, and these conditions have not often been met in the available collections. For the most profitable study of single bodies of mythology, folktales should hold an important place in the tribal life, not being relegated, for example, to children's amusement or used solely as word-perfect recitations of magical formulae; a large body of tales should have been recorded, and over as long a period as possible; the culture of

---

[6] Ed. note: Johannes Bolte (1858-1937) and Georg Polívka (1858-1933), compilers of the *Anmerkungen zu den Kinder-und Hausmärchen der Brüder Grimm* (5 vols., Leipzig, 1913-32), exhaustive comparative notes to the folktale texts collected and published by the Grimm brothers.

[7] Franz Boas, *Tsimshian Mythology,* 31st Annual Report, Bureau of American Ethnology (1916), pp. 393-477; Franz Boas, *Kwakiutl Culture as Reflected in Mythology,* Memoirs of the American Folklore Society, No. 28 (1935); Clara Ehrlich, "Tribal Culture in Crow Mythology," *Journal of American Folklore* [Vol. 50 (1937), 307-408].

[8] Franz Boas, "The Folklore of the Eskimo," *Journal of American Folklore,* Vol. 17 (1904), 1-13. See also Ralph S. Boggs, "The Hero in the Folk Tales of Spain, Germany, and Russia," *Journal of American Folklore,* Vol. 44 (1931), 27-42.

[9] See, for a comparative study, D. Demetracopoulou, "The Loon Woman Myth: A Study in Synthesis," *Journal of American Folklore,* Vol. 46 (1933), 101-28.

the people who tell the tales should be well known; and folklore among that people should be a living and functioning culture trait.

These optimum conditions are fulfilled in the folklore of Zuni, the largest pueblo of the Southwest of the United States. Even compared with other North American tribes, mythology is a highly developed and serious art in Zuni, and the great number of tales that have been collected by many different persons extend over a period of fifty years. The culture of Zuni is well known, and in discussing the tales I have been able to use my own first-hand acquaintance with Zuni beliefs and behavior, as well as detailed accounts by other students. Finally, in contrast to that of almost all other tribes of the North American continent, folklore in Zuni is not moribund. The processes that can be studied in it are not reconstructed in a kind of folkloristic archaeology but are open to observation and experiment.

When these conditions can be fulfilled, intensive study of a single body of folklore is of first-rate theoretical importance, whether the problem at issue is historical reconstruction, the study of culture, or literary problems in the development of oral traditions. It seems obvious enough that studies in the two latter problems can be carried out best by careful intensive study, and that the students of symbolism, for example, have overlooked in favor of misleading comparative studies a method of work which can yield definite results. Even in the matter of historical reconstruction, also, which is the chief end of comparative studies of folklore, intensive study has also much to contribute. The usual library-trained comparative student works with standard versions from each locality; in primitive cultures, usually one from a tribe. This version arbitrarily becomes "the" tribal tale, and is minutely compared with equally arbitrary standard tales from other tribes. But in such a body of mythology as that of Zuni, many different variants coexist, and the different forms these variants take cannot be ascribed to different historical levels, or even in large measure to particular tribal contacts, but are different literary combinations of incidents in different plot sequences. The comparative student may well learn from intensive studies not to point an argument that would be invalidated if half a dozen quite different versions from the same tribe were placed on record.

The two problems which I shall consider at the present time from the analysis of Zuni mythology are: I, the themes which their folklore elaborates and the relation of these to their culture; II, the literary problems of the Zuni narrator.

I

No folktale is generic. It is always the tale of one particular people with one particular livelihood and social organization and religion. The final form that a tale takes in that culture is influenced, often fundamentally, by attitudes and customs that cannot be discovered except with full knowledge of life and behavior among that people. It has always been obvious to students of every theoretical persuasion that folklore tallied with culture and yet did not tally with it, and the majority of students have agreed upon one convenient explanation of those instances where the two are at odds. Folklore, it is said, reflects not the customs and beliefs of the narrators of the tales, but those of many generations past; cultural survivals of earlier ages are perpetuated in folklore, and these, it is often felt, are the chief reasons for the study of oral traditions. Even conditions of barbarism in which fathers are supposed to have eaten their children, and conditions of primal life when man first gained ascendancy over animals, have been said to be embalmed in folklore.

A conservatism that perpetuates long-discarded customs, however, is characteristic of a dead lore rather than a living one, and the great emphasis on the importance of survivals in the interpretation of folklore is evidently due to certain characteristics of oral tradition in Western civilization. European folklore was rescued from the memories of old men and women much as that of the Plains Indians is rescued today. It was recorded by collectors long after its heyday. Grimm's tales are found to reflect the manners and customs of the feudal age, not contemporary contacts with industrialism or with urban civilization, and the belief has become current that survivals of old customs are perpetuated in folklore through great lapses of time. This, however, is to generalize the senescence of folklore into a law by means of which mythology is elaborately interpreted. Folklore often remains current and can be adequately collected when it is no longer a living trait. North American Indians can almost always relate their folktales long after their aboriginal cultural life is in abeyance, and many valuable bodies of mythology have been collected in dead cultures from old men who learned the stories in their youth. The functioning of myth in culture and the processes of cultural adaptation, however, cannot be adequately studied in these cases. Comparison of variants under such conditions indicates mainly how much or how little different informants have forgotten of a dead culture trait, and such comparison is comparatively unrewarding. In Zuni tales are constantly told, and recounting folktales is an habitual occupation of a great number of the most important members of the community.

A living folklore, such as that of Zuni, reflects the contemporary interests and judgments of its tellers, and adapts incidents to its own cultural usages. Like any cultural trait, folklore tends, of course, to perpetuate traditional forms, and there is a certain lag in folklore as there is in contemporary statecraft or in morals. But the scope of this conservatism is limited in folklore as in other traits. It is never sufficient to give us license to reconstruct the items of a racial memory; and contemporary attitudes are always to be reckoned with, rather than those that have been superseded in that culture. In the present collection the cultural lag is apparent in many details of overt behavior. In the folktales, for example, except in those recognized by the tellers as Mexican, entrance to the house is by means of a ladder to the roof and down another ladder from the hatchway, yet doors have been common in Zuni since 1888 and are today universal except in the kivas. Old conditions, therefore, have been equally retained in the ceremonial house and in the folktale. The same may be said of the use of stone knives. Stone knives are still laid upon altars and used in ceremonies; and in folktales also heroes use stone knives instead of the omnipresent contemporary store knife. More elaborate modern innovations are also unrecognized in folklore. At present sheep herding occupies much of the life of Zuni men, and hunting is in abeyance. In the tales, however, all heroes are hunters, and there is no mention of sheep herding except in tales recognized as Mexican. In like manner men do not now come courting with a bundle of gifts for the girl, but in folklore this is a convention usually observed. Similarly, at the present time the activity of the medicine societies is centered in their great all-night ceremony at the winter solstice, the individual planting of prayer-sticks at full moon, and in not very exacting incidental activities. In the myths, on the other hand, every member goes every night to his medicine society and returns home when others are in bed.

The cultural lag that is represented by these differences between custom in contemporary life and in folktales covers, however, a short period, and by no means gives indication of an early cultural horizon such as can be reconstructed, for instance, from comparative studies of culture, still less from studies of comparative linguistics. The agreement between the conduct of contemporary life and the picture of life in the folktales is very close. The roles of men and women in Zuni life, the role of the priesthoods, the conduct of sex life, the concern with witchcraft, are all faithfully indicated.

Where there is a contrast between Zuni custom and literary convention, the divergence commonly rests upon other considerations than survival of older customs. Even in the divergences just mentioned, cultural lag is not a sufficient explanation. It may well be, as any native will assure you, that, in times not long past, men spent every night in their medicine society meetings. On the other hand, it is possible that in those times as in these, this was a conventional description of a golden age, and golden ages have often existed only in the imagination. The impulse to idealize must be reckoned with in folkloristic contrasts with contemporary life even when it is also possible to set the difference down to cultural lag. Similarly, courting with bundles may not be a survival of an older custom but a borrowed incident which is a folkloristic convention. Stone knives and entrance through the hatchway also have become conventional attributes of a less troubled and ideal age, and from this point of view should be considered along with the fabulous prowess of heroes as runners in the stick race.

This tendency to idealize in folklore has often been pointed out. There is another set of discrepancies in Zuni folklore that cannot so easily be disposed of. The most striking instance is that of the constant recurrence of polygamy in the tales. Zuni institutions are thoroughly monogamous. It is of course conceivable that the folkloristic pattern reproduces earlier conditions. Polygamy is allowed almost everywhere in North America outside the Southwest and even polyandry is accepted in certain nearby tribes. The absence of any taboo against multiple spouses is an old and general North American Indian trait. To assign the Zuni folkloristic pattern, however, to such a reflection of an earlier background is difficult for two reasons. In the first place, all pueblo cultures have the Zuni taboo on polygamy and pueblo culture is exceedingly old and stable, as one may judge from archaeological evidence in material culture. It is doubtful whether any folklore can be cited from any part of the world that reflects cultural conditions as remote as those before pueblo culture took form, and there is, therefore, good reason for dissatisfaction with this explanation. In the second place, even if it were possible to interpret the Zuni folkloristic pattern of polygamy as a survival, we should still have to explain why the marriage with eight wives or with two husbands is prominent in Zuni mythology and not generally over North America. The simultaneous marriage with many wives was culturally allowed over most of the continent, but it does not figure in their tales as it does in pueblo folklore. The presumption that is indicated by a study of the distribution of this folkloristic pattern in North America is that in the pueblos polygamy is a grandiose folkloristic convention partaking on the one hand of usual mythological exaggeration and on the other of a compensatory daydream. Just as the hero of folktales kills a buck every day, or four in a single day, so he also is courted by eight maidens and marries them. When a hero is given supernatural power by his supernatural father, he signalizes it by accepting all eight of the priests' daughters who had flouted him, killing them, and resuscitating them to serve his triumph. It is a grandiose demonstration of power, and of the same nature as the rain-blessing the eight wives bring back to the pueblo after their resuscitation, a blessing so great that the consequent flood fills the whole valley and the people have to escape to the top of the mesa. In the same way the hunter whose sister uses her supernatural power in his behalf marries wives from all the seven towns, and in his witch wife's reprisal she has him abducted by eight Crane girls who keep him as their husband for four years. Marriage with many wives is a Zuni fantasy of the same order as raising the dead or travelling with seven-league boots in other bodies of folklore. It plays a fairy-tale role in Zuni mythology which is automatically rendered impossible in those areas of North America where tales of polygamy and polyandry have bases in fact. What compensatory elements the tale embodies it is hard to prove, but it seems likely that these are present.

Other contrasts between custom and folkloristic conventions must be explained as fundamentally compensatory. The abandonment of children at birth is a constantly recurring theme and is alien to Zuni custom. In real life it does not come up for consideration at all. Illegitimate children are cared for in their mothers' homes, and present-day gossips, though they specialize in outrageous libels, do not tell of any instance in which an infant has been done away with. All men and women, not only the parents, give children the fondest care. There is no cultural background for the abandonment of illegitimate children. It is harder to judge about the abandonment of young children in famine. The tales of migrations to pueblos where crops have not failed are based on fact and such incidents as *Children deserted in famine*[10] may possibly have occurred, where children too large to carry and too young to make the journey were left behind, though actual reminiscences are always of tender protection of the child.[11] The incidents, however, of the girl in childbed who overtakes her party, leaving the baby in the grinding stone, are regarded as fabulous by contemporary Zunis, like all tales of women who are able to get up immediately after childbirth as if nothing had happened. The abandonment of the child and the impossible physical recovery are grouped in one category. When the story of babies abandoned at birth is used in explanation of Zuni custom, the narrator concludes from the incident: "That's why girls who become pregnant before marriage conceal their condition,"—which is true,—not "That's why they expose their babies."

The fact remains that abandonment of children is an extraordinarily popular theme in Zuni folklore. The clue lies in the fact that the hearers' identification is with the child, not with the mother. Even women, who would be expected to identify with the mother in telling these tales, comment on the reunion of the abandoned child with his mother from the point of view of the child. "He made her cry all right," a woman said with heat, and, "Oh, she (the mother) was *ashamed.*" The plots are all concerned with the supernatural assistance and human success of the poor child, and often the whole plot is directed toward the triumph of the abandoned child over the mother or the parents. In Deer Boy B,[12] when the child claims his relationship to his mother, she weeps while all her family scorn her. In the popular tale of the *Deserted children protected by dragonfly* the parents return in poverty and miserably sue their children for favors. The daydream, from the point of view of the child, is completed by the final largess of the children and their appointment to priestly rank. In two versions of the Twin Children

---

[10] Ed. note: Benedict offers the following explanation for italicized citations of the kind found here: "Italicized captions of incidents refer to the form in which these are listed in the Index of Incidents, Vol. II" (I, xi, n. 1). The entries in her Index of Incidents (Vol. II, 334-45) are similar to what folklorists call *motifs*—i.e., recurring content elements (e.g., "ghost pursuit," "heart of wrongdoer removed," "separable soul," "snake husband").

[11] Ed. note: Readers wishing to peruse actual Zuni folktale texts which contain this and other motifs mentioned by Benedict should consult the original version of her work, where such examples are provided in considerable numbers. See the explanation in n. 1 above.

[12] Ed. note: Benedict's reference here is to the second (B) text of two texts of a similar story, printed and referred to in the second volume of her study as "Deer Boy" (Vol. II, 12-20).

of the Sun, the twins return, make a laughingstock of their mother, and force her to confess. These two versions, which tell of the children's abandonment at birth, contrast strongly with the other two versions in which the girl does not expose her children but is killed by a witch or by the priests as a punishment for her unconfessed pregnancy. Her sons therefore do not humiliate her, but vindicate their mother's memory. The point of the story is entirely different.

The popularity of the theme of abandoned children in Zuni has a psychological significance that parallels the familiar daydreams of children in our civilization which detail their parents' suffering at their imminent death. That is, it is the expression of a resentment directed by children against their parents and worked out into a day-dream of the childrens' imagined vantage.

This resentment, and the narrator's identification with the child, is still clearer in the tales of boys whose gambling ruins them, and of children who are scolded. At least the deserted children are pitiful innocents and the identification of the Zuni audience with them might be on the basis of their lack of any wrongdoing. But the same attitude is taken toward girls who will not do their share of the work, and boys who gamble away all their mother's valuable possessions. Their triumph is not only recounted, but those who scolded them are held up to criticism and suffering is brought upon them. "Even though they saw them doing wrong, they should not have scolded them."[13]

Another popular theme in Zuni folklore which reflects culture somewhat obliquely is that of *Death sought by summoning the Apache*. These tales must be understood against the cultural fact that suicide is unknown and even inconceivable to the Zuni mind, and violence is culturally taboo.[14] There is no cultural channel for taking vengeance upon an unfaithful spouse,[15] and no idea of the possibility of ending one's own life. Folkloristic daydreams, however, provide for both. One of these is *Death sought by summoning the*

---

[13] Ed. note: Quotations such as the one given here are taken directly from folktale texts collected either by Benedict or other investigators.

[14] Ruth Benedict, "Psychological Types in the Cultures of the Southwest," *Proceedings of the Twenty-third International Congress of Americanists, September 1928* (New York, 1930), pp. 572-81 (see p. 581).

[15] The one situation where physical violence is institutionalized in Zuni, as in other pueblos, is the conflict between the wife and the husband's mistress. The two women may meet in a fist fight, in contemporary custom as in folklore. The man does not take part.

Apache. The abandoned wife sends a message to the Apache to come to destroy the pueblo. She washes herself for ceremonial cleanness and dances in her finest costume. She goes out to meet the Apache and is the first to be killed. Her faithless husband and his mistress are said to be the next victims. The daydream is particularly characteristic of Zuni in that it provides a means of achieving the imagined end without the necessity of any violent act save on the part of the Apache.

The same incident occurs at the behest of the priestly families, when they regard themselves as wronged by their people; they, too, dress themselves in their best and go out to meet death at the hands of outsiders. The most aberrant use of the situation is that in the tale of the young husband who thought his wife protested her love too much—demonstrativeness is suspect in Zuni custom—and called the Apache so that her indifference to his death could be exposed. In each case the story is a daydream motivated by resentment, and maneuvers the daydreamer into the martyr's position.

The other compensations which serve the wronged spouse as folkloristic daydreaming are available only to persons who have access to supernatural power and these are told consequently only for priests and witches. They approach simple situations of revenge more nearly than the tales we have been considering. Revenge tales are not differentiated according to sex, since if women have witch power they attempt to kill, as men do also when they use the power of the priests. The witch stories are analogous to European witch stories, as Zuni ideas of witchcraft also are analogous to European witch beliefs. They mirror Zuni culture to the extent that the jilted woman kills or transforms the woman who has supplanted her more often than her lost husband or lover. Similarly the faithful wife kills her faithless co-spouse.

The folktales of deserted husbands who have supernatural power at their command are tales of calamities brought about by priestly power. They are similar to the tale of the wronged wife, *Death sought by summoning the Apaches,* in that the objective they have in view is not a simple vengeance against the spouse or the present lover but a general destruction of innocent and guilty alike. It is specifically stated that the wronged spouse is miserable and wants other people to be miserable too. There is no singling out of the guilty such as constitutes the whole point of modern moral tales of infidelity, and which is retained to a limited extent in the more derivative witch tales. The characteristic daydream of Zunis who are unhappy is that others should suffer likewise.

Another theme, which also reflects Zuni culture but with a difference, is that of violent action based upon secret enmity. Grudges are cherished in Zuni. They are usually the rather generalized expression of slights and resentments in a small community. In actual life they give rise to malicious aspersions, but in folklore they are usually satisfied by nothing less than the death of the offender. People grudge others their prosperity and set about to destroy them; they grudge a man his success in hunting and attempt to do away with him; they are jealous of a supernatural who has brought a new dance to Zuni, and try to bewitch him; a priest who has not been paid for instruction kills the delinquent; the child who is scolded for shirking satisfies her grudge by leaving so that her family fear she is dead and recover her only after search by the supernaturals; people are angry because a [witch] girl will not lend a dipper [to another girl] and . . . therefore a feud starts and both girls are killed. Men and women both resent any slight in courtship; the woman tries to kill the man who has refused her a piece of his game (a usual courtship gesture in the tales), and men kill or bewitch girls who have laughed at them or refused them a drink (a courtship preliminary today as well). The deserted husband ritualistically causes a drought, an earthquake, or an epidemic, which threatens to wipe out the whole pueblo. The deserted wife similarly summons the Navahos or Apaches to demolish the village, or attempts to kill her husband. Unlike those of the Plains, Zuni folkways have no place for an ideal of character which overlooks slights, however small, and their folktales provide exaggerated fantasies of reprisal. In a culture in which homicide occurs with such extraordinary rarity that instances are not even remembered, the compensatory violence of these reprisals is the more striking.

True to the peculiar ideology of Zuni these reprisals are easily phrased as "teaching people to love you," i.e. to act decently toward you. The despised children, whom the people spit at, throwing refuse and urine into their grandmother's house, get the help of Salt Mother who takes away all the clothing in the pueblo. They tell her: "The people at Itiwana hate us. We want them to learn to love us." The people have to stay in bed all the time and in their shame are brought to the point of begging work from the poor children. The latter remove the curse when the people promise to "love them." The whole story is an excellent illustration of the strange way in which, according to Zuni notions, you teach people to love you.

Zuni folklore therefore in those cases where it does not mirror contemporary custom owes its distortions to various fanciful exaggerations and compensatory mechanisms. The role of daydreams, of wish fulfillment, is not limited to these cases of distortion. It is equally clear in the tales that most minutely reflect the contemporary scene. Zuni folklore differs from most North American Indian mythology in that the usual daydream is little concerned with prowess in warfare. Nor are there in Zuni accounts of supernatural encounters and the acquisition of power, such as fill the folktales of the Plains Indians. Zuni folktales are as faithful to Zuni fantasies in what they exclude as in what they include. Their most popular theme is the triumph of the despised and weak and previously worsted. The poor orphan boy is victorious in hunting, in stick races, in gambling, and in courtship; those who do not have witch power are triumphant over those who have; the stunted ragamuffin Ahaiyute win first place in everything. The detailed story is a generic daydream of the Zuni male, and is interwoven with the woman's daydream, which is more specifically presented in the tale.

Zuni folktales give an extraordinary place to women. Except for one point which will be discussed presently, the sexes of the protagonists are constantly reversed. Men or women may equally take the initiative in courtship. In these tales, when the man is the suitor, the women impose tests upon their suitors and refuse marriage, and when the woman is the suitor, the men do likewise. Men and women equally are taught marriage by supernaturals; and either men or women follow their spouses or sweethearts to the world of the dead. This evenhandedness in the role of the sexes, however, has one great exception. Women are thought to be more erotic than men are. Sex is not well understood nor its values rated high in Zuni, and they have not the cultural background which makes the "masculine protest" so common an element of male behavior in our civilization. Women are not thought to rate higher than men because they are more highly sexed; rather, it is felt that they make a dangerous demand upon men; and men fear this demand. This is strongly emphasized in the tales. The sexes are reversed in the rape tales. It is always the theme of the timid man that is developed, not of the frightened virgin. There is a group of tales in which the hunter flees from women who want sexual intercourse. He takes refuge all along the way; the woman catches up with him and again pursues him. He

is in a panic of terror. Even when he retraces his steps next day after
the fabulous Goat Man has killed his pursuer, "he saw the footprints
of Toothed Vagina Woman and his own footprints escaping from
her. His heart beat to see them." Even the powerful little Ahaiyute,
the patrons of war, are saved from their terror only by the institution
of the scalp dance; upon having intercourse with the Navaho girl
they summarily kill her, and she pursues them as a corpse from
refuge to refuge until they are taught the ceremonial of purification.

The corresponding theme for women is differently developed. Except for [the example cited by] Parsons,[16] it is not sexual advances
that are offered to women in such tales. The monsters offer to cut
off their heads, gore them, wrap them in their snake's coil, or to eat
them as they over and over again eat men and boys also.

One of the most popular stories in Zuni is that of the Rabbit
Huntress, of which four versions are recorded. Atocle, the scare
kachina, swallows all the girl's clothing so that she is shamed in her
nakedness, and tries to get at her to swallow her too, but Atocle is
a female kachina and the girl is afraid because the ogress is going to
eat her. Similarly in the tale of two girls trapped by an ogre with
black and white scales over his body, the indignity he offers them is
a stew of baby's bodies, and when he makes them louse him he is
preparing in turn to louse them by biting them in the neck, as in
other tales where people are killed for food.

Even in such a story as that of the girl who bathes and is made
pregnant by the Horned Serpent, the tale has not the affect we might
expect. All Zuni girls are taught that they will be entered by the
mythical Serpent if they immerse their bodies in bathing—actually
they never do so—but in folklore the stories that employ this taboo
are not nightmare tales. The girl merely acquires a supernatural
husband and is sent ceremonially to accompany him to his home as
any girl may be who marries a supernatural.

When the subject is of proposed sexual intercourse, women are
not pictured as frightened. The *Abduction* tales in Zuni, where the
woman is enticed by a man who meets her casually and takes her to
his house, contrast strongly with the stories of the frightened man.
The man with supernatural powers, the abductor, uses his powers to
bless her and to endow her children with power as often as he uses
his powers to force her to do hard work. But the tales in neither case

---

16 Elsie Clews Parsons, "Zuni Tales," *Journal of American Folklore*, Vol. 43 (1930),
1-58 (see p. 25).

are stories of fear of sexual violence on the part of the women; when the abductor uses her harshly the tale is a realistic reflection of the fact that men can require certain obedience from women when they have the power. Abduction stories in Zuni, in contrast to similar stories even in other pueblos, are handled as tales of the triumph of the husband (or of the supernaturals whose aid he secures) in recovering something that has been taken from him. From the point of view of the man, they become stories of the triumph of the weak and of the settling of a grudge. From the point of view of the woman, they are stories of handsome men they admire and desire; or if fear is suggested it is because of a threat to cut off their heads or eat them, see above. In the tale of Winter Man who accosted a maiden at the spring, took her to his home in his kickstick and treated her cruelly, the girl herself is successful in all encounters and finally kills him. She is thoroughly adequate in the situation, and Winter Man's sexual demands are not mentioned. "Oh, a woman wouldn't be afraid," men have answered when I asked for a tale corresponding to the group, The Hunter is pursued by Women, but with a woman as the victim.

Even when the story is of the violation of women the women take matters into their own hands. The idea that men take advantage [of] women in their sleep is not only folkloristic in the pueblos, it is current scandal, and I have been told of living Lotharios in Zuni and in Cochiti who have been successful in the practice. It is extraordinarily consistent with the man's clandestine subterfuges in sex expression. Bat Youth violates four girls in this way, but upon waking, their reaction is not one of fear. All they say is, "It is Bat Youth who has done this. Let us run after him and pay him back." They caught him before he reached the ladder of his house, and it was he who was so frightened he could not climb it. They tore off his clothing and shamed him in his nakedness. "That is why nobody thinks bats are pretty. Nobody says when he sees a bat, 'Oh, see that pretty bat flying!' And because of Bat Youth's shame bats still carry bedbugs."

Similarly erotic invitation is ascribed to women, not to men. Women doublecross their husbands and make assignations with lovers, and the lovers are reluctant and they take the initiative in sex play. A woman's ruse to secure sexual intercourse is the theme of The Thunder Knives. It is told of Badger Woman and of Horned-Toad Man, who was a doctor. She groaned terribly in pretended pain, begging him to massage her further and further down her body. When she got what she wanted, her pain was all gone. Since Horned Toad is the progenitor of the ancient stone knives called thunder knives in Zuni, she bore a pile of these knives, and the conclusion is, "That's why women don't want to conceive when they have intercourse."

The timid man figures constantly, also, in tales of courtship evasions. Courtship evasions are of course not peculiar to men; both men and women exhibit their superiority by turning down suitors. It is an occasion for pride almost as common in the tales as prowess in hunting. It proves superiority, as well for the woman as for the man. In two versions of the same tale, the girl in one humiliates the suitors, in the other, the youth. These tales of tests imposed in marriage, now upon women, now upon men, are not reflections of Zuni culture. Women are scrupulously taught not to be dilatory in accepting an offer, and men are proverbially eager to get a wife. They are daydreams of power and they are almost equally available to either sex. Only the poor and despised may not exhibit this form of pride in folktales.

Pride, however, must be curbed, and in all tales of reluctant suitors the role of the supernaturals is much in evidence. It is regarded as a specific function of supernaturals to teach the joys of intercourse, and without such teaching, virgins, both men and women, will be guilty of rejecting marriage. Even the Rabbit Huntress, who has had no suitors, and whose only irregular behavior was to assume the masculine prerogative of hunting to feed her aged parents, is punished by the encounter with Atocle, and her rescue by the Ahaiyute is in all versions the occasion of her instruction in marriage. In three versions, one of the heroes marries her himself, and, when he has taught her, instructs her to marry the first human man who asks her. In another group of tales, reluctant suitors, either men or women, hide game so that men fail while seeking a deer as a marriage test; the supernaturals finally release the deer and win the bride or bridegroom, turning their temporary spouses over to human suitors when they have been instructed. This theme is illustrative of the role of supernaturals in Zuni. They are thought of as stepping in to keep people from making mistakes, and one of the most likely of these mistakes is that of reluctance in regard to cohabitation.

The girl, however, is never portrayed in these tales as fearing the wedding night and circumventing it, but this is a familiar incident for the man. In "The Mannikin Wife" the boy makes himself a figure of a woman out of grass and a blanket, and lies with it. "He was ashamed with all the nice-looking girls who wanted to marry him and so he had to make this mannikin for a wife." The supernaturals step in as usual and teach him how to face the difficult situation of taking a human wife. In "The Man who married a Donkey" the son of the village priest is afraid of marriage and of the girls who court him and tries bestiality. "He thought how much better this was than taking a wife. . . . He thought all the time how sensible he had been not to take a wife and have all that trouble. He thought that this way he would never have any trouble." He is disillusioned only when he finds that the animal's period of heat is short, and retribution descends upon him when his donkey offspring discloses the truth to his father. His father gets the help of the Ahaiyute and they kill the half-human offspring and the youth has the good fortune to win a human wife whom he now knows how to value. The supernaturals tell his father that he is to blame for not having given his son sex instruction and trained him to accept the proper responsibilities: "You are a priest and you have not done these things."

The theme of the man's fear of submitting to a woman is developed also by means of several fantasies. Two of these are obvious: the hide and seek game proposed to a wandering man by a woman who demands that they stake their lives on the game, and the fantasy that brides appear as hags or as corpses in the morning. In the *Hide and Seek Game* the man always loses and is killed by the woman. "She seized him by the hair and cut off his head. She twisted his hair together, and she cut open his chest and took out his heart. She dug a hole in the earth and put his body in it and covered it with earth." The dangerous maiden and her sister are of course punished.

The incident, *Brides appear old in the morning,* is a courtship test which men must surmount. In case they do so they are rewarded with a successful marriage; but the nightmare is transparent: "He was lying with an old, old woman. Her eyes were almost shut. She was skin and bones. She was too weak to sit up and she scratched herself all the time."

The brides who appear as corpses in the morning, *Corpse Girls,* is used in a somewhat different connection. It appears in several tales, and points the moral that men who yield to feminine blandishments are really yielding to corpses, and will find skeleton arms wound about them in the morning. In three versions of Eagle Man, the wife tells her husband that he is not to smile at the girls who come to dance for him. They look very pretty, however, and he disobeys his wife. Instantly he is in their power and they spirit him away to their village of the dead, which is alive only at night. He goes to bed with them, but they smell like rotten meat so that he does not have intercourse with them. "At sunrise he woke up and the roof of that house was all falling down around them and a dead girl lay on each side of him with their arms over his chest. He jumped up and threw aside their arms and ran as fast as he could."

Witch tales also develop this masculine fear of women. They are fantasy, since actual witchcraft techniques are apparently not owned and taught in Zuni. Witchcraft is terribly feared, but it is a Zuni anxiety neurosis, and actual witch practices, in the Melanesian manner, are unrecorded. There are no stories of witch husbands; but the fear is directed toward the wife, or the sweetheart whom the youth has passed over. She betrays him by leaving him upon the top of a rock from which he cannot descend, or she calls the rest of the witches and attempts the life of the hunter.

The man's fear of sex which is constantly turned to the wedding night may be illustrated from still other stories. The Zuni noodle tales are especially told to describe the discomfiture of the suitor and the young husband, and some of these stories make use of a transparent symbolism. In one of them the girl he has just slept with sets meat before him and gives him the little salt pot. He cannot reach the salt at first and gets his whole fist stuck in the pot. He runs to his grandmother who tries to make him go back, work his hand out of the pot and give her property back to the girl. " 'No, I won't do it,' says the young man, and strikes the salt pot against the wall and breaks it, spilling salt all around." In another, a kitten scratches him between the legs while he is eating and he screams. When he sees it is only a kitten, he covers his shame by admiring the kitten and proposing that he take it to show to his grandmother. As soon as he gets around the corner, he swings the kitten against a wall and kills it. His grandmother tries to make him go back. " 'No, I'm out of it,' and he would not go back." The images of killing the kitten and breaking the salt pot are apt.

In all these tales it is evident that it is the Zuni boy, not the girl, who fears the wedding night and has to be fortified for marriage. This theme is fully developed in "The Boy who had to learn to marry." Zuni does not celebrate the innocence of the young girl but that of the young boy. It is he who is so naive that he runs home to his grandmother at the advances of a young girl. He tells his grandmother, "I like her in the daytime but nights I think I shall run away from her." His grandmother lets him sleep with her and fortified with his newly acquired knowledge he accepts the girl on the next occasion. "They always lived happily because the boy married before he knew anything about girls." It is a story of the ideal marriage, like the stories in our own romances of the sweet innocent girl who makes the most acceptable wife.

Another popular theme in Zuni is that of the reunion of families. This favorite Zuni conclusion had often been apparent in tales already discussed. The Deserted Children, in contrast to the usual form of this tale in other parts of North America, ends with a happy reunited family; the story of the ruined gambler ends with the happy reunion when he is welcomed back; tales of girls who are chastised and leave home end with the reconciliation when they are at last discovered after great search; men who are taken in marriage in the sky land get homesick and return happily. This is thoroughly in keeping with the strength of the matrilineal family bond in Zuni. In the conjugal relationship the theme takes a more unusual form. In these tales the favorite theme is that of the return of the husband to the first wife whom he has abandoned. This is strongly felt in Zuni, and the motivation may easily be missed by readers of another civilization to whom the theme is not familiar. It is a common interpretation of death, i.e. the husband returns in death to the wife to whom he had long since been false. The incidents may readily seem confused without an understanding of the force of the traditional conclusion. The man sleeps with a girl whose mother has entertained him when he is overtaken by night on the hunt; in the morning he finds skeleton arms wound about him and the mother pursues him as a rolling skull. Porcupine helps him to overcome Skull and he marries Porcupine Girl. After four years he meets Eagle Girl and goes with her as her husband to her home in the sky. He is faithless to her with Chicken Hawk Girl, but is reconciled to his Eagle Wife who warns him against Corpse Girls who try to play with him as they dance. He is snatched off by them, and he is stripped by his outraged Eagle Wife and falls, which brings about his return in death to his first wife, the ghost girl. All the erotic adventures merely give point to the favorite theme.

The same theme is felt in the story of the deserted wife who calls the Apache to destroy the pueblo. The first to be killed are the wife who has summoned the enemy, her faithless husband, and his mistress. After the story was ended, I asked, "What then?" and the narrator said, "Oh, she got him back again. She was his first wife."

There is a singular mildness in Zuni tales, and this mildness is strangely at variance with the compensatory violence we have already discussed in the reprisal stories which have cherished grudges as their theme. In these latter the violence of the daydream is fabulous, and the very fact that it is not a reflection of Zuni behavior allows the vengeance to take the most extreme forms. In other tales the mildness of actual Zuni life and institutions are accurately reflected. The idea of trapping all the witches into an ambush from which they could kill Apaches and must therefore have to become bow priests is a curious one. "So A·lucpa caught all the witches in the bow priesthood. They were forced to go into retreat and be purified. They were bow priests. Only one witch had not been able to go out. So one witch was left. That is why there is no witch society any more, because A·lucpa made them all bow priests." This tale in no way calls in question the great prestige of the bow priesthood in Zuni, nor the fear and hatred of witches. Nevertheless the conclusion is felt as adequate. In a case of personal vengeance, the priest's son who has been distressed at his wife's demonstrativeness, calls the Apache to kill him in order to test his wife's faithfulness to his memory. She is merely left to enjoy herself at the favorite yaya dance, by which he proves her affection was too shallow to allow for proper respect for her husband. "He turned into an eagle, and that is why we value eagle feathers."

Similarly, bestiality and sexual fetishism, in the tales already discussed, are regarded as shameful, but the erring youths are aided by the supernaturals and protected by human beings and their misstep is corrected, not punished. In the former tale, it is the father of the boy who is rebuked because, though he was a priest, he had not given his boy the education which would have prevented the moral breach.

All the tales of abandoned children are similarly mild, and we have spoken before of the revision of the "Deserted Children" story in Zuni, whereby instead of killing the parents, they are only humiliated for four days, even for only one day. Pautiwa's rebuke to the proud maiden who has refused her lovers because she required them to bring her scalps is typical: "Perhaps if you had been wise, you might have been beloved, but now you have wished for evil days," as is also the comment on the girl who has scolded her lazy sister who did not do her share of the housework: "For even though these were children of a priest they did not love one another, and so they (the supernaturals) tried them for a while. They hid their sister from them. Even though they used to see her doing wrong, they should not have scolded her." And narrators keep introducing into plots which demand revenge: "Let's not kill her. She's quite nice." "Let's stop now. Don't let's kill so many people."

II

The literary problems which confront a primitive narrator are easily misunderstood. The gap between the traditionalism of primitive mythology and the emphasis upon originality in our own literature is so great that the reader from our civilization confronted by a collection of folktales is often led to false conclusions. Many students have assumed that the fixity of tales is absolute or almost so, that the individual narrator has no literary problems, and that the tales originated in a mystical source called communal authorship. On the other hand, it would be as easy to interpret the tales as far more fortuitous than they really are, for from the point of view of the outsider the incidents out of which the tale is built might just as well be other incidents, the stylistic elements might as well be omitted or amplified in any imaginable direction. In fact, because of the diffuseness and ease of prose, it is far easier to mistake the problems of the artist in this field than, for instance, in the plastic arts.

There is no more communal authorship in folklore than there is a communal designer in ironwork or a communal priest in religious rites. The whole problem is unreal. There is no conceivable source of any cultural trait other than the behavior of some man, woman or child. What is communal about the process is the social acceptance by which the trait becomes a part of the teaching handed down to the next generation. The role of the narrator in such a body of folklore as that of Zuni remains as real as that of any story teller in any civilization though its scope is somewhat changed by the role of the audience.

On the other hand, even more serious misunderstanding of folklore is introduced by the outsider's inability to appreciate the fixed limits within which the narrator works. The artist works within definite traditional limits as truly in folklore as in music. The first requisite in understanding any folk literature is to recognize the boundaries within which he operates.

In Zuni, tales fall into no clearly distinguishable categories. The divisions I have used in this volume are for convenience of reference only, and have little to do with the literary problems of the narrator. Even the Emergence story, which is the Zuni scripture, is not reserved for the priests nor owned by them. It is freely repeated by any fireside by any layman, and all versions differ markedly, not so much in order of incidents as in the details introduced. Incidents of it, moreover, can be lifted and used as the basis of entertaining stories.

Tales of kachinas, also, form no special group. Kachinas are freely introduced even into European tales, and are heroes of romances who marry several wives, contest with witches, and win in stick races. Much of the stock saga of the Ahaiyute has evidently been ascribed to them since Cushing's day,[17] and these little supernatural twins figure as supernatural helpers in tales of every kind. They make themselves a "kapitan" and buy a dog from a Mexican in a patently Mexican tale. In other cases the Ahaiyute tales are direct transcriptions of Zuni daydreams, and represent the wish fulfillments most desired by the people. A variety of stories are attributed to the Ahaiyute in one of several versions, and it seems probable that this tendency is still operative in Zuni. If that is true, still other stories that were not yet told of the twins ten years ago when these stories were collected may become Ahaiyute stories in the future.

It is in keeping with the fact that folklore is such a living and popular trait in Zuni at the present time that tales of European derivation are so little differentiated from others. The ones that are popular or have been told for some time or are retold by a good narrator often mirror the details of Zuni life to the last degree. Cushing fifty years ago published an excellent example of this in his day in the tale of "The Cock and the Mouse," which adapted an Italian accumulative tale he had himself repeated in Zuni.[18] In this volume "The Man who married the Donkey," is an excellent example of such acculturation, as is also "Tail by Tail."

Animal trickster tales, which form so large a bulk of many North American mythologies, are little told. Children's tales, usually a few

---

[17] Ed. note: Frank Hamilton Cushing (1857-1900), American anthropologist who lived for five years among the Zunis and who published numerous works on Zuni ethnography, including studies of mythology.

[18] Ed. note: This is reported in Frank Hamilton Cushing, *Zuni Folk Tales* (New York, 1901), pp. 411-22. It has been reprinted recently in *The Study of Folklore,* ed. Alan Dundes (Englewood Cliffs, N.J., 1965), pp. 269-76.

sentences that go with a nursery song, are little represented in this collection but they exist in greater numbers.

In all tales, therefore, since the short animal incident occurs so rarely, roughly the same objectives are present to the narrator. Of these stylistic aims, probably the one most relied upon is the endless incorporation of cultural details. In most mythologies the picture of cultural life that can be abstracted from the tales, as in the studies of the Tsimshian, Kwakiutl, and Crow, is a comparatively adequate description of most phases of social life, but in Zuni there is in addition a loving reiteration of detail that is over and above this faithful rendition. The most extreme examples are the long descriptions of ceremonies which are reserved for another volume of Zuni Ceremonial Tales. These have practically no plot but are strung together on some thread such as that of the Pekwin who grieved for his dead wife and was comforted by each of the three religious organizations of Zuni, which each brought out a dance in turn, and finally by the great ceremony of the Corn Dance. In one of these ceremonies more than forty participants in the dance are severally invited by the bow priests to take part. In each of the forty retellings the priests go to the individual's house, greet those who live there with the conventional greeting, "How have you lived these days, my fathers, my mothers, my children?" are answered, fed, thank them for the food, explain the part in the dance they wish them to assume and conduct them back to the priests' chamber or leave them to prepare for the occasion. In each case, also, the moment's occupation of the principal occupants of the room are described as the priests enter. Practice for the dancing and the great occasion itself are meticulously described in the same fashion.

The excess of cultural detail is similarly apparent in the present collection. The Corn Maidens, The Rabbit Huntress, Ahaiyute marries the Bow Priest's Daughter, Lazy Bones, The Deserted Husband causes an Epidemic, and The Navaho come against Zuni are all good examples. The tale does not merely assume the cultural background, as the tale of any people must; it itemizes each detailed observance and encounter.

The Zuni narrator, besides this general preoccupation, has a special obligation to relate certain details. The greeting formulas, with the offer of food to the visitor and his thanks, recur constantly. Localization is imperative, and certain places are the scenes of certain kinds of incidents, as Cunte'kaia is the scene of witch tales and Hecokta of ogre tales. Indication of points of the compass is marked, but is much less of a stylistic necessity than in the pueblo tales from Laguna, for instance.[19] The introduction of helpful animals is marked in all tales where such incidents are relevant. Such animals, according to their abilities, fly, gnaw, or kill, for the hero. Stylistic obliviousness to incisiveness or condensation is obvious in all the tales and if anything is only the more marked in the text translations.

The Zuni narrator is almost always free to incorporate his special knowledge in a tale. If he has taken part in a Corn Dance, his incidents of the Corn Dance practice reproduce his own experience, which is then of course retold by others. Men, as well as women, incorporate accounts of woman's childbirth ritual, or of cooking techniques. The Emergence tale is used as a basis for the incorporation of a variety of ritual with which a narrator is familiar.

Cushing's tale of "The Cock and the Mouse" has already been mentioned. It is a striking example of the extent to which Zuni stylistic requirements operate to remodel a borrowed tale. He himself told a group of native friends a European accumulative tale and a year later recorded the same tale as he heard it told by one of his listeners. The European tale tells simply of the joint nut-gathering adventure of the cock and the mouse. When the cock had tried in vain to reach the nuts he asked the mouse to throw some down to him, and the nut cut the cock's head. He ran to an old woman to get it bandaged, and she asked two hairs for payment. He ran to the dog for these, who asked bread. He went to the baker who asked wood, to the forest which asked water. He went to the fountain, which gave him water, and so he retraced his steps and got his head bound up. The story is bare of all further details. In keeping with Zuni narrative standards, the adapted version begins with a description of the old woman and her turkey yard, "like an eagle cage against a wall." The cock of the original story has appropriately enough become a Zuni pet turkey, and the fact that the turkey has a beard while the cock has not, is capitalized in the resulting story. The old woman had only the one turkey and she was too poor to give it meat, so that the turkey was always meat-hungry. One day he caught sight of Mouse's tail disappearing in his hole and snapped it up for a worm. Now the mouse's tail was his "sign of manhood" and he vowed vengeance. So

---

[19] Franz Boas, *Keresan Texts,* Publications of the American Ethnological Society, Vol. 8 (2 vols., New York, 1926-28).

far the additions are by way of supplying the traditional literary motivation of the despised and put-upon who set out to overcome their enemies. The mouse, therefore, made friends with the cock, who allowed him to eat crumbs thrown him by the old woman, and finally brought the turkey a nut out of his own hoard. The turkey lamented that he was not free like the mouse to gather such nuts and the mouse offered to gnaw the fastening of his corral. This incident is the familiar *Helpful Animals:* rodent (mouse, gopher, etc.) gnaws (ropes, wall, tree roots, etc.). When the nut hit the turkey he was stunned, fell "dead" as the Zunis say, and the mouse avenged himself by gnawing off his neck bristles, his "signs of manhood," in exact compensation for what he had himself suffered. This is the familiar incident and is especially connected in Zuni with *Underground to the Monster,* where the rodent shaves the monster directly over his heart. When the turkey could get up he went to the old woman to have his head bound and she asked him for four neck bristles, i.e. his signs of manhood. But they had been gnawed off. He therefore went to the dog, etc., until at last he got to the spring to ask for water, and the spring asked for prayersticks which should pay the gods for rain. It came and he retraced his steps and was healed. The story is easily a better story than its original; it has been thoroughly adapted to its new cultural setting by the incorporation of all sorts of observations of Zuni life, motivation has been skillfully built up, and well-known Zuni incidents have been appropriately introduced in a thoroughly workmanlike manner.

The second ideal of the Zuni stylist is in the building up [of] plot sequences out of large numbers of incidents. A Zuni audience likes very long tales, and the majority of stories combine in different ways several well-marked incidents. These incidents are stock property, and their outlines are known to all the audience. It is impossible to understand Zuni stylistic problems without this realization of what is traditional material. The collections of Zuni folklore that are now available do not reproduce all the tales that are told or may be told, but they give at least the elements out of which these would be built up. The study of the different variants indicates the principles of composition, and the way in which these elements, and new ones when they are introduced, are handled by the native narrators.

The stock incidents available in the composition of Zuni tales are indicated in the Index of Incidents, and those which are used in any given story are listed in the footnote to each tale. The principle themes in the service of which these incidents are combined have been discussed above in this introduction. The narrator's skill is shown in his use of these stock incidents in elaborating these stock themes, and an examination of the tales shows clearly that this is no mean role. The way in which incidents are combined is certainly a main interest of the Zuni audience, and the skill with which this is done by the narrator can be illustrated over and over again.

Certain of these combinations of incidents are very stable, and such complex stories as the Box Boat and the Sun's Twins follow the same sequence in Cushing's versions and in the present collection. Cushing's tales were recorded fifty years ago, and from families with quite different ceremonial affiliations and clan relationships. The sequences of incidents in these cases had very likely become popular and fairly fixed long before Cushing's time, and they may well hold firm until folktales are no longer told in Zuni.

Even in such a tale as the Sun's Twins, however, the scope of the narrator in building plot is clearly marked. Version A in this collection reproduces the Cushing tale; it is the theme of the proud maiden magically impregnated by a supernatural, publicly killed because she was about to bear illegitimate children, and vindicated by her two sons at the direction of their supernatural father. The great contrast between these two versions is the cleverness with which the thoroughly non-Southwestern ceremony of the Cushing version (this part of Cushing's story has many Shoshonean analogues) has been transformed into the familiar ceremony of the Zuni scalp dance in the present tale. This present version, moreover, has dropped the concluding incidents of the Cushing tale: the death of the two sons as a consequence of their disobedience to their supernatural father, the resurrection of one of them as the Skull Husband and the repetition of the original supernatural pregnancy of the priest's daughter with her death, also by a fall from the sky, in a public retribution. This omission of the concluding incidents consolidates the plot, just as the changes in the ceremony bring it into agreement with Zuni cultural behavior.

The difference between these two versions, however, and versions B and C in this collection is more drastic. The same incidents have been used in these latter versions to elaborate a different theme: that of the sons' humiliation of the mother who abandoned them at birth. By introducing into these versions this stock incident of abandonment in childbirth, the narrator is under obligation to develop his story differently. He uses the old Cushing situation of the yaya dance to which the twins come at the direction of their father to dance in the pueblo, but instead of vindicating their dead mother by honoring the eight "mothers" with whom they dance, they dazzle their proud mother who abandoned them, make her select them as her chosen husbands, and humiliate her by announcing their relationship and her act in abandoning them. Version C is concluded at this point, but Version B continues with the concluding incidents of the Cushing tale which were dropped in Version A.

This role of the Zuni narrator in adapting incidents to different themes is apparent in many tales. The narrator must follow out the implications of the new sequence he has chosen. The same informant tells a like series of incidents, the Eagle Wife story with the broken taboo on laughing at the dance of the corpse girls, but he has dropped the *Borrowed feathers* incident which Cushing gives also in his version, according to which Eagle Wife brings about her husband's death when he attempts to return to earth and leave her, and has substituted a series of miracles by means of which he overcomes all obstacles and is ceremonially returned with gifts by the Eagles. The story has been adapted therefore to the theme of the blessings acquired through marriage with the supernaturals.

In his other version he retains the *Borrowed feathers* incident, but he builds up to it by relating a series of faithless adventures with other women to motivate his wife's retribution, introducing especially an initial incident of an affair with a ghost girl so that the whole story is told to the favorite theme of the husband's reunion in death with his first wife, i.e. the ghost girl.

Another version is a still different treatment of these incidents. The initial incident is the *Bungler's Instruction in Hunting.* The character of the hero is set in this incident; he is a bungler, and throughout the story he is true to this character. He ignores a supernatural's directions; he is an inept lover; he is laughed at by his Eagle Wife for offering his rabbits to the skeleton which was his Ghost Wife; when he leaves her, he deceives Eagle Girl instead of asking for her help. In motivating the husband's death in this way, the narrator has had to reverse the order of the two marriages, but he has achieved as the others have in different ways, an integrated story. The interpreter said at the end of this tale, "He had all this trouble because of what he did to the rabbits," i.e., the rabbits whose killing he had bungled at the beginning of the tale.

The incident of the *Butterfly pursuit* is another illustration of the implications recognized by Zuni narrators in plot combinations. Three versions combine this incident with the *Hide and seek game with a dangerous maiden.* The kachina identifications are quite different in Versions A and B, and in the former since the hero assumes the form of the Ne'we·kwe, the licentious clown, he summons Coyote and both of them punish the girls with intercourse; in the latter since he is Paiyatamu, the gracious impersonation associated with sun and flowers, flute music and love, he transforms the sisters into butterflies, which are here associated with eroticism, and sends them to the four directions to call the rain, i.e. instruments of fertility magic. In the Bunzel version the narrator has carried out still further the associations with Ne'we·kwe, suppressing details which do not belong to this cult and emphasizing details that are in character.

These three versions contrast strongly with the Bunzel ms version. In this case the *Butterfly pursuit* has been used alone, without introducing the *Hide and seek game.* The story is of a proud maiden who had no time for suitors but occupied herself with her basket making. She wanted to catch the butterfly to copy its marking in her basket patterns, and she pursued it till it disappeared in the Ne'we·kwe spring. She followed and was taken in marriage by the Ne'we·kwe who had shown himself as a butterfly. When he had taught her the human role of marriage, she returned home and married, but eventually returned to her first husband, and her children were the Ne'we·kwe society. The incident, therefore, has been used to point [out] two favorite Zuni themes, *Marriage taught by supernaturals to those who refuse it,* and the *Return in death to the first husband.*

Other examples of the recognition by Zuni narrators of the literary problems involved in various transpositions are discussed in the notes: the two versions of the Bridegroom is required to kill a Deer, in which the courtship test is imposed in one case by a girl and in the other by a youth; the three versions in which the test is possible of accomplishment and the two in which the unwilling youth or maiden supernaturally render it impossible; the consequences of substituting a human husband for the Ahaiyute, in the version of the Girl who requires a Scalp of her Suitors; the Tarantula steals the Youth's Clothing which is told in the present collection to the theme of the humiliation of a youth who refuses marriage and in the Cushing version without reference to this theme; the versions of Parrot Girl, of Deer Boy, of the Deserted Child guided by Awl, of the incident *Transformation into Coyote* which in three out of four versions is the regular conclusion of Deer Boy in Zuni, and is used as conclusion also in a similar tale of a despised boy who gains a patron in Coyote, but which is transferred to the initial incident of a plot which allows the development of the theme of the hunter's revenge upon his false friend.

The freedom with which plots may be built up is made clear also by a consideration of certain incidents which serve as stock introductions or conclusions to a variety of tales. Whenever the plot allows its use, the incident of *Supernaturals are sent to shrines* may be called in requisition. The *Orpheus* incident is popular in a similar capacity, as well as the *Contests to retain a wife,* and *Witch contests.* The *Apparation impersonated to punish evildoers or enemies* is used both as introduction and conclusion to several tales. The *Kachinas at Kachina Village provide food or clothing* is requisitioned in almost any tale in which it is appropriate. The *Marriage taught by supernaturals to those who refuse it,* the *Magical impregnations* by Sun or Horned Serpent, the *Famine is caused by misuse of corn in a game* are popular introductions in tales the plots of which differ completely.

These elements (incidents) are often cleverly adapted to serve the plot. This can be most clearly illustrated in tales from other peoples adopted in Zuni. The story of the *Mare Wife* becomes in Zuni a means of stating quite completely the native views of marriage and the necessary sex education of the boy. The story of *Tail by Tail* is completely and elaborately assimilated to the favorite theme of kachina origins. The popular Shoshonean incident of *Odors as deadly* (usually identified with bullets) is adapted to a tale of famine caused by too much rainfall and a priest's device for overpowering and driving away the rain gods. The noodle tales are adapted to the situation of the reluctant and self-conscious bridegroom.

It is obvious that where such freedom in handling incidents is expected of a good story teller, it will often become impossible to trace with assurance a tale's genetic relationship with tales of other peoples. The likelihood that Cushing's satire on the scalp dance is a Zuni handling of the Turtle's War Party, and the Little Girl and the Turkeys of the Cinderella story is discussed in the notes,[20] and in both cases the ease and freedom of the Zuni adaptation to its native themes and ceremonies is complete.

---

[20] Ed. note: Benedict refers here to her own notes in *Zuni Mythology,* Vol. I, 294; and Vol. II, 259.

The Zuni narrator is also allowed freedom in the use of stock folkloristic devices. The loads made magically light, the runners who carry straws or gourds or feathers to run lightly, the inexhaustible meals provided by helpful animals, the magically surmounted precipices, are all legion. Good story tellers usually incorporate these devices at any appropriate point.

The greatest freedom allowed the Zuni narrator, however, is in the adaptation of the tale to explanations and origins. Such "that's why's" are a stylistic requirement in Zuni, and no American Indian folklore presents such a prodigality of explanatory elements. They are seldom standardized, so that the same explanatory elements occur in different versions even of the same tale, and good story tellers often give several to one tale. The explanatory elements attached to the story of the Deserted Children in four versions illustrates the freedom with which they are habitually inserted:

Hence to this day the dragonfly comes in early summer humming from one plant to another, yet never content with its resting place.
For this reason the dragonfly is painted on the priests' ceremonial bowls.
Hence we have today Guardians of the Corn, i.e. priesthoods.
Hence to this day the priests or hosts of Zuni cast a morsel of food into the fire with a prayer to the ancestors.
That is why the yellow wolves who live on animals they kill are in hills in every direction.
That is why we worship the dragonfly and why we are not allowed to kill it.
That is why we always choose honest people for the priesthoods.[21]

Explanatory elements are added to European tales quite as readily as to old indigenous ones. The conclusion to an accumulative tale is: "And that is why medicine men never serve without pay." The familiar *Tail by Tail* is concluded in all versions with different kachina origins, including always the coyote collars of the Saiyalia. The *Substitute Race* gives the origin of ceremonial offerings to animals on the occasion of stick races. Explanatory elements are in Zuni the recognized mark of a good story teller, and the Zuni audience delights in the ingenuity which the narrator displays in inventing them.

----

[21] Ed. note: The first four explanatory elements in this list are quoted from Frank Hamilton Cushing, *Zuñi Breadstuff,* Museum of the American Indian, Heye Foundation, Indian Notes and Monographs, Vol. 8 (New York, 1920), 121, 121, 124, 115, respectively. The fifth item is quoted from Elsie Clews Parsons, "Notes on Zuni, Parts I, II," *Memoirs of the American Anthropological Association,* Vol. 4 (1917), 321. Items six and seven in the list are quoted from *Zuni Mythology,* Vol. II, 9 and 12 respectively.

The scope allowed the individual narrator in Zuni folklore is evident also from the comparison of versions told by the different narrators. The tales were told in English by Informant 7 [22] and those of the other informants were interpreted by a woman of the household. Both Informant 7 and the interpreter were asked to translate the stories literally. They were faithful in their rendition as can be seen by comparing actual text translations in Bunzel AES 15, and I have not retained their inadequate English in the translation, any more than if I were translating from text. Informants 3 and 6 are brother and sister, resident of course in different households, but members of the same major priesthood and tied by all the bonds which hold the matrilineal group together in Zuni. Informant 4 is their mother, and Informant 8 their father, resident in the clan household for nearly forty years. This group had heard the same tales told constantly around the same fireside and contrasts between them are therefore due in large measure to individual preferences and to different individual experience. Informant 7 was of a rival faction, a man of more independent activities and psychologically more aberrant than the members of the other family. He was a medicine society headman who in his young manhood was condemned by the priests as a witch and hung by the thumbs until he confessed. He turned informant against the priests and caused the elder brother bow priest to be imprisoned in a government penitentiary. The story is told [in] Bunzel.[23] He was a person of great ability, of commanding presence, and with a great personal need for achieving eminence, which he had primarily sought in the medicine societies. He knew incredible masses of ritual and song as well as tales. Earlier in his life he had sought prominence in trading and making money, but, as he said, "That was no good." He had used this wealth to build one of the annually required new houses for entertaining the Ca'lako, and he was no longer active in trading. More lately he had gained position as the

---

[22] Ed. note: In the "Foreword" to *Zuni Mythology*, Benedict gives the following explanation of the system used to refer to informants (e.g., as "Informant 7"): "The informants are numbered as in Bunzel AES 15:VIII"—i.e., as they are numbered by Ruth Bunzel in her *Zuni Texts*, Publications of the American Ethnological Society, Vol. 15 (New York, 1933), viii. Benedict and Bunzel worked with many of the same informants. Bunzel (*b*. 1898), who was also a student of Boas', arrived at Zuni during August of 1925 on the day before Benedict left after a period of fieldwork there (see Margaret Mead, *An Anthropologist at Work: Writings of Ruth Benedict*, Boston, 1959, p. 293). Benedict utilized a number of Bunzel's texts for comparative purposes in *Zuni Mythology*.

[23] *Zuni Texts*, p. 44. See also Ruth Benedict, *Patterns of Culture* (New York, 1934), p. 260.

Zuni representative in transactions with the Whites, and at the time
these stories were recorded was governor of Zuni, a secular office. It
is clear that he likes elaborate plot better than the other informants,
who prefer to indulge rather in cultural details. This is of course only
relative, and Informant 7 gave long ceremonial accounts which will
be published in "Zuni Ceremonial Tales." However, the wilder combinations of incidents are his, and the others stick closer to the beaten
track in plot combinations.

There is also a contrast in ceremonial emphasis between Informant 7 and the other story tellers. The former was a headman of
Little Fire Society, and had set himself to learn the tales and rituals
of the medicine societies, those of which he was not a member as
well as of Little Fire. His emphasis upon the medicine societies in
his tales is very marked, though the emphasis is apparent also in tales
of other informants. On the other hand, all the long tales of tenatsali
divination, and all statements of its great power, "that is why people
who have tenatsali always have the best of everything," are from the
tales of the other family, which possesses tenatsali and plants prayer-
sticks for it regularly.

It is characteristic of Informant 7 that he tells the only tales of
skeptics and their conversion. The skeptic doubts whether the Sun
receives the prayersticks planted for him and sets out on the journey
to the Sun to assure himself; the Ahaiyute doubt the power of the
medicine societies and are humiliated until they are convinced. The
point in another instance is that the skeptic is successful because he
does not accept the oracle he is given: the gambler takes offerings to
an Ahaiyute shrine and is told he is too late. He says, "I don't care
for omens," and goes back to his patron, to whom he says, "Somebody spoke to me, 'My boy, you are too late.' And I said, 'What do
I care for omens?' I said that." He challenged his opponents and was
successful.

On the other hand it is characteristic of the family of the other
informants that they carry the general mildness of Zuni tales to
characteristic lengths. In her version of The Deserted Child guided
by Awl, one of the women of this family tells how Awl spoke to the
child and guided him to his parents. Informant 7, on the other hand,
tells how his foster mother, Coyote Woman, was fattening him for a
feast, chased him as he fled, and was only prevented from overtaking
him by helpful animals who detained her with offers of intercourse
and finally humiliated her. In two versions of the Twin Children of

the Sun, Informant 7 introduces the incident of the mother's abandonment of her children at birth and makes the point of the tale the
children's humiliation of their mother; Informant 8 tells of no abandonment and makes his conclusion the twins' vindication of their
mother's memory. In accounts of the origin of the scalp dance,
Informant 7 tells of the fight between the two brothers to possess
the girl and "in the morning they took their bows and shot her."
Informant 8 gives the story: "Elder Brother said, 'Let's not kill her.
She is quite nice. We will come back some day and enjoy her again.'
Younger Brother said, 'No, we will kill her as we planned. If we
come back again to play with her, she might like me best, and then
you would be angry again.' Elder Brother said, 'No, I shan't be
angry.'" Among all the versions of the Ahaiyute's rain-making game
in which their grandmother is killed, Informant 8 is alone in saving
the grandmother alive, and she says, "Please don't play those games
any more, my grandchildren. If you go on, you won't have any grandmother any more."

The most striking way in which the importance of personal bias
and experience is shown in Zuni tales is in the contrast between tales
told by men and by women. There is no taboo in Zuni which restricts
such choice. The differences that exist are the result of unconscious
preference on the part of the narrators. Men tell the tales which
feature extended accounts of the stick races, of gambling, and of
hunting. Women tell those which detail cooking techniques.[24] The
Cinderella story is told by a woman, and the stories of women
assisting in childbirth who discover that the mother has initiated her
baby as a witch. Women also tell the only tales of poor little girls
who are overworked. "Every day the little girl worked all day long.
She ground flour and baked corncakes. One night she was tired. Her
mother said to her, 'There is no water. Go fetch a jar of water.' The
little girl cried, she was so tired she could not go for water." A Moth
takes pity on her [,takes her away,] and her mother grieves. Even
when the little girl is brought back she [the mother] cannot restrain
her tears and so [she] loses her [daughter] again. The little girl who
becomes the founder of the Crane Clan, lives with her uncle and says,
"My uncle is always away in his fields, my aunt treats me badly, and I
always have to grind and carry water. My jar is heavy and I am almost

---

[24] See, however, in tales by men the bride's teaching cooking to the Ahaiyute grandmother *([Zuni Mythology,]* Vol. I, 119), and the good corncakes Lazy Bones makes *([Zuni
Mythology,]* Vol. I, 149). These are less elaborate.

starved." The kind of detail that distinguishes the women's stories is characteristic; women give the only account of childbirth observances; women add to a description of a picnic, "The mothers nursed their babies and laid them down comfortably," to an account of girls grinding for the priests, "Their sweethearts waited to see in which house the girls were grinding. They drew their shawls over their faces and went in to husk for them." In Informant 3's tale of the Deserted Wife, the mother, before she sends her children away from the doomed pueblo, tells them, "My dears, I shall wake you before sunrise. You alone I do not wish them to kill. On no account turn back home when you see dust and smoke rising. Don't think perhaps your mother is not dead, for I shall be the first one to be killed. But I shall have ways to help you. I shall go to Kachina Village and become a uwanami." Thereafter the tale follows the fortunes of the children, not of the doomed village. Two tales by women informants relate at great length the good time people have staying at other pueblos during famine. The one case of a mother's regret in abandoning her child at birth and her care of it is in a tale told by a woman. When the baby was born she picked it up. "She liked that baby, but she was ashamed to take it home. She broke the soft leaves off the weeds and made a nest to put it in. She broke the weeds and branches and made a shelter over the baby. She nursed it," and returned next day to renew the shelter and nurse the child again. "The third day his mother went out in the evening to see if the baby was still there. He was gone. She saw the deer tracks. She was sorry."

In two cases tales are told from the point of view of the men actors or of the woman according to the sex of the narrator. The version of The Deserted Husband told by a woman expatiates on the woman's grievance; her husband did not compliment her on her cooking, "he never said, 'How good!'" It details the wife's determination to cook at other people's feasts and arrange a meeting with a man; it tells how she made herself beautiful, and how she went home to look after her little daughter; "she was making dolls out of rags." It follows through her arrangements with her lover and her handling of her suspicious husband. The men's versions omit all this; they tell the story from the point of view of the man. They begin with the husband's proposal to bring calamity upon the pueblo because of his faithless wife, and relate the details of the kiva conversations, the ritual which causes the earthquake, the friend who informs on him, and the help of the Hopi priests.

In the Rabbit Huntress, the woman's version tells how the resourceful girl gets more than a man's good catch in her hunting and expends itself in an account of the making of the sand bed and presentation of the child and role of the father's mother in the birth of the child of her marriage with Ahaiyute. The man's version tells how the girl has no success in hunting and gets only two rabbits; instead of the women's details of the other version, it goes on to describe a second marriage to a human husband and how the latter followed her to the land of the dead.

The fear of sex on the part of men that is evident in Zuni folklore has been discussed as a dominant theme in their mythology. Nothing could make this point clearer than the distinctions between the tales told by men and women. All the witch tales in which this theme is embodied, all the Ahaiyute tales, all the *Hide and Seek Games,* all the stories of sexual fetishism and bestiality, are told by men. One out of the five *Pursuits by a dangerous woman* is told by a woman, but that is the single appearance of this theme in a woman's tale. There is no tale of a woman who fears intercourse. In addition a man tells the tale of the husband's fear of demonstrativeness on the part of his wife and his arrangements to call the Apache, and a man tells of the six Corn Maidens who trap their husbands and kill them.

One minor point remains for discussion in connection with the Zuni tales, and that is in regard to their accuracy as history. The historical reconstructions of early ethnological students in Zuni and in Hopi were based in large measure upon the statements in folklore. Thus Fewkes interpreted the history of the Hopi as a gathering of diverse groups, now represented by the clans, from the four points of the compass; he interpreted their social organization as a consequence of these originally distinct groups. Cushing similarly, though less insistently, interpreted Zuni migration legends. The comparison of the different versions makes it clear that the often-repeated migration incident, the *Choice of eggs,* is told with almost as many "that's why's" as any other Zuni tale and that these explanatory elements are strictly comparable to those in courtship or witch tales. They certainly give no basis for reconstruction of history. In other examples of "that's why's" that have historic reference, the same truth is obvious. Thus the tale of Tupe kills the Apaches is given as the origin of the scalp dance, an origin accounted for by half a dozen other tales, and recounts a scalp dance said to have been held two generations before the tale was told to me. Obviously the scalp dance in Zuni has no such recent origin, and the narrator himself scouted the suggestion. His "origin" was a literary flourish. In the same way a true story of treachery against Navaho visitors which happened two generations ago is told by the grandson of the chief actor as an origin of albinos in Zuni; yet immediately after telling the tale he named albinos who had been born considerably before the date of the incident. I did not point out to him the inconsistency and he saw none. The tale did not even represent history according to his own personal knowledge.

The lack of historicity in the tales is apparent in other ways than in the explanatory elements. In the albino story a comparison with the historical account of the incident recorded by Dr. Bunzel shows that even in so short a time the tale has been built up to a climax with repetitive incidents and otherwise modified. The story of the battle which took place on Corn Mountain, at which time a friendship pact was made with the Lagunas, and the Big Shell cult vanquished the enemy, is told in two historical settings, once as the tale of a quarrel with the eastern pueblos, and the other, the catastrophe of the Rebellion against the Spaniards in 1670.[25] To the latter tale, as is indicated also by Cushing,[26] is added the story of the Spanish priest who saved the people and who elected to stay in Zuni rather than return to his own people. It is obvious that standard literary versions of battles may do service in different connections, and that it is impossible to trust their historical accuracy.

---

[25] Franz Boas, "Tales of Spanish Provenience from Zuni," *Journal of American Folklore*, Vol. 35 (1922), 62-98 (see p. 97).

[26] *Outlines of Zuni Creation Myths,* 13th Annual Report, Bureau of American Ethnology, 1891-1892 (1896), p. 331.

Myths and Rituals: A General Theory[*][1]

CLYDE KLUCKHOHN

I

NINETEENTH century students strongly tended to study mythology apart from associated rituals (and indeed apart from the life of the people generally). Myths were held to be symbolic descriptions of phenomena of nature.[2] One prominent school, in fact, tried to find an astral basis for all mythic tales. Others, among whom Andrew Lang was prominent, saw in the myth a kind of primitive scientific theory. Mythology answered the insistent human *how?* and *why?* How and why was the world made? How and why were living creatures brought into being? Why, if there was life must there be death? To early psychoanalysts such as Abraham[3] and Rank[4] myths were "group phantasies," wish-fulfillments for a society strictly analogous to the dream and day-dream of individuals. Mythology for these psychoanalysts was also a symbolic structure par excellence, but the

*Reprinted from the *Harvard Theological Review,* Vol. 35 (1942), 45-79, by permission of the *Harvard Theological Review.*

[1] Based upon a paper read at the Symposium of the American Folklore Society at Chicago in December, 1939. My thanks are due to W. W. Hill, Florence Kluckhohn, A. H. Leighton, Arthur Nock, E. C. Parsons, and Alfred Tozzer for a critical reading and a number of suggestions, to Ruth Underhill and David Mandelbaum for supplying unpublished material on the Papago and Toda respectively.

[2] Professor Nock has called my attention to the fact that the naturalistic theory actually works very well for the Vedic material.

[3] See *Traum und Mythus* (Vienna, 1909). Rank's final conclusion was that "myths are relics from the infantile mental life of the people, and dreams constitute the myths of the individual" (*Selected Papers of Karl Abraham,* London, 1927, p. 32). Cf. also *Traum und Mythus,* pp. 69, 71.

[4] See Otto Rank, *Psychoanalytische Beiträge zur Mythenforschung* (Vienna and Leipzig, 1919), and *Der Mythus von der Geburt des Helden* (2d ed., Leipzig and Vienna, 1922). Rank attempts to show that hero myths originate in the delusional structures of paranoiacs.

symbolism which required interpretation was primarily a sex symbolism which was postulated as universal and all-pervasive. Reik[5]
recognized a connection between rite and myth, and he, with Freud,[6]
verbally agreed to Robertson Smith's proposition that mythology was
mainly a description of ritual. To the psychoanalysts, however, mythology was essentially (so far as what they did with it is concerned)
societal phantasy material which reflected impulse repression.[7] There
was no attempt to discover the practical function of mythology in
the daily behaviors of the members of a society[8] nor to demonstrate
specific interactions of mythology and ceremonials. The interest was
in supposedly pan-human symbolic meanings, not in the relation of a
given myth or part of a myth to particular cultural forms or specific
social situations.[9]

To some extent the answer to the whole question of the relationship between myth and ceremony depends, of course, upon how
wide or how restricted a sense one gives to "mythology." In ordinary
usage the Oedipus tale is a "myth," but only some Freudians believe
that this is merely the description of a ritual! The famous stories of
the Republic are certainly called "$\mu\tilde{\upsilon}\theta o\varsigma$," and while a few scholars[10]
believe that Plato in *some* cases had reference to the Orphic and/or
Eleusinian mysteries there is certainly not a shred of evidence that
all of Plato's immortal "myths" are "descriptions of rituals." To be
sure, one may justifiably narrow the problem by saying that in a
technical sense these are "legends," and by insisting that "myths"
be rigorously distinguished from "legends," "fairy-tales," and "folk-

---

[5] Theodor Reik, *Das Ritual* (Leipzig, Vienna, Zurich, 1928).

[6] Cf. Freud's statement in his introduction to Reik, *op. cit.*, p. 11.

[7] Many psychoanalysts today consider myths simply "a form of collective daydreaming."
I have heard a prominent psychoanalyst say, "Creation myths are for culture what early
memories (true or fictitious) are to the individual."

[8] This has been done, even by anthropologists, only quite recently. Boas, as early as
1916 (*Tsimshian Mythology,* Bureau of American Ethnology, Annual Report for 1909-10,
Vol. 31, 29-1037) did attempt to show how the origin of all folklore must be sought in
imaginings based upon the ordinary social life of the society in question. But in this (as in
his later publication on the Kwakiutl) he showed how mythology reflected social organization—*not* how mythology preserved social equilibrium or symbolized social organization.

[9] Dr. Benedict in her *Zuni Mythology* (New York, 1935) follows a form of explanation
which draws heavily from psychoanalytic interpretations. Thus, in discussing the compensatory functions of mythology, she speaks of "folkloristic daydreaming." But her treatment
lacks the most objectionable features of the older psychoanalytic contributions because she
does not deal in universalistic, *pan*-symbolic "meanings" but rather orients her whole presentation to the richly documented Zuni materials and to the specific context of Zuni
culture. [Ed. note: The discussion to which Kluckhohn refers is Ruth Benedict's "Introduction to Zuni Mythology," reprinted in this volume on pp. 102-136.]

[10] Cf. e.g., R. H. S. Crossman, *Plato Today* (London, 1937), p. 88.

tales." If, however, one agrees that "myth" has Durkheim's connotation of the "sacred" as opposed to the "profane" the line is still
sometimes hard to draw in concrete cases. What of "creation myths"?
In some cases (as at Zuni) these are indeed recited[11] during ritual
performances (with variations for various ceremonies). In other cases,
even though they may be recited in a "ritual" attitude, they do not
enter into any ceremonial. Nevertheless, they definitely retain the
flavor of "the sacred." Moreover, there are (as again at Zuni) exoteric
and esoteric forms of the same myth. Among the Navaho many of
the older men who are not ceremonial practitioners know that part
of a myth which tells of the exploits of the hero or heroes but not
the portion which prescribes the ritual details of the chant. Granting
that there are sometimes both secular and sacred versions of the same
tale and that other difficulties obtrude themselves in particular cases,
it still seems possible to use the connotation of the sacred as that
which differentiates "myth" from the rest of folklore.[12] At least,
such a distinction appears workable to a rough first approximation
and will be followed throughout this paper.

But defining "myth" strictly as "sacred tale" does not carry with
it by implication a warrant for considering mythology purely as a
description of correlative rituals. Rose[13] quite correctly says "among
myths there are many whose connection with any rite is a thing to
be proved, not assumed." What is needed is a detailed comparative
analysis of actual associations. Generally speaking, we do seem to

---

[11] There are Aranda, Fijian, and Winnebago chants which are almost purely recitals of
an origin myth.

[12] This covers the differentia which is often suggested: namely, that myth is distinguished
from legend or folktale by the circumstances that some (or perhaps most) of the actors in
a myth must be supernatural beings—not simply human beings of however great a legendary
stature. There are, of course, other distinctions which could—for other purposes—profitably
be entered into. Thus, Professor Nock has suggested to me that there are differences of
some consequence between an oral mythology and a written theology. "A true myth," he
says, "never takes form with an eye to the pen or to the printed page."

These refinements are undoubtedly interesting and important, but they do not seem
directly relevant to the issues dealt with in this paper. Here only the major contrast of sacred
and profane appears to be crucial. Any segregation of myth from folktale, legend, fairy
tale, etc., which rests upon hair-splitting or upon special premises must be avoided. Thus
[Géza] Roheim's recent stimulating discussion ("Myth and Folk-Tale," *American Imago*,
Vol. 2, 1941, 266-79) is acceptable only insofar as one grants the major postulates of
orthodox Freudian psychoanalysis. Roheim says: "A folk tale is a narrative with a happy
end, a myth is a tragedy; a god must die before he can be truly divine" (p. 276). "In the
folk tale we relate how we overcome the anxiety connected with the 'bad parents' and grew
up, in myth we confess that only death can end the tragic ambivalence of human nature.
Eros triumphs in the folk-tale, Thanatos in the myth" (p. 279).

[13] H. J. Rose, Review of "The Labyrinth," *Man*, Vol. 36 (1936), No. 87, 69.

find rich ritualism and a rich mythology together. But there are cases (like the Toda)[14] where an extensive ceremonialism does not appear to have its equally extensive mythological counterpart and instances (like classical Greece) where a ramified mythology appears to have existed more or less independent of a comparatively meagre rite-system.[15] For example, in spite of the many myths relating to Ares the rituals connected with Ares seem to have been few in number and highly localized in time and space.[16] The early Romans, on the other hand, seemed to get along very well without mythology. The poverty of the ritual which accompanies the extremely complex mythology of the Mohave is well known.[17] Kroeber indeed says "Public ceremonies or rituals as they occur among almost all native Americans cannot be said to be practised by the Mohave."[18] The Bushmen likewise had many myths and very little ritual. On the other hand, one can point to examples like the Central Eskimo, where every detail of the Sedna myth has its ritual analogue in confessional, other rites, or hunting tabus, or, for contrast, to the American Indian tribes (especially some Californian ones) where the creation myth is never enacted in ceremonial form. In different sectors of one culture, the Papago, all of these possibilities are represented. Some myths are never ceremonially enacted. Some ceremonies emphasize content foreign to the myth. Other ceremonies consisting only of songs have some vague place in the mythological world; between these and the myths "there is a certain tenuous connection which may be a rationalization made for the sake of unity. . . ."[19]

---

[14] Dr. [David] Mandelbaum writes me: "For the Todas do not have complex myths; myth episodes which take hours and days in the telling among Kotas, are told by Todas in less than three minutes." Cf. M. Emeneau, "The Songs of the Todas," *Proceedings of the American Philosophical Society,* Vol. 77 (1937), 543-60: ". . . the art of story-telling is almost non-existent. In fact, imaginative story-telling hardly exists and the stories of traditional events in the life of the tribe do not seem to be popular. . . . Some of the songs are based on legendary stories, but even in the case of these some of my informants knew the songs without knowing the stories" (p. 543).

[15] I am thinking here of public (noncultist) mythology and of official and public ritual. Orphic ritual may have been more closely connected to the complicated Orphic myth. Cf. W. K. C. Guthrie, "Who Were the Orphics?" *Scientia,* Vol. 67 (1937), 110-21 (esp. pp. 119-20).

[16] Cf. L. R. Farnell, *The Cults of the Greek States,* Vol. IV (Oxford, 1909), 396-407.

[17] A. L. Kroeber, *Handbook of the Indians of California* (Washington, D.C., 1925), p. 660.

[18] *Ibid.,* p. 755. The Mohave are, of course, also a classic case where myths, at least according to cultural theory, are dreamed. But even though we recognize the cultural patterning of the "dreaming," this in no sense justifies the inference that the myths are derived from the meagre rituals. Indeed, Kroeber points out (p. 770) that some myths are not sung to–i.e., are not even ritualized to the extent of being connected with song recitals.

[19] Personal communication from Dr. Ruth Underhill.

The anthropology of the past generation has tended to recoil sharply from any sort of generalized interpretation. Obsessed with the complexity of the historical experience of all peoples, anthropologists have (perhaps over-much) eschewed the inference of regularities of psychological reaction which would transcend the facts of diffusion and of contacts of groups. Emphasis has been laid upon the distribution of myths and upon the mythological patterning which prevailed in different cultures and culture areas. Study of these distributions has led to a generalization of another order which is the converse of the hypothesis of most nineteenth century classical scholars [20] that a ritual was an enactment of a myth. In the words of Boas: [21] "The uniformity of many such rituals over large areas and the diversity of mythological explanations show clearly that the ritual itself is the stimulus for the origin of the myth. . . . The ritual existed, and the tale originated from the desire to account for it."

While this suggestion of the primacy of ritual over myth is probably a valid statistical induction and a proper statement of the modal tendency of our evidence, it is, it seems to me, as objectionably a simple unitary explanation (if pressed too far) as the generally rejected nineteenth century views. Thus we find Hocart [22] recently asking: "If there are myths that give rise to ritual where do these myths come from?" A number of instances will shortly be presented in which the evidence is unequivocal that myths did give rise to ritual. May I only remark here that — if we view the matter objectively — the Christian Mass, as interpreted by Christians, is a clear illustration of a ritual based upon a sacred story. Surely, in any case, Hocart's question can be answered very simply: from a dream or a waking phantasy or a personal habit system of some individual in the society. The basic psychological mechanisms involved would seem not dissimilar to those whereby individuals in our own (and other) cultures construct private rituals [23] or carry out private divination [24] —

---

[20] Certain contemporary classical scholars take a point of view which is very similar to that adopted in this paper. Thus H. J. Rose (*Modern Methods in Classical Mythology,* St. Andrews, 1930, p. 12) says: ". . . I postulate . . . a reciprocal influence of myth and ceremony. . . ." Cf. also L. R. Farnell, *The Value and the Methods of Mythologic Study* (London, 1919), p. 11: ". . . occasionally myth is the prior fact that generates a certain ritual, as for instance the offering of horses to St. George in Silesia was suggested by the myth of St. George the horseman. . . ."

[21] F. Boas and others, *General Anthropology* (New York, 1938), p. 617.

[22] A. M. Hocart, "Myth and Ritual," *Man,* Vol. 36 (1936), No. 230, 167.

[23] Cf. A. M. Tozzer, *Social Origins and Social Continuities* (New York, 1934), pp. 242-67 (esp. p. 260 ff.).

[24] R. R. Willoughby gives good examples and discussions of these culturally unformalized

e.g. counting and guessing before the clock strikes, trying to get to a given point (a traffic light, for instance) before something else happens. As DuBois[25] has suggested, "the explanation may be that personal rituals have been taken over and socialized by the group." These "personal rituals" could have their genesis in idiosyncratic habit [26] formations (similar to those of obsessional neurotics in our culture) or in dreams or reveries. Mrs. Seligman [27] has convincingly suggested that spontaneous personal dissociation is a frequent mechanism for rite innovations. The literature is replete with instances of persons "dreaming" that supernaturals summoned them, conducted them on travels or adventures, and finally admonished them thereafter to carry out certain rites (often symbolically repetitive of the adventures).

Moreover, there are a number of well documented actual cases where historical persons, in the memory of other historical persons, actually instituted new rituals. The ritual innovations of the American Indian Ghost Dance cult [28] and other nativistic cults of the New World [29] provide striking illustration. In these cases the dreams or phantasies—told by the innovators before the ceremonial was ever actualized in deeds—became an important part of traditionally accepted rite-myths. Lincoln [30] has presented plausible evidence that dreams are the source of "new" rituals. Morgan,[31] on the basis of Navaho material, says:

---

divinatory practices. See "Magic and Cognate Phenomena: An Hypothesis," in *A Handbook of Social Psychology*, ed. Carl Murchison (Worcester, Mass., 1935), pp. 461-520 (pp. 480-82).

[25] C. DuBois, "Some Anthropological Perspectives on Psychoanalysis," *Psychoanalytic Review*, Vol. 24 (1937), 246-64 (p. 254).

[26] In other words, in terms of patterns of behavior which are distinctive of an individual, not as a representative of a particular cultural tradition, but as a differentiated biological organism who—either because of inherited constitutional differences or because of accidents of the conditioning process—behaves differently in major respects from most individuals of the same age, sex, and status acculturated in the same culture.

[27] B. Z. Seligman, "The Part of the Unconscious in Social Heritage," in *Essays Presented to C. G. Seligman* (London, 1934), pp. 307-19.

[28] I am, of course, well aware that the rites of the Ghost Dance were not by any means identical in all tribes. But in spite of wide variations under the influence of preexistent ideal and behavioral patterns, *certain* new ritual practices which must be connected with the visions of the founder may be found in almost every tribe.

[29] See A. F. Chamberlain, "New Religions among the North American Indians," *Journal of Religious Psychology*, Vol. 6 (1913), 1-49.

[30] J. S. Lincoln, *The Dream in Primitive Culture* (Baltimore, 1935).

[31] William Morgan, *Human Wolves among the Navaho*, Yale University Publications in Anthropology, No. 11 (1936), p. 40. Dr. Henry A. Murray of Harvard Psychological Clinic informs me that there is clinical evidence that an individual can be conditioned (in the technical psychological sense) by a dream.

. . . delusions and dreams . . . are so vivid and carry such conviction that any attempt to reason about them afterwards on the basis of conscious sense impressions is unavailing. Such experiences deeply condition the individual, sometimes so deeply that if the experience is at variance with a tribal or neighborhood belief, the individual will retain his own variation. There can be no doubt that this is a very significant means of modifying a culture.

Van Gennep [32] asserts that persons went to dream in the sanctuary at Epidaurus as a source for new rites in the cult of Asclepius. To obtain ceremony through dream is, of course, itself a pattern, a proper traditional way of obtaining a ceremony or power. I do not know of any cases of a society where dreaming is generally in disrepute, as at Zuni, and where ceremony has yet demonstrably originated through dream. But where dreaming is accepted as revelation it must not be assumed that the content (or even, entirely, the structure) of a new myth and its derived ceremony will be altogether determined by pre-existent cultural forms. As Lowie [33] has remarked, "That they themselves (dreams) in part reflect the regnant folklore offers no ultimate explanation." Anthropologists must be wary of what Korzybski calls "self-reflexive systems"—here, specifically, the covert premise that "culture alone determines culture."

The structure of new cultural forms (whether myths or rituals) will undoubtedly be conditioned by the pre-existent cultural matrix. But the rise of new cultural forms will almost always be determined by factors external to that culture: pressure from other societies, biological events such as epidemics, or changes in the physical environment. Barber [34] has recently shown how the Ghost Dance and the Peyote Cult represent alternative responses of various American Indian tribes to the deprivation resultant upon the encroachment of whites. The Ghost Dance was an adaptive response under the earlier external conditions, but under later conditions the Peyote Cult was the more adaptive response, and the Ghost Dance suffered what the stimulus-response psychologists would call "extinction through non-reward." At any rate the Ghost Dance became extinct in some tribes; in others it has perhaps suffered only partial extinction.

---

[32] A. van Gennep, *La Formation des Légendes* (Paris, 1910), p. 255. The peyote cult is, of course, an outstanding case where dreams determine variation in ritual.

[33] R. H. Lowie, *The History of Ethnological Theory* (New York, 1937), p. 264.

[34] Bernard Barber, "Acculturation and Messianic Movements," *American Sociological Review,* Vol. 6 (1941), 663-70; "A Socio-Cultural Interpretation of the Peyote Cult," *American Anthropologist,* Vol. 43 (1941), 673-76.

There are always individuals in every society who have their private rituals; there are always individuals who dream and who have compensatory phantasies. In the normal course of things these are simply deviant behaviors which are ridiculed or ignored by most members of the society. Perhaps indeed one should not speak of them as "deviant"—they are "deviant" only as carried to extremes by a relatively small number of individuals, for everyone probably has some private rituals and compensatory phantasies. When, however, changed conditions happen to make a particular type of obsessive behavior or a special sort of phantasy generally congenial, the private ritual is then socialized by the group, the phantasy of the individual becomes the myth of his society. Indeed there is evidence [35] that when pressures are peculiarly strong and peculiarly general, a considerable number of different individuals may almost simultaneously develop substantially identical phantasies which then become widely current.

Whether belief (myth) or behavior (ritual) changes first will depend, again, both upon cultural tradition and upon external circumstances. Taking a very broad view of the matter, it does seem that behavioral patterns more frequently alter first. In a rapidly changing culture such as our own many ideal patterns are as much as a generation behind the corresponding behavioral patterns. There is evidence that certain ideal patterns (for example, those defining the status of women) are slowly being altered to harmonize with, to act as rationalizations for, the behavioral actualities. On the other hand, the case of Nazi Germany is an excellent illustration of the ideal patterns ("the myth") being provided from above almost whole cloth and of the state, through various organizations, exerting all its force to make the behavioral patterns conform to the standards of conduct laid down in the Nazi mythology.

Some cultures and sub-cultures are relatively indifferent to belief, others to behavior. The dominant practice of the Christian Church, throughout long periods of its history, was to give an emphasis to belief which is most unusual as seen from a cross-cultural perspective. In general, the crucial test as to whether or not one was a Christian was the willingness to avow belief in certain dogmas. [36] The term

---

[35] See Marie Bonaparte, Princess of Greece, "The Myth of the Corpse in the Car," *American Imago,* Vol. 2 (1941), 105-27.

[36] Ruth Benedict in the article "Myth," *Encyclopaedia of the Social Sciences,* Vol. IX (1933), makes a similar point but distorts it by the implication that belief in a certain *cosmology* was the single crucial test of Christianity.

"believer" was almost synonymous with "Christian." It is very possibly because of this cultural screen that until this century most European scholars selected the myth as primary.

II

To a considerable degree, the whole question of the primacy of ceremonial or mythology is as meaningless as all questions of "the hen or the egg" form. What is really important, as Malinowski has so brilliantly shown, is the intricate interdependence of myth (which is one form of ideology) with ritual and many other forms of behavior. I am quite aware that I have little to add conceptually to Malinowski's discussion in "The Myth in Primitive Psychology." [37] There he examines myths not as curiosa taken out of their total context but as living, vitally important elements in the day to day lives of his Trobrianders, interwoven with every other abstracted type of activity. From this point of view one sees the fallacy of all unilateral explanations. One also sees the aspect of truth in all (or nearly all) of them. There are features which seem to be explanatory of natural phenomena. [38] There are features which reveal the peculiar forms of wish fulfillments characteristic of the culture in question (including the expression of the culturally disallowed but unconsciously wanted). There *are* myths which are intimately related to rituals, which may be descriptive of them, but there are other myths which stand apart. If these others are descriptive of rituals at all, they are, as Durkheim (followed by Radcliffe-Brown and others) suggested, descriptions of rituals of the social organization. That is, they are symbolic representations of the dominant configurations [39] of the

---

[37] London, 1926.

[38] [A. R.] Radcliffe-Brown's explanation, though useful, strikes me as too narrow in that it seems to deny to nonliterate man *all* bare curiosity and any free play of fancy, undetermined by societal necessities. He says (*The Andaman Islanders,* Cambridge, 1933, pp. 380-81): "Natural phenomena such as the alternation of day and night, the changes of the moon, the procession of the seasons, and variations of the weather, have important effects on the welfare of the society . . . a process of bringing within the circle of the social life those aspects of nature that are of importance to the well-being of the society." [Ed. note: The chapter of *The Andaman Islanders* from which Kluckhohn quotes is reprinted in part in this volume on pp. 46-71. The specific quotation cited in this note can be found on pp. 50-51 above.]

[39] "Configuration" is here used as a technical term referring to a structural regularity of the covert culture. In other words, a configuration is a principle which structures widely varying contexts of culture content but of which the culture carriers are minimally aware. By "configuration" I mean something fairly similar to what some authors have meant by "latent culture pattern" as distinguished from "manifest culture pattern." The concept is

particular culture. Myths, then, may express not only the latent content of rituals but of other culturally organized behaviors. Malinowski is surely in error when he writes [40] "... myth ... is not symbolic. ..." Durkheim and Mauss [41] have pointed out how various non-literate groups (notably the Zuni and certain tribes of southeastern Australia) embrace nature within the schema of their social organization through myths which classify natural phenomena precisely according to the principles that prevail in the social organization. Warner [42] has further developed this type of interpretation.

Boas,[43] with his usual caution, is sceptical of all attempts to find a systematic interpretation of mythology. But, while we can agree with him when he writes "... mythological narratives and mythological concepts should not be equalized; for social, psychological, and historical conditions affect both in different ways,"[44] the need for scrupulous inquiry into historical and other determinants must not be perverted to justify a repudiation of all attempts to deal with the symbolic processes of the all-important covert culture. At all events, the factual record is perfectly straightforward in one respect: neither myth nor ritual can be postulated as "primary."

This is the important point in our discussion at this juncture, and it is unfortunate that Hooke and his associates in their otherwise very illuminating contributions to the study of the relations between myth and ritual in the Near East have emphasized only one aspect of the system of interdependences which Malinowski and Radcliffe-Brown have shown to exist. When Hooke [45] points out that myths are constantly used to justify rituals this observation is quite congruent with the observed facts in many cultures. Indeed all of these

---

also closely akin to what Sumner and Keller call a cultural "ethos." For a fuller discussion of "configuration" and "covert culture," see Clyde Kluckhohn, "Patterning as Exemplified in Navaho Culture," in *Language, Culture, and Personality,* ed. L. Spier (Menasha, 1941), pp. 109-31 (esp. pp. 109, 124-29). [Ed. note: Reference is made to Kluckhohn's concept of myths as "symbolic representations of the dominant configurations of the particular culture" by Raymond Firth in his "Oral Tradition in Relation to Social Status," reprinted in this volume. See p. 168.]

[40] *Op. cit.,* p. 19.

[41] [Émile Durkheim and Marcel Mauss,] "De Quelques formes primitives de classification," *L'Année Sociologique,* Vol. 6 [(1901-2), 1-72.]

[42] W. L. Warner, *A Black Civilization* (New York, 1937), esp. pp. 371-411.

[43] See especially F. Boas, Review of G. W. Locher, "The Serpent in Kwakiutl Religion: A Study in Primitive Culture," *Deutsche Literaturzeitung* (1933), pp. 1182-86; reprinted in *Race, Language and Culture* (New York, 1940), pp. 446-50.

[44] *Ibid.,* p. 450.

[45] S. H. Hooke, *The Origins of Early Semitic Ritual* (London, 1938), pp. 2, 3, 8. See also *Myth and Ritual* (London, 1933).

data may be used toward a still wider induction: man, as a symbol-using animal, appears to feel the need not only to act but almost equally to give verbal or other symbolic "reasons" for his acts.[46] Hooke[47] rightly speaks of "the vital significance of the myth as something that works," but when he continues "and that dies apart from its ritual" he seems to imply that myths cannot exist apart from rituals and this, as has been shown, is contrary to documented cases. No, the central theorem has been expressed much more adequately by Radcliffe-Brown:[48] "In the case of both ritual and myth the sentiments expressed are those that are essential to the existence of the society." This theorem can be regarded as having been well established in a general way, but we still lack detailed observations on change in myths as correlated with changes in ritual and changes in a culture generally.[49] Navaho material gives certain hints that when a culture as a whole changes rapidly its myths are also substantially and quickly altered.

In sum, the facts do not permit any universal generalizations as to ritual being the "cause" of myth or vice versa. Their relationship is rather that of intricate mutual interdependence, differently structured in different cultures and probably at different times in the same culture. As Benedict[50] has pointed out, there is great variation in the extent to which mythology conditions the religious complex—"the small role of myth in Africa and its much greater importance in religion in parts of North America." Both myth and ritual satisfy the needs of a society and the relative place of one or the other will depend upon the particular needs (conscious and unconscious) of the individuals in a particular society at a particular time. This principle covers the observed data which show that rituals are borrowed without their myths,[51] and myths without any accompanying ritual. A ritual may be reinforced by a myth (or vice versa) in the donor

---

[46] This statement is not to be interpreted as credence in "the aetiological myth" if by this one means that a myth "satisfies curiosity." We are not justified, I believe, in *completely* excluding the aetiological (in this sense) motive in every case, but Whitehead's statement (*Religion in the Making,* New York, 1926) probably conforms to a rough induction: "Thus the myth not only explains but reinforces the hidden purpose of the ritual which is emotion" (p. 25).

[47] S. H. Hooke, ed., *The Labyrinth* (New York, 1935), p. ix.

[48] *Op. cit.,* p. 405.

[49] The best documentation of the fact that myths are constantly undergoing revision is probably to be found in various writings of Boas. See, for example, *Race, Language and Culture* (New York, 1940), pp. 397-525, *passim.*

[50] *Op. cit.,* p. 180.

[51] This appears to be the Papago case. (Underhill, personal communication.)

culture but satisfy the carriers of the recipient culture simply as a
form of activity (or be rationalized by a quite different myth which
better meets their emotional needs).[52] In short, the only uniformity
which can be posited is that there is a strong tendency for some sort
of interrelationship between myth and ceremony and that this interrelationship is dependent upon what appears, so far as present information goes, to be an invariant function of both myth and ritual: the
gratification (most often in the negative form of anxiety reduction)
of a large proportion of the individuals in a society.

If Malinowski and Radcliffe-Brown (and their followers) turned
the searchlight of their interpretations as illuminatingly upon specific
human animals and their impulses as upon cultural and social abstractions, it might be possible to take their work as providing a fairly
complete and adequate general theory of myth and ritual. With
Malinowski's notion of myth as "an active force" which is intimately
related to almost every other aspect of a culture we can only agree.
When he writes: [53] "Myth is a constant by-product of living faith
which is in need of miracles; of sociological status, which demands
precedent; of moral rule which requires sanction," we can only
applaud. To the French sociologists, to Radcliffe-Brown, and to
Warner we are indebted for the clear formulation of the symbolic
principle. Those realms of behavior and of experience which man
finds beyond rational and technological control he feels are capable
of manipulation through symbols.[54] Both myth and ritual are sym-
bolical procedures and are most closely tied together by this, as well
as by other, facts. The myth is a system of word symbols, whereas

---

[52] There are many striking and highly specific parallels between Navaho and Hopi ceremonial practices. For example, the mechanical equipment used in connection with the Sun's
House phase of the Navaho Shooting Way chants has so much in common with similar
gadgets used in Hopi ceremonials that one can hardly fail to posit a connection. Dr. [Elsie
Clews] Parsons has documented the intimate resemblances between the Male Shooting Way
chant and Hopi Flute and Snake-Antelope ceremonies ("A Pre-Spanish Record of Hopi
Ceremonies," *American Anthropologist,* Vol. 42, 1940, 541-43, fn. 4, 541). The best guess
at present would be that the Hopi was the donor culture, but the direction of diffusion is
immaterial here: the significant point is that the supporting myths in the cases concerned
show little likeness. For instance, Dr. Parsons regards the Flute Ceremony as a dramatization
of the Hopi emergence myth, but the comparable ritual acts in Navaho culture are linked
to chantway legends of the usual Holy Way pattern and not to the emergence story. In
contrast, the White Mountain Apache seem to have borrowed *both* Snake myth and ritual
from the Hopi. See E. C. Parsons, *Pueblo Indian Religion* (Chicago, 1939), p. 1060, and
G. Goodwin, *Myths and Tales of the White Mountain Apache,* Memoirs of the American
Folklore Society, Vol. 33 (New York, 1939), vii.

[53] *Op. cit.,* p. 92.

[54] That is, forms of behavior whose value or meaning is assigned by human beings—not
inherent in the intrinsic properties of the words or acts.

ritual is a system of object and act symbols. Both are symbolic processes for dealing with the same type of situation in the same affective mode.

But the French sociologists, Radcliffe-Brown, and — to a lesser extent — Malinowski are so interested in formulating the relations between conceptual elements that they tend to lose sight of the concrete human organisms. The "functionalists" do usually start with a description of some particular ritualistic behaviors. Not only, however, do the historical origins of this particular behavioral complex fail to interest them. Equally, the motivations and rewards which persons feel are lost sight of in the preoccupation with the contributions which the rituals make to the social system. Thus a sense of the specific detail is lost and we are soon talking about myth in general and ritual in general. From the "functionalist" point of view specific details are about as arbitrary as the phonemes of a language are with respect to "the content" of what is communicated by speech. Hence, as Dollard [55] says, "What one sees from the cultural angle is a drama of life much like a puppet show in which 'culture' is pulling the strings from behind the scenes." The realization that we are really dealing with "animals struggling in real dilemmas" is lacking.

From this angle, some recent psychoanalytic interpretations of myth and ritual seem preferable. We may regard as unconvincing Roheim's [56] attempts to treat myths as historical documents which link human phylogenetic and ontogenetic development, as we may justly feel that many psychoanalytic discussions of the latent content of mythology are extravagant and undisciplined. Casey's [57] summary of the psychoanalytic view of religion ". . . ritual is a sublimated compulsion; dogma and myth are sublimated obsessions" may well strike us as an over-simplified, over-neat generalization, but at least our attention is drawn to the connection between cultural forms and impulse-motivated organisms. And Kardiner's [58] relatively sober and controlled treatment does "point at individuals, at bodies, and at a rich and turbulent biological life"—even though that life is admittedly

---

[55] John Dollard, "Culture, Society, Impulse, and Socialization," *American Journal of Sociology,* Vol. 45 [1939-40], 50-64 (p. 52).

[56] G. Roheim, *The Riddle of the Sphinx* (London, 1934), esp. pp. 173-74.

[57] R. P. Casey, "The Psychoanalytic Study of Religion," *Journal of Abnormal and Social Psychology,* Vol. 33 (1938), 437-53 (p. 449).

[58] A. Kardiner, *The Individual and His Society* (New York, 1939), esp. pp. 182-94, 268-70.

conditioned by social heredity: social organization, culturally defined symbolic systems, and the like.

In a later section of this paper, we shall return to the problem of how myths and rituals reinforce the behavior of individuals. But first let us test the generalities which have been propounded thus far by concrete data from a single culture, the Navaho.[59]

III

The Navaho certainly have sacred tales which, as yet at all events, are not used to justify associated rituals. A striking case, and one where the tale has a clear function as expressing a sentiment "essential to the existence of the society," is known from different parts of the Navaho country.[60] The tales differ in detail but all have these structural elements in common: one of "the Holy People" visits one or more Navahos to warn them of an impending catastrophe (a flood or the like) which will destroy the whites — but believing Navahos will be saved if they retire to the top of a mountain or some other sanctuary. It is surely not without meaning that these tales became current at about the time that the Navahos were first feeling intensive and sustained pressure (they were not just prisoners of war as in the Fort Sumner epoch) from the agents of our culture.[61]

---

[59] Some Navaho material has, of course, already been presented.

[60] E. L. Hewitt (*The Chaco Canyon and Its Monuments,* Albuquerque, 1936, p. 139) records the dissemination of this tale among the Chaco Canyon Navaho. Drs. A. and D. Leighton and I have obtained independent evidence that the same story was told, and believed by many, among the Ramah Navaho (two hundred odd miles away) at the same time. Those who believed the tale carried out ceremonials but not new ceremonials. Rather the old ceremonials (especially Blessing Way rites) were carried out in unusual frequency. In 1936 in the Huerfano country a young woman reported that she had been visited by White Shell Woman who had been given instructions for Blessing Ways to be held—but with special additional procedures. These rites were widely carried out in the northeastern portion of the Navaho area. (See article by Will Evans in the Farmington, N. M., *Times Hustler,* under date-line of February 21, 1937.) Also in 1936 a woman in the Farmington region claimed to have been visited by Banded Rock Boy (one of the Holy People) and a similar story spread over the Reservation. A famous singer, Left-handed, refused to credit the tale and many Navahos attributed his death (which occurred soon thereafter) to his disbelief. See *Mesa Verde Notes,* Vol. 7 (March, 1937), 16-19. Frances Gillmor has used a story of the same pattern, obtained from the Navaho of the Kayenta, Arizona, region as a central episode in a novel (*Windsinger,* New York, 1930).

[61] Jane Harrison (*Themis,* Cambridge, 1912), says: "It is this collective sanction and solemn purpose that differentiate the myth alike from the historical narrative and the mere *conte* or fairy-tale . . ." (p. 330), and many agreeing with her will doubtless assert that my argument here is invalid because these tales though unquestionably having "solemn purpose" lack "collective sanction." Some would also contend that since living persons claim to have seen the supernatural beings these stories must be called "tales" or, at any rate, not "myths." I see these points and, since I wish to avoid a purely verbal quarrel, I would agree, so far as present data go, that Navaho myths (in the narrow sense) are uniformly associated with ritual behaviors. Actually, *the* myth which most Navaho call their most sacred (the emer-

Father Berard Haile[62] has recently published evidence that Navaho ceremonials may originate in dreams or visions rather than being invariably post hoc justifications for existent ritual practices. A practitioner called "son of the late Black Goat" instituted a new ceremonial "which he had learned in a dream while sleeping in a cave." Various informants assured Father Berard that chantway legends originated in the "visions" of individuals.[63] We have, then, Navaho data for (*a*) the existence of myths without associated rituals, (*b*) the origin of both legends and rituals in dreams or visions.

It is true that all ceremonial practice among the Navaho is, in cultural theory, justified by an accompanying myth. One may say with Dr. Parsons[64] on the Pueblos: "Whatever the original relationship between myth and ceremony, once made, the myth supports the ceremony or ceremonial office and may suggest ritual increments." One must in the same breath, however, call attention to the fact that myth also supports accepted ways of secular behavior. As Dr. Hill[65] has pointed out, "Women are required to sit with their legs under them and to one side, men with their legs crossed in front of them, because it is said that in the beginning Changing Woman and the Monster Slayer sat in these positions." Let this one example suffice for the many which could easily be given.[66] The general point is that in both sacred and secular spheres myths give some fixity to the ideal patterns of cultures where this is not attained by the printed word.

gence story) is associated with rites only in a manner which is, from certain points of view, tenuous. The emergence myth (or some part of it) *is* often prefaced to the chantway legend proper. In any case, I must insist (granting always that the line between secular and sacred folk literature must not be drawn too sharply) that the stories dealt with above are not part of the "profane" folklore of the Navaho in the sense in which the Coyote tales, for example, are. The origin legends of the various clans are certainly not secular literature, but I imagine that a purist would maintain that we must call these "legends" as lacking "solemn purpose" (in Harrison's sense). Nevertheless, I repeat that "myths" in the broad sense of "sacred tale" are, among the Navaho, found quite dissociated from ritual.

[62] "A Note on the Navaho Visionary," *American Anthropologist,* Vol. 42 (1940), 359. This contains still another reference to the flood motif.

[63] The assertion that ceremonials sometimes have their genesis in dreams and the like does not imply that this, any more than that between myth and ritual, is a one-way relationship. One can by no means dispose of the matter simply by saying "dreams cause myths and myths cause ceremonies." William Morgan ("Navaho Dreams," *American Anthropologist,* Vol. 34, 1932, 390-406), who was convinced that some Navaho myths derive from dreams (p. 395), has pointed out the other aspect of the interdependence: ". . . myths . . . influence dreams; and these dreams, in turn, help to maintain the efficacy of the ceremonies. . . . Repetitive dreams do much to strengthen the traditional beliefs concerning dreams" (p. 400).

[64] E. C. Parsons, *Pueblo Indian Religion* (Chicago, 1939), fn., p. 968.

[65] W. W. Hill, *The Agricultural and Hunting Methods of the Navaho Indians* (New Haven, 1938), p. 179.

[66] Dr. Parsons has suggested (personal communication) an analogue from our own culture: "It was argued that because Eve was made from Adam's rib women should not have the vote."

The existence of rituals has a similar effect. Although I cannot agree with Wissler [67] that "the primary function" of rituals is "to perpetuate exact knowledge and to secure precision in their application," there can be no doubt that both myths and rituals are important agencies in the transmission of a culture and that they act as brakes upon the speed of culture change.

Returning to the connections between myth and rite among the Navaho, one cannot do better than begin by quoting some sentences from Washington Matthews: [68]

> In some cases a Navajo rite has only one myth pertaining to it. In other cases it has many myths. The relation of the myth to the ceremony is variable. Sometimes it explains nearly everything in the ceremony and gives an account of all the important acts from beginning to end, in the order in which they occur; at other times it describes the work in a less systematic manner. . . . Some of the myths seem to tell only of the way in which rites, already established with other tribes, were introduced among the Navajos. . . . The rite-myth never explains all of the symbolism of the rite, although it may account for all the important acts. A primitive and underlying symbolism which probably existed previous to the establishment of the rite, remains unexplained by the myth, as though its existence were taken as a matter of course, and required no explanation.

To these observations one may add the fact that knowledge of the myth is in no way prerequisite to carrying out of a chant. Knowledge does give the singer or curer prestige and ability to expect higher fees, and disparaging remarks are often heard to the effect "Oh, he doesn't know the story," or "He doesn't know the story very well yet." And yet treatment by a practitioner ignorant of the myth [69] is regarded as efficacious. Navahos are often a little cynical about the variation in the myths. If someone observes that one singer did not carry out a procedure exactly as did another (of perhaps greater repute) it will often be said "Well, he says *his* story is different."

---

[67] C. Wissler, "The Function of Primitive Ritualistic Ceremonies," *Popular Science Monthly,* Vol. 87 [1915], 200-204 (p. 203).

[68] Washington Matthews, "Some Illustrations of the Connection between Myth and Ceremony," *International Congress of Anthropology, Memoirs* (Chicago, 1894), pp. 246-51 (p. 246).

[69] How much a practitioner knows of both legend and ceremonial depends upon the demands he made upon his instructor during his apprenticeship. The instructor is not supposed to prompt his pupil. Many practitioners are satisfied with quite mechanical performances, and there is no doubt that much information (both legendary and ritualistic) is being lost at present owing to the fact that apprentices do not question their instructors more than superficially.

Different forms of a rite-myth tend to prevail in different areas of the Navaho country and in different localities. Here the significance of the "personality" of various singers may sometimes be detected in the rise of variations. The transvestite [70] "Left-handed" who died a few years ago enjoyed a tremendous reputation as a singer. There is some evidence [71] that he restructuralized a number of myths as he told them to his apprentices in a way which tended to make the hermaphrodite *be?gočidí* a kind of supreme Navaho deity—a position which he perhaps never held in the general tradition up to that point. [72] I have heard other Navaho singers say that sandpaintings and other ceremonial acts and procedures were slightly revised to accord with this tenet. If this be true, we have here another clear case of myth-before-ritual.

Instances of the reverse sort are also well documented. From a number of informants accounts have been independently obtained of the creation (less than a hundred years ago) of a new rite: Enemy Monster Blessing Way. All the information agreed that the ritual procedures had been devised by one man who collated parts of two previously existent ceremonials and added a few bits from his own fancy. And three informants independently volunteered the observation "He didn't have any story. But after a while he and his son and another fellow made one up." [73] This is corroborated by the fact that none of Father Berard's numerous versions of the Blessing Way myth mention an Enemy Monster form. [74]

Besides these notes on the relations between myth and rite I should like to record my impression of another function of myth—one which ranges from simple entertainment to "intellectual edification." Myth among the Navaho not only acts as a justification, a rationale for ritual behavior and as a moral reinforcement for other customary behaviors. It also plays a role not dissimilar to that of literature (especially sacred literature) in many literate cultures. Navahos have a keen expectation of the long recitals of myths (or

---

[70] A transvestite is an individual who assumes the garb of the other sex. Transvestites are often, but apparently not always, homosexuals.

[71] See W. W. Hill, "The Status of the Hermaphrodite and Transvestite in Navaho Culture," *American Anthropologist*, Vol. 37 (1935), 273-80 (p. 279).

[72] For a hint, however, that *be?gočidí* was so considered at an earlier time, see W. Matthews, *Navaho Legends* (New York, 1897), fn. 78, p. 226.

[73] Cf. Clyde Kluckhohn and Leland C. Wyman, *An Introduction to Navaho Chant Practice*, Memoir 53, American Anthropological Association (1940), pp. 186-87.

[74] Personal communication.

portions of them) around the fire on winter nights.[75] Myths have all the charm of the familiar. Their very familiarity increases their efficacy, for, in a certain broad and loose sense, the function of both myths and rituals is "the discharge of the emotion of individuals in socially accepted channels." And Hocart [76] acutely observes: "Emotion is assisted by the repetition of words that have acquired a strong emotional coloring, and this coloring again is intensified by repetition." Myths are expective, repetitive dramatizations—their role is similar to that of books in cultures which have few books. They have the (to us) scarcely understandable meaningfulness which the tragedies had for the Greek populace. As Matthew Arnold said of these, "their significance appeared inexhaustible."

IV

The inadequacy of any simplistic statement of the relationship between myth and ritual has been established. It has likewise been maintained that the most adequate generalization will not be cast in terms of the primacy of one or the other of these cultural forms but rather in terms of the general tendency for the two to be interdependent. This generalization has been arrived at through induction from abstractions at the cultural level. That is, as we have sampled the evidence from various cultures we have found cases where myths have justified rituals and have appeared to be "after the fact" of ritual; we have also seen cases where new myths have given rise to new rituals. In other words, the primary conclusion which may be drawn from the data is that myths and rituals tend to be very intimately associated and to influence each other. What is the explanation of the observed connection?

The explanation is to be found in the circumstance that myth and ritual satisfy a group of identical or closely related needs of individ-

---

[75] Why may the myths be recited only in winter? In Navaho feeling today this prohibition is linked in a wider configuration of forbidden activities. There is also, as usual, an historical and distributional problem, for this same prohibition is apparently widely distributed in North America. For example, it is found among the Berens River Salteaux (see A. I. Hallowell, "Fear and Anxiety as Cultural and Individual Variables in a Primitive Society," *Journal of Social Psychology*, Vol. 9, 1938, 25-48, esp. p. 31) and among the Iroquois (Dr. William Fenton: personal conversation). But I wonder if in a certain "deeper" sense this prohibition is not founded upon the circumstance that only winter affords the leisure for telling myths, that telling them in summer would be unfitting because it would interfere with work activities?

[76] A. M. Hocart, "Ritual and Emotion," *Character and Personality*, Vol. 7 (1939), 201-11 (p. 208).

uals. Thus far we have alluded only occasionally and often obliquely to myths and rituals as cultural forms defining individual behaviors which are adaptive or adjustive[77] responses. We have seen how myths and rituals are adaptive from the point of view of the society in that they promote social solidarity, enhance the integration of the society by providing a formalized statement of its ultimate value-attitudes, afford a means for the transmission of much of the culture with little loss of content—thus protecting cultural continuity and stabilizing the society. But how are myth and ritual rewarding enough in the daily lives of individuals so that individuals are instigated to preserve them, so that myth and ritual continue to prevail at the expense of more rational responses?

A systematic examination of this question, mainly again in terms of Navaho material, will help us to understand the prevailing interdependence of myth and ritual which has been documented. This sketch of a general theory of myth and ritual as providing a cultural storehouse of adjustive responses for individuals is to be regarded as tentative from the writer's point of view. I do not claim that the theory is proven—even in the context of Navaho culture. I do suggest that it provides a series of working hypotheses which can be tested by specifically pointed field procedures.

We can profitably begin by recurring to the function of myth as fulfilling the expectancy of the familiar. Both myth and ritual here provide cultural solutions to problems which all human beings face. Burke has remarked, "Human beings build their cultures, nervously loquacious, upon the edge of an abyss." In the face of want and death and destruction all humans have a fundamental insecurity.[78] To some extent, all culture is a gigantic effort to mask this, to give the future the simulacrum of safety by making activity repetitive, expective—"to make the future predictable by making it conform to the past." From one angle our own scientific mythology is clearly related to that motivation as is the obsessive, the compulsive tendency which lurks in all organized thought.

When questioned as to why a particular ceremonial activity is

---

[77] This useful distinction I owe to my colleague, Dr. Hobart Mowrer. "Adaptation" is a purely descriptive term referring to the fact that certain types of behavior result in survival. "Adjustment" refers to those responses which remove the motivation stimulating the individual. Thus suicide is adjustive but not adaptive.

[78] Cf. Malinowski (*op. cit.,* p. 78): "They would screen with the vivid texture of their myths, stories, and beliefs about the spirit world, the vast emotional void gaping beyond them."

carried out in a particular way, Navaho singers will most often say "because the diɣin diné—the Holy People—did it that way in the first place. The *ultima ratio* of non-literates [79] strongly tends to be "that is what our fathers said it was." An Eskimo said to Rasmussen: [80] "We Eskimos do not concern ourselves with solving all riddles. We repeat the old stories in the way they were told to us and with the words we ourselves remember." The Eskimo saying "we keep the old rules in order that we may live untroubled" is well-known. The Navaho and Eskimo thus implicitly recognize a principle which has been expressed by Harvey Ferguson [81] as follows:

> ... man dreads both spontaneity and change, ... he is a worshipper of habit in all its forms. Conventions and institutions are merely organized and more or less sanctified habits. These are the real gods of human society, which transcend and outlive all other gods. All of them originate as group expedients which have some social value at some time, but they remain the objects of a passionate adoration long after they have outlived their usefulness. Men fight and die for them. They have their high priests, their martyrs, and their rituals. They are the working gods, whatever the ostensible ones may be.

These principles apply as well to standardized overt acts as to standardized forms of words. Thus Pareto considered the prevalence of ritual in all human cultures as perhaps the outstanding empirical justification for his thesis of the importance of non-logical action. Merton [82] writes:

> ... activities originally conceived as instrumental are transmuted into ends in themselves. The original purposes are forgotten and ritualistic adherence to institutionally prescribed conduct becomes virtually obsessive ... Such ritualism may be associated with a mythology which rationalizes these actions so that they appear to retain their status as means, but the dominant pressure is in the direction of strict ritualistic conformity, irrespective of such rationalizations. In this sense ritual has proceeded farthest when such rationalizations are not even called forth.

Goldstein, [83] a neurologist, recognizes a neurological basis for the persistence of such habit systems and writes: "The organism tends to

---

[79] There is, to be sure, at least a rough parallel in our own culture in "the Bible says so" and similar phrases.

[80] Knud Rasmussen, *Intellectual Culture of the Hudson Bay Eskimos* (Copenhagen, 1938), p. 69.

[81] *Modern Man* (New York, 1936), p. 29.

[82] R. K. Merton, "Social Structure and Anomie," *American Sociological Review,* Vol. 5 (1938), 672-83 (p. 673).

[83] Kurt Goldstein, *The Organism* (New York, 1939), p. 57.

function in the accustomed manner, as long as an at least moderately effective performance can be achieved in this way."

Nevertheless, certain objections to the position as thus far developed must be anticipated and met. It must be allowed at once that the proposition "man dreads both spontaneity and change" must be qualified. More precisely put, we may say "most men, most of the time, dread both spontaneity and change in most of their activities." This formulation allows for the observed fact that most of us *occasionally* get irked with the routines of our lives or that there are certain sectors of our behavior where we fairly consistently show spontaneity. But a careful examination of the totality of behavior of any individual who is not confined in an institution or who has not withdrawn almost completely from participation in the society will show that the larger proportion of the behavior of even the greatest iconoclasts is habitual. This must be so, for by very definition a socialized organism is an organism which behaves mainly in a predictable manner. Even in a culture like contemporary American culture which has made an institutionalized value of change (both for the individual and for society), conformity is at the same time a great virtue. To some extent, this is phrased as conformity with the latest fashion, but Americans remain, by and large, even greater conformists than most Europeans.

Existence in an organized society would be unthinkable unless most people, most of the time, behaved in an expectable manner. Rituals constitute a guarantee that in certain societally organized behaviors touching upon certain "areas of ignorance" which constitute "tender spots" for all human beings, people can count upon the repetitive nature of the phenomena. For example, in Zuni society (where rituals are highly calendrical) a man whose wife has left him or whose crops have been ruined by a torrential downpour can yet look forward to the Shalako ceremonial as something which is fixed and immutable. Similarly, the personal sorrow of the devout Christian is in some measure mitigated by anticipation of the great feasts of Christmas and Easter. Perhaps the even turn of the week with its Sunday services and mid-week prayer meetings gave a dependable regularity which the Christian clung to even more in disaster and sorrow. For some individuals daily prayer and the confessional gave the needed sense of security. Myths, likewise, give men "something to hold to." The Christian can better face the seemingly capricious reverses of his plans when he hears the joyous words "lift up your hearts." Rituals and myths supply, then, fixed points in a world of bewildering change and disappointment.

If almost all behavior has something of the habitual about it, how is it that myths and rituals tend to represent the maximum of fixity? Because they deal with those sectors of experience which do not seem amenable to rational control and hence where human beings can least tolerate insecurity. That very insistence upon the minutiae of ritual performance, upon preserving the myth to the very letter, which is characteristic of religious behavior must be regarded as a "reaction formation" (in the Freudian sense) which compensates for the actual intransigeance of those events which religion tries to control.

To anticipate another objection: do these "sanctified habit systems" show such extraordinary persistence simply because they are repeated so often and so scrupulously? Do myths and rituals constitute repetitive behavior par excellence not merely as reaction formations but because the habits are practiced so insistently? Perhaps myths and rituals perdure in accord with Allport's "principle of functional autonomy"[84] — as interpreted by some writers? No, performances must be rewarded in the day to day lives of participating individuals. Sheer repetition in and of itself has never assured the persistence of any habit. If this were not so, no myths and rituals would ever have become extinct except when a whole society died out. It is necessary for us to recognize the somewhat special conditions of drive and of reward which apply to myths and rituals.

It is easy to understand why organisms eat. It is easy to understand why a defenceless man will run to escape a charging tiger. The physiological bases of the activities represented by myths and rituals are less obvious. A recent statement by a stimulus-response psychologist gives us the clue:[85] "The position here taken is that human beings (and also other living organisms to varying degrees) can be motivated either by organic pressures (needs) that are currently felt *or* by the mere anticipation of such pressures and that those habits tend to be acquired and perpetuated (reinforced) which effect a reduction in either of these two types of motivation." That is, myths and rituals

[84] As a matter of fact, Allport has made it plain ("Motivation in Personality: Reply to Mr. Bertocci," *Psychological Review,* Vol. 47, 1940, 533-55) that he contends only that motives may be autonomous in respect to their origins but never in respect to the satisfaction of the ego (p. 547).

[85] O. H. Mowrer, "A Stimulus-Response Analysis of Anxiety and Its Role as a Reinforcing Agent," *Psychological Review,* Vol. 46 (1939), 553-66 (p. 561).

are reinforced because they reduce the anticipation of disaster. No living person has died—but he has seen others die. The terrible things which we have seen happen to others may not yet have plagued us, but our experience teaches us that these are at least potential threats to our own health or happiness.

If a Navaho gets a bad case of snow-blindness and recovers after being sung over, his disposition to go to a singer in the event of a recurrence will be strongly reinforced. And, by the principle of generalization, he is likely to go even if the ailment is quite different. Likewise, the reinforcement will be reciprocal—the singer's confidence in his powers will also be reinforced. Finally, there will be some reinforcement for spectators and for all who hear of the recovery. That the ritual treatment rather than more rational preventatives or cures tends to be followed on future occasions can be understood in terms of the principle of the gradient of reinforcement. Delayed rewards are less effective than immediate rewards. In terms of the conceptual picture of experience with which the surrogates of his culture have furnished him, the patient *expects* to be relieved. Therefore, the very onset of the chant produces some lessening of emotional tension—in technical terms, some reduction of anxiety. If the Navaho is treated by a white physician, the "cure" is more gradual and is dependent upon the purely physico-chemical effects of the treatment. If the native wears snow goggles or practices some other form of prevention recommended by a white, the connection between the behavior and the reward (no soreness of the eyes) is so diffuse and so separated in time that reinforcement is relatively weak. Even in those cases where no improvement (other than "psychological") is effected, the realization or at any rate the final acceptance that no help was obtained comes so much later than the immediate sense of benefit [86] that the extinction effects are relatively slight. [87]

Navaho myths and rituals provide a cultural storehouse of adjus-

---

[86] I have attended hundreds of Navaho ceremonials and I have never yet seen a case where the patient at some point, at least, during the ceremonial did not profess to feel an improvement. This applies even to cases where the patient was actually dying.

[87] The theory of this paragraph has been stated in the language of contemporary stimulus-response psychology. But it is interesting to note that E. S. Hartland (*Ritual and Belief*, New York) expressed essentially the same content in 1916: "Recurrence of the emotional stress would tend to be accompanied by repetition of the acts in which the reaction has been previously expressed. If the recurrence were sufficiently frequent, the form of the reaction would become a habit to be repeated on similar occasions, even where the stress was less vivid or almost absent. It can hardly be doubted that many rites owe their existence to such reactions" (pp. 116-17).

tive [88] responses for individuals. Nor are these limited to the more obvious functions of providing individuals with the possibility of enhancing personal prestige through display of memory, histrionic ability, etc. Of the ten "mechanisms of defence" which Anna Freud[89] suggests that the ego has available, their myths and rituals afford the Navaho with institutionalized means of employing at least four. Reaction-formation has already been briefly discussed. Myths supply abundant materials for introjection and likewise (in the form of witchcraft myths) suggest an easy and culturally acceptable method of projection of hostile impulses. Finally, rituals provide ways of sublimation of aggression and other socially disapproved tendencies, in part, simply through giving people something to *do*.

All of these "mechanisms of ego defence" will come into context only if we answer the question "adjustive with respect to what?" The existence of motivation, of "anxiety" in Navaho individuals must be accounted for by a number of different factors. In the first place—as in every society—there are those components of "anxiety," those "threats" which may be understood in terms of the "reality principle" of psychoanalysis: life *is* hard—an unseasonable temperature, a vagary of the rainfall does bring hunger or actual starvation; people *are* organically ill. In the second place, there are various forms of "neurotic" anxiety. To some extent, every society tends to have a type anxiety. In our own society it is probably sexual, although this may be true only of those segments of our society who are able to purchase economic and physical security. In most Plains Indians sexual anxiety, so far as we can tell from the available documents, was insignificant. There the basic anxiety was for life itself and for a certain quality of that life (which I cannot attempt to characterize in a few words).

Among the Navaho the "type anxiety" is certainly that for health. Almost all Navaho ceremonials (essentially every ceremonial still carried out today) are curing ceremonials. And this apparently has

---

[88] It is not possible to say adaptive here because there are not infrequent occasions on which ceremonial treatment aggravates the condition or actually brings about death (which would probably not have supervened under a more rational treatment or even if the patient had simply been allowed to rest). From the point of view of the society, however, the rituals are with little doubt adaptive. Careful samples in two areas and more impressionistic data from the Navaho country generally indicate that the frequency of ceremonials has very materially increased concomitantly with the increase of white pressure in recent years. It is tempting to regard this as an adaptive response similar to that of the Ghost Dance and Peyote Cult on the part of other American Indian tribes.

[89] Anna Freud, *The Ego and the Mechanisms of Defence* (London, 1937).

a realistic basis. A prominent officer of the Indian Medical Service stated that it was his impression that morbidity among the Navaho is about three times that found in average white communities. In a period of four months' field work among the Navaho Drs. A. and D. Leighton found in their running field notes a total of 707 Navaho references to "threats" which they classified under six headings.[90] Of these, sixty per cent referred to bodily welfare, and are broken down by the Leightons as follows:

Disease is responsible for sixty-seven per cent, accidents for seventeen per cent, and the rest are attributed to wars and fights. Of the diseases described, eighty-one per cent were evidently organic, like smallpox, broken legs, colds, and sore throats; sixteen per cent left us in doubt as to whether they were organic or functional; and three per cent were apparently functional, with symptoms suggesting depression, hysteria, etc. Of all the diseases, forty per cent were incapacitating, forty-three per cent were not, and seventeen per cent were not sufficiently specified in our notes to judge. From these figures it can easily be seen that lack of health is a very important concern of these Navahos, and that almost half of the instances of disease that they mentioned interfered with life activities.

While I am inclined to believe that the character of this sample was somewhat influenced by the fact that the Leightons were white physicians—to whom organic illnesses, primarily, would be reported— there is no doubt that these data confirm the reality of the health "threat." In terms of clothing and shelter which are inadequate (from our point of view at least), of hygiene and diet which similarly fail to conform to our health standards, it is not altogether surprising that the Navaho need to be preoccupied with their health.[91] It is unequivocally true in my experience that a greater proportion of my Navaho friends are found ill when I call upon them than of my white friends.

The Navaho and Pueblo Indians live in essentially the same physical environment. But Pueblo rituals are concerned predominantly with rain and with fertility. This contrast to the Navaho preoccupation with disease cannot (in the absence of fuller supporting facts) be laid to a lesser frequency of illness among the Pueblos, for it seems well documented that the Pueblos, living in congested towns, have

---

[90] See A. H. and D. C. Leighton, "Some Types of Uneasiness and Fear in a Navaho Indian Community" [*American Anthropologist*, Vol. 44, 1942, 194-209].

[91] It remains amazing that their population could have increased at such an extraordinary rate if health conditions have been so poor. Dr. A. Leighton suggests to me that it is conceivable that when the land was less crowded their health was better.

been far more ravaged by endemic diseases than the Navaho. The explanation is probably to be sought in terms of the differing historical experience of the two peoples and in terms of the contrasting economic and social organizations. If one is living in relative isolation and if one is largely dependent (as were the Navaho at no terribly distant date) upon one's ability to move about hunting and collecting, ill health presents a danger much more crucial than to the Indian who lives in a town which has a reserve supply of corn and a more specialized social organization.

That Navaho myths and rituals are focussed upon health and upon curing has, then, a firm basis in the reality of the external world. But there is also a great deal of uneasiness arising from inter-personal relationships, and this undoubtedly influences the way the Navaho react to their illnesses. Then, too, one type of anxiousness always tends to modify others. Indeed, in view of what the psychoanalysts have taught us about "accidents" and of what we are learning from psychosomatic medicine about the psychogenic origin of many "organic" diseases we cannot regard the sources of disease among the Navaho as a closed question.[92]

Where people live under constant threat from the physical environment, where small groups are geographically isolated and "emotional inbreeding" within the extended family group is at a maximum, inter-personal tensions and hostilities are inevitably intense. The prevalence of ill health which throws additional burdens on the well and strong is in itself an additional socially disrupting force.[93] But if the overt expression of aggressive impulses proceeds very far the whole system of "economic" co-operation breaks down and then sheer physical survival is more than precarious. Here myths and rituals constitute a series of highly adaptive responses from the point

---

[92] It does not seem implausible that some disorders (especially perhaps those associated with acute anxieties) are examples of what Caner has called "superstitious self-protection." See G. C. Caner, "Superstitious Self-Protection," *Archives of Neurology and Psychiatry*, Vol. 44 (1940), 351-61.

[93] Dr. A. Leighton has pointed out to me that these disruptive tendencies are reinforced by one of the techniques for survival which those Navahos who have intimate and competitive relations with whites have developed. He writes: "A group threatened by a stronger group can swing to one of two poles. (*a*) They can coalesce and form a highly efficient, highly integrated unit that can act with swiftness, power, and precision, and in which all individuals stand or fall together. (*b*) They can disperse like a covey of quail so as never to present a united target to the foe. This is the Navaho method of dealing with the whites. It is every man for himself, and though individuals may fall, enough escape to survive. You don't rush to help your tribesman when trouble comes, you stay out of it, you 'let it go.' Such an attitude, however, does lead to mutual mistrust."

of view of the society. Recital of or reference to the myths reaffirms the solidarity of the Navaho sentiment system.[94] In the words of a Navaho informant: "Knowing a good story will protect your home and children and property. A myth is just like a big stone foundation—it lasts a long time." Performance of rituals likewise heightens awareness of the common system of sentiments. The ceremonials also bring individuals together in a situation where quarrelling is forbidden. Preparation for and carrying out of a chant demands intricately ramified co-operation, economic and otherwise, and doubtless thus reinforces the sense of mutual dependency.

Myths and rituals equally facilitate the adjustment of the individual to his society. Primarily, perhaps, they provide a means of sublimation of his anti-social tendencies. It is surely not without meaning that essentially all known chant myths take the family and some trouble within it as a point of departure. Let us look at Reichard's [95] generalization of the chant myth:

A number of chant legends are now available and all show approximately *the same* construction. People are having a hard time to secure *subsistence or have some grievance. A boy of the family is forbidden* to go somewhere or to do some particular thing. He does not observe the warnings and does that which was forbidden, whereupon he embarks upon a series of adventures which keep him away from home so long that *his family despairs of his return.* . . . After the dramatic episodes, the hero returns to his home bringing with him the ritualistic lore which he teaches to *his brother.* He has been away so long and has become so accustomed to association with deity that *his own people seem impure* to him. He corrects that fault by teaching them the means of purification. . . . He has *his brother* conduct the ritual over *his sister* . . . he vanishes into the air.

While as a total explanation the following would be over-simple, it seems fair to say that the gist of this may be interpreted as follows: the chant myth supplies a catharsis for the traumata incident upon the socialization of the Navaho child. That brother and sister are the principal *dramatis personae* fits neatly with the central conflicts of the Navaho socialization process. This is a subject which I hope to treat in detail in a later paper.

Overt quarrels between family members are by no means infrequent, and, especially when drinking has been going on, physical

---

[94] Cf. Radcliffe-Brown (*op. cit.,* p. 330): ". . . tales that might seem merely the product of a somewhat childish fancy are very far indeed from being merely fanciful and are the means by which the Andamanese express and systematize their fundamental notions of life and nature and the sentiments attaching to those notions."

[95] Gladys Reichard, *Navajo Medicine Man* (New York, 1939), p. 76. Italics mine.

blows are often exchanged. Abundant data indicate that Navahos have a sense of shame [96] which is fairly persistent and that this is closely connected with the socially disapproved hostile impulses which they have experienced toward relatives. It is also clear that their mistrust of others (including those in their own extended family group) is in part based upon a fear of retaliation (and this fear of retaliation is soundly based upon experience in actual life as well as, possibly, upon "unconscious guilt"). Certain passages in the myths indicate that the Navaho have a somewhat conscious realization that the ceremonials act as a cure, not only for physical illness, but also for anti-social tendencies. The following extract from the myth of the Mountain Top Way Chant will serve as an example: "The ceremony cured Dsiliyi Neyani of all his strange feelings and notions. The lodge of his people no longer smelled unpleasant to him." [97]

Thus "the working gods" of the Navaho are their sanctified repetitive ways of behavior. If these are offended by violation of the culture's system of scruples, the ceremonials exist as institutionalized means of restoring the individual to full rapport with the universe: nature and his own society. [98] Indeed "restore" is the best English translation of the Navaho word which the Navaho constantly use to express what the ceremonial does for the "patient." The associated myths reinforce the patient's belief that the ceremonial will both truly cure him of his illness and also "change" him so that he will be a better man in his relations with his family and his neighbors. An English-speaking Navaho who had just returned from jail where he had been put for beating his wife and molesting his stepdaughter said to me: "I am sure going to behave from now on. I am going to be changed—just like somebody who has been sung over."

Since a certain minimum of social efficiency is by derivation a biological necessity for the Navaho, not all of the hostility and un-

---

[96] This is significantly reflected in ceremonial lore. Torlino, a singer of Beauty Way, said to Washington Matthews: "I am ashamed before the earth; I am ashamed before the heavens; I am ashamed before the dawn; I am ashamed before the evening twilight; I am ashamed before the blue sky; I am ashamed before the sun; *I am ashamed before that standing within me which speaks with me (my conscience).* Some of these things are always looking at me. I am never out of sight." Washington Matthews, *Navaho Legends,* Memoirs of the American Folklore Society, No. 5 (1897), pp. 58-59. Italics are mine.

[97] W. Matthews, "The Mountain Chant," *Annual Report of the Bureau of American Ethnology,* Vol. 5 (1887), 379-467 (p. 417).

[98] Cf. A. R. Radcliffe-Brown, *Taboo* (Cambridge, 1939), p. 44: "The primary value of ritual . . . is the attribution of ritual value to objects and occasions which are either themselves objects of important common interests linking together the persons of a community or are symbolically representative of such objects."

easiness engendered by the rigors of the physical environment, geographical isolation, and the burdens imposed by illness is expressed or even gets into consciousness. There is a great deal of repression and this leads, on the one hand, to projection phenomena (especially in the form of phantasies that others are practicing witchcraft against one [99]) and, on the other hand, the strong feelings of shame at the conscious level are matched by powerful feelings of guilt at the unconscious level. Because a person feels guilty by reason of his unconscious hostilities toward members of his family (and friends and neighbors generally), some individuals develop chronic anxieties. Such persons feel continually uncomfortable. They say they "feel sick all over" without specifying organic ailments other than very vaguely. They feel so "ill" that they must have ceremonials to cure them. The diagnostician and other practitioners, taking myths as their authority, will refer the cause of the illness to the patient's having seen animals struck by lightning, to a past failure to observe ritual requirements or to some similar violation of a cultural scruple. But isn't this perhaps basically a substitution of symbols acceptable to consciousness, a displacement of guilt feelings?

It is my observation that Navahos other than those who exhibit chronic or acute anxieties tend characteristically to show a high level of anxiety. It would be a mistake, however, to attribute all of this anxiety to intra-familial tensions, although it is my impression that this is the outstanding pressure. Secondary drives resultant upon culture change and upon white pressure are also of undoubted importance. And it is likewise true, as Mr. Homans [100] has recently pointed out, that the existence of these ritual injunctions and prohibitions (and of the concomitant myths and other beliefs) gives rise to still another variety of anxiety which Homans has well called secondary anxiety. In other words, the conceptual picture of the world which Navaho culture sets forth makes for a high threshold of anxiety in that it defines all manner of situation as fraught with peril, and individuals are instigated to anticipate danger on every hand.

But the culture, of course, prescribes not only the supernatural

---

[99] This view is developed with full documentation in a forthcoming publication to be issued by the Peabody Museum of Harvard University in the spring of 1942. [Ed. note: The study to which Kluckhohn refers here is apparently *Navaho Witchcraft,* which was published by the Peabody Museum in 1944.]

[100] G. C. Homans, "Anxiety and Ritual," *American Anthropologist,* Vol. 43 (1941), 164-73.

dangers but also the supernatural means of meeting these dangers or of alleviating their effects. Myths and rituals jointly provide systematic protection against supernatural dangers, the threats of ill health and of the physical environment, anti-social tensions, and the pressures of a more powerful society. In the absence of a codified law and of an authoritarian "chief" or other father substitute, it is only through the myth-ritual system that Navahos can make a socially supported, unified response to all of these disintegrating threats. The all-pervasive configurations of word symbols (myths) and of act symbols (rituals) preserve the cohesion of the society and sustain the individual, protecting him from intolerable conflict. As Hoagland[101] has recently remarked:

Religion appears to me to be a culmination of this basic tendency of organisms to react in a configurational way to situations. We must resolve conflicts and disturbing puzzles by closing some sort of a configuration, and the religious urge appears to be a primitive tendency, possessing biological survival value, to unify our environment so that we can cope with it.

V

The Navaho are only one case.[102] The specific adaptive and adjustive responses performed by myth and ritual will be differently phrased in different societies according to the historical experience of these societies (including the specific opportunities they have had for borrowing from other cultures), in accord with prevalent configurations of other aspects of the culture, and with reference to pressures exerted by other societies and by the physical and biological environment. But the general nature of the adaptive and adjustive responses performed by myth and ritual appears very much the same in all human groups. Hence, although the relative importance of myth and of ritual does vary greatly, the two tend universally to be associated.

For myth and ritual have a common psychological basis. Ritual is an obsessive repetitive activity—often a symbolic dramatization of

---

[101] Hudson Hoagland, "Some Comments on Science and Faith," in *Conference on Science, Philosophy, and Religion* (New York, 1941, mimeographed), p. 5.

[102] But I was very much struck in reading Dr. Hallowell's recent article (A. I. Hallowell, "The Social Function of Anxiety in a Primitive Society," *American Sociological Review*, Vol. 6, 1941, 869-82)—which I read only when this paper was in proof—at the similarity not only in the interpretations he reached but at that in the data from the Saulteaux, when he says "fear of disease is a major social sanction" (p. 871) that fits the Navaho case precisely— as does "illness due to having done bad things or to transgression of a parent" (p. 873).

the fundamental "needs" of the society, whether "economic," "biological," "social," or "sexual." Mythology is the rationalization of these same needs, whether they are all expressed in overt ceremonial or not. Someone has said "every culture has a type conflict and a type solution." Ceremonials tend to portray a symbolic resolvement of the conflicts which external environment, historical experience, and selective distribution of personality types[103] have caused to be characteristic in the society. Because different conflict situations characterize different societies, the "needs" which are typical in one society may be the "needs" of only deviant individuals in another society. And the institutionalized gratifications (of which rituals and myths are prominent examples) of culturally recognized needs vary greatly from society to society. "Culturally recognized needs" is, of course, an analytical abstraction. Concretely, "needs" arise and exist only in specific individuals. This we must never forget, but it is equally important that myths and rituals, though surviving as functioning aspects of a coherent culture only so long as they meet the "needs" of a number of concrete individuals, are, in one sense, "supra-individual." They are usually composite creations; they normally embody the accretions of many generations, the modifications (through borrowing from other cultures or by intra-cultural changes) which the varying needs of the group as a whole and of innovating individuals in the group have imposed. In short, both myths and rituals are cultural products, part of the social heredity of a society.

---

[103] This selective distribution of personality types may become established biologically, through the operation of genetic mechanisms or through the processes of child socialization operative in the particular culture.

Oral Tradition in Relation to Social Status*

RAYMOND FIRTH

I TURN now to another type of interpretation . . . It consists essentially in the establishment of relations between two contemporary sets of material, between the body of traditional tales as I received them in 1928-29 (and again in 1952) and the body of other data concerned with the social, economic, political and ritual position of narrators and other members of the Tikopia society at those same times. The kinds of relationships sought for are those which will help to explain why the Tikopia who tell these tales, listen to them and comment upon them, behave in that way. For the tales are not just preserved. In a community which can communicate tradition only orally, the act of imparting it is invested with meaning for two parties, teller and recipient, in a manner different from that of imparting knowledge by written communication. Comment also may be stimulated by some different factors. In being imparted, the tales are told with an object—for recreation; for money—or the Tikopia equivalent, in goods; for self-assertion, to draw attention to oneself and control the reactions of others; for demonstration of some social position. They are heard, judged, commented upon, in the same light. Primarily, I am concerned here with the analysis of those relationships in the situation which depend upon the position of people as members of social groups.

Let us look at these traditional tales first of all as a kind of resource. They are part of the resources of the whole community, a sort of cultural furniture on a par with the customs of dressing, the

*Reprinted from *History and Traditions of Tikopia,* Memoir No. 33, The Polynesian Society (Wellington, New Zealand, 1961), Chapter 10, pp. 168-83, by permission of the author and the Polynesian Society.

institutions of initiation and marriage, or the patterns of kinship behaviour. They constitute a kind of entity, with boundaries rather vaguely defined, but with a very definite well-marked core, and much formal structure of incident and manner of recital. They have a cultural character of their own, distinguished from the traditional tales of Anuta, of Vanikoro and other islands known to the Tikopia. *Tara tupua o fenua nei* — "traditional information of this land," is something significant to a Tikopia, serving to differentiate him and his society from others within his ken. From this point of view the recital of any of these tales can be a source of satisfaction; whether it is believed to be true or not, it is something which belongs to the Tikopia alone.

The traditions are also important as a value referent, as a background for estimating the quality of contemporary behaviour. They do so in terms of a very general morality—they validate the institutions of the present day, arguing by implication that they are right and proper because they have endured so long. Persistence in itself is assumed to be a test of worth. For the great mass of institutions this is validation by projection back. But there is also validation by projection forward. One implication is that customs which have continued for so long will continue still longer. The assertion of continuity is thus also an assertion of security.

Yet to this there are qualifications. Some incidents in the traditional tales are repeated not for their continuity but for their discontinuity with the modern state. As Radcliffe-Brown pointed out long ago, they emphasise a present value by contrast.[1] This is so with cannibalism in the Tikopia tales, and to a less extent with physical violence. Tikopia stress the man-eating by the Tongans and by their own ancestors, with the explicit boast that they do not do this nowadays, and they plume themselves by the comparison more than they denigrate their ancestors. With physical violence, including killing, the situation is more complex. What the traditions about the fighting with the Tongans do is to assert the aggression of the strangers, the capacity of some Tikopia to cope with this aggression, and the special valour of the Taumako siblings in doing so. In this sense tradition helps to maintain Tikopia pride. It also helps to sanction the modern exercise of executive, almost "police" functions by representatives of the Taumako chiefly lineage, who cite with

---

[1] Ed. note: Radcliffe-Brown discusses this point in the excerpt from *The Andaman Islanders* which is reprinted in this volume. See pp. 46-71.

approval the doings of their ancestors. It supports the *maru* (execu-
tant) role in modern internal administration in Tikopia. As regards
the internal violence in the traditions something of the same is true.
But here it is more like whistling in the dark to keep their courage
up. Even in the contemporary Tikopia scene, physical violence has
lain too near the surface at times for them to feel quite sure it will
not occur again on some scale. Yet it is reprobated by both government and Christian mission, and its recurrence would be generally
deplored and feared. Such was the situation in 1952, and the tales of
olden times then had a kind of fearful warning in them—an "it could
happen here!" kind of quality.[2]

There is a further point—the emphasis on non-violence as a proper
mode of action by the Atua i Kafika. This may be interpreted as a
moral argument. I am not satisfied that it is so; I think it is to be
interpreted as a technical argument. Traditionally, and at least until
the end of Tikopia paganism, most Tikopia chiefs, especially the
Ariki Kafika, have stood aloof from the exercise of physical force.
Their basic power was the antithesis of this; it was superhuman, and
ran the risk of being contaminated by their use of human force.
Hence the attitude expressed in the tradition is that it is good to
abjure the use of violence for technical reasons, in order that other
techniques of power may be more effective. It is possible to interpret
this further, and to see in the prescription of non-violence for a chief,
especially for the premier chief, a statement on the level of ritual
techniques of what is essentially a precaution on the level of political
techniques. If a chief is allowed the use of violence, he may invite
violence in return. Hence his position may be more assured by ruling
out violence completely from the sphere of his authority – and it
must be remembered that the physical force is still at his command
in the person of his next-of-kin, his agnates, his *maru.*

The breach of continuity between past and present by the citation
of physical violence in the traditional tales is then more apparent
than real—it is a superficial contrast in a field of shared values. But
a more fundamental breach of continuity occurs when the traditional
tales no longer describe the kind of society which is generally desired
by the people, and the continuity itself either has ceased to have

---

[2] Raymond Firth, "Rumor in a Primitive Society," *Journal of Abnormal and Social
Psychology,* Vol. 53 (1956), 122-32. The tales may also give expression to more positive
aggressive impulses, satisfied otherwise only in small-scale mundane acts of insult in epithet
or song.

meaning or is actively opposed. In some cases a traditional tale itself may be revised, or a new one brought into being to handle the new situation, as must have happened with a Tikopia traditional tale about the origin of iron from the Tikopia gods.[3] But for the most part the reaction of a people is to let the traditional tales go altogether, not bothering to impart them or to listen to them any more; or alternatively to shift to the sphere of recreation, with a reduction in emotional level, the material formerly imparted as necessary apparatus. In this process, what was formerly the exclusive possession of [sic; read *or*] the prized property of individuals or restricted social groups, may well become the property of the community—just as on a wider scene the stories of Maui and the gods of the Maori pantheon have become the property of every New Zealand schoolchild.

But the process may also assume a cyclic form. A group that ignores its traditional tales because they do not correspond to their changed social system may come to find in time that they want these tales again, not as a validating resource for specific institutions but as a validating resource for their own general continued existence as a society. To maintain their social identity in a wider social universe, where so many pressures and attractions lead them to merge themselves in that universe completely, they want to call on any aids. Traditional tales are helpful here since they are relatively neutral from an action point of view. Maintenance of them, imparting of them, either within the specific society or in the whole social universe of which the society is a part, does not mean any very specific committal. The tales can be maintained as true, they can be held to have a symbolic character, with their true meaning ascertainable only to those who are patient to inquire, and sympathetic to the interpretation, or they can be regarded as simple recreation. Or they can be maintained as overtly or symbolically true by the community concerned, and issued to the world outside as recreational or aesthetic products. In any case, as a property that is indubitably belonging to the group concerned, the traditions can serve as an identity badge, and a social rallying point.

So far I have considered the traditional material mainly as a general resource for the community. But the contrast I have drawn

---

[3] Ed. note: The tale to which Firth refers here is discussed in some length in his article "The Plasticity of Myth," *Ethnologica*, Vol. 2 (1960), 181-88. This article has also been reprinted as Chapter 13 of Firth's book *Tikopia Ritual and Belief* (London, 1967), pp. 284-92.

earlier indicates also how significant may be the traditions as a resource specifically for individuals and sectional groups. This has been
very much the case in Tikopia. This is so in three ways. Firstly, the
traditions relating to the origins of a social group are regarded as
being very much their own property, known to others, repeatable
perhaps by others, but primarily at the discretion of the group they
mainly concern, both as regards occasion of telling, and acceptance
of authenticity of variant versions. Secondly, the leader of the group,
whether ritual elder or not, regards it as his particular right to control
the traditional material. On the one hand he is the representative
and trustee of it for the group; he is the guardian of its preservation
and of its correctness. On the other hand, the control of it is a
function of his status; if someone other than himself, or a person
designated by him, is regarded as the proper authority to maintain
and impart the tradition, then this is derogatory to him. This a
Tikopia usually resists strongly. Thirdly, in the pagan Tikopia system
one basic reason for this jealous attitude towards the traditional
materials relating specifically to a social group, i.e. a lineage, was its
ritual value. In giving the origins of the group the traditions gave
also information about the gods of the group, including their names
and their ancestry. This was believed to be information of ritual
power, involving the prosperity and health of the leader and other
members of the group. Prosperity, to the Tikopia, is not a chance
phenomenon; it comes from the gods. Also, it is not of an infinite
content, but may well be limited, and obtained in competition with
others. If they can use the same set of information—the same set of
gods, with the same names—then they too can appeal for prosperity
with the same force, and possibly distract some of it from its rightful
destination. Moreover, the gods can bring evil as well as good, and
most of them have aspects, activities or titles which can be used
against enemies. Hence, again, there is reluctance to hand over property in traditional information which may be turned against the
imparter.

Now I turn to an aspect of the interpretation which is perhaps
rather more novel. It concerns the relation of the traditional material to the Tikopia social structure, but in particular, its instrumental
use.

The conventional way of treating this traditional material is to
show how it reflects the institutions of a society, maintaining the
integration and solidarity of the system by providing a charter from

the past for the structure and actions of the present. This can be shown for the Tikopia. Among the primary features of the structure of the society are the division of the island community into two major districts; the system of four clans, each composed of lineages, and each with its chief, seconded by the lineage ritual elders; the system of land-holding by lineages under the general control of the clan chief; and (formerly) the elaborate religious rituals performed to gods and ancestors, and culminating in the great collective cycle of the Work of the Gods twice a year in which the chief of Kafika clan has the ritual leadership. Each of these features has its reflection and support in the system of traditional tales. The tale of the birth of the Brethren and their struggle with Tikorau reflects the clan structure and the ritual preoccupations of its chief with his clan god and with a major foodstuff. It also indicates by the symbol of sibling-ship among the gods the integrative fraternal relationships that obtain among the chiefs. The tales of the origins of lineages verify their authenticity, and link them in various ways with other lineages, with clan membership, and with a ritual system. The apportionment of lands among clans and lineages is reflected and legitimized by the tales of the destruction of Nga Ravenga and Nga Faea, which also give a basis for the modern distribution of population between the districts of Faea and Ravenga. The religious leadership and much of the social primacy of the Ariki Kafika are legitimized by the tales of the energizing role of the Atua i Kafika, and the citation of the rites he instituted also provides the outline for the pattern of the Work of the Gods, and for the intricate socio-economic relationships of the Tikopia chiefs therein. If we stop there, it could be argued with considerable cogency that in general, the body of Tikopia tradition serves to reflect, and support, and legitimize the framework of the Tikopia society.[4]

But we cannot stop there. Not all of the major features of Tikopia society are reflected in the traditional tales, or if they are so, it is only indirectly. The institution of chieftainship is one of the cardinal features of the Tikopia social structure, but while there are plenty of tales about chiefs, there is no account of how they came into being as a social category. The Tikopia have apparently never asked themselves the question: why are there chiefs at all; what is the

---

[4] I would distinguish here between *validation*—situations where material offered or used by a group is held to be valid evidence of their claims by themselves alone; and *legitimization*—in situations where other units also accept, or the whole society accepts, the evidence.

justification for their existence in this differential position? So also with the institution of ritual elders *(matapure)* in the pagan religious system. There may be then some major elements in a social system which are not reflected and solidarised by tradition. Is this because they are so fundamental to the nature of the system that they need no validation? Or is it because they are too sensitive—on the principle of "let well alone," no attempt has been made in the process of working the social system to provide a statement of origins. This may be so with the role of chiefs vis-à-vis commoners. Rather than try to explain why you have come into being, it may be better to assume that you have always been there!

Again, the traditional tales may not reflect a unitary society. They may reflect the social structure, but in its competitive, opposition aspects rather than in its integrative ones. As Leach has shown for the Kachin,[5] there may be conflicting principles involved in the sets of stories which all refer to the constitution of the society. This is so in Tikopia. One set of stories, about the birth of the Brethren, validates a clan and lineage grouping at the beginning of things from which Kafika is excluded. Another set, in a narrative specifically entitled the Sacred Story, accounts for the origin of Pu Ma, the prime Kafika deities, and locates them squarely in Tikopia. A third set, by an identification process—a favourite device of Tikopia story-tellers—brings Pu Ma right in back at the beginning by making them in the form of Metikitiki responsible for pulling up Tikopia with the parent of the Brethren sitting there. Even on the most liberal interpretation, these stories put together cannot all promote the unity of Tikopia social relations. They are rather as Kluckhohn has put it ". . . symbolic representations of the dominant configurations" of the social organization.[6]

What then do these stories do? Do they simply cancel one another out? I suggest that their function is much more positive than this. They may, as Leach has shown, be used as alternative principles according to circumstances, each being employed to justify a course of action which has seemed appropriate from other circumstances.[7] The society as a whole may be served by this. But I think the inter-

---

[5] Ed. note: The discussion by Leach to which Firth refers is found in Edmund R. Leach, *Political Systems of Highland Burma* (London, 1954), and is reprinted in this volume on pp. 184-98.

[6] Ed. note: The source of Firth's quotation is Clyde Kluckhohn, "Myths and Rituals: A General Theory," reprinted in this volume. See pp. 145-46 above.

[7] Ed. note: See pp. 186-98 below.

ests of specific groups and even of individuals may be served also, in an instrumental way.

The Tikopia traditional tales are an important mnemonic for perpetuating social relationships. These may be relationships of union, as the story of the Path of Our Ancestor[8] has shown for Kafika and Taumako, or as many other tales describing marriages are used in the organization of funeral and other assemblies requiring contributions of food and labour. But they may also perpetuate relations of disunity, as the tale of the slaying of Kaitu continues to serve—though apparently with diminishing vigour—as a reminder of division and suspicion between Tafua and Taumako chiefly lineages. It could be held that the disunity in the tales may be a kind of outlet for pressures, and that the basic integration of Tikopia society is ultimately strengthened by fantasy elaboration which can be pursued without maladaptative consequences. Yet with more cogency, I think it can be argued indeed that *very often traditional tales are divisive, not unitive* for the society at large, and that social integration is accomplished by the practical requirements of economic and social co-operation, such as are involved in marriage, or by the political requirements of obedience to authority. The function of the traditional tales here is of another order—they are pressure instruments for keeping alive competing claims of varying kind, in particular claims to social status. Or in other circumstances they may serve as a mechanism for compensation, a surrogate for benefits of a more substantial kind. My argument here is that the lack of agreement between these different versions, often in conflict, is due not so much to differential memory as to differential interests. Even one informant may give stories which are inconsistent with one another and this I interpret as resulting from the particular theme he is concerned to discuss at the moment. If he is explaining the creation of land he gives one version; if he is defending his own claims he gives another which does not completely fit.[9]

---

[8] *Te Ara O Pu,* in Raymond Firth, *The Work of the Gods in Tikopia,* London School of Economics Monograph (London, 1940), pp. 84-90.

[9] If these traditions had been obtained separately from representatives of different group interests whose versions were never compared (except by the anthropologist) but existed side by side, each denying the other only by implication, they could not be said to conflict, not merely to be discrepant. But in Tikopia, while there was rarely any direct confrontation and public dispute, there was much private comparison, critical appraisal and attempt at refutation through third parties. In this sense the term conflict may be properly used.

Paul Radin, *Primitive Man as Philosopher* (New York, 1927), pp. 46-48, points out that far-reaching variants in a myth may be found by adequate research. But he seems to attrib-

This bears on the general function of the oral tradition. It does not simply back up the present social system, giving validation of it item for item by reference to previous similar conditions. Rather it denies vigorously other people's mythical bases, compensating present inequalities by assertion of past conditions when things were different. The result is no general body of agreed tales but a series of competing tales from which it is impossible to extract a coherent reality in the distant past.

One finds also a grading of inconsistency. One might expect a somewhat misty description of the remote past in terms of a uniformity agreed to by all, with discrepancies becoming manifest the nearer the approach to existing social conditions with their clash of interests. The opposite is the case. The nearer the scene is shifted to the present day the closer do the accounts of victors and vanquished correspond and the more remote the scene the greater the conflict of opinion. Why? As a hypothesis I suggest that the facts of the present day, the supremacy of Kafika, the poverty of Fangarere, the attachment of Torokinga, etc., to the chiefs are indisputable as such and that there is less room for dispute about how they immediately occurred. But about ultimate origins and former prestige, which can be treated as quite independent of the present structure, there is much more opportunity for conflict.

Note also that the period of probably great internal struggle (the later period) has the most consistent scheme of stories whereas that of possibly internal peace has the greatest conflict in its stories.

Historically the interpretation is that different groups at different times brought their stories and an amalgamation has taken place. But this has not resulted in a fusion and unanimity. The absence of unanimity cannot be attributed to a simple persistence of ancient struggle but must be interpreted rather as due to present clash of interests. That this is so is seen from the fact that persons who have no particular axe to grind have achieved a fairly coherent synthesis of the stories and the conflict is maintained by the heads of the different kinship groups.

From this point of view it is interesting to examine Tikopia traditional tales of the origins of various lineage groups, setting these against the social status of their leaders. I take here the complete set of lineages having either a chief (4 in all) or a ritual elder (19 in all),

---

ute such variation primarily to "the free play of participants and story-tellers," i.e. to individual initiative and fancy, not to any more permanent interests or structural elements.

making a grand total of 23 groups. These lineages can be ranked in their clans by the relative status of their ritual elder in each case, and though the elders in different clans cannot be ranked closely against one another, the four chiefs have a clear order of rank. So a rough cross-clan comparison can be made. Imagine the lineages set out in order by clans and in intra-clan terms (Table 1). What might plausibly be said in advance of the field-information about expectations in regard to the traditional tales of origins of these lineages? Put bluntly, the question is: If traditional tales reflect the social structure, in a status-ranked system of lineages such as Tikopia, in what way will the lineage origin tales reflect their relative rank? Will A 1 in present social or ritual status have A 1 ranking in the origins scale, or what?

TABLE 1
Major Lineages Ranked by Relative Status of Ritual Leaders

	Ranking Number in Clan	Clan and Lineage			
		A	*B*	*C*	*D*
(chiefly)	1	Kafika	Tafua	Taumako	Fangarere
(commoner)	2	Rarovi	Fusi	Niumano	Rangimakini
	3	Raropuka	Sao	Fatumaru	.
	4	Porima	Korokoro	Farekofe	.
	5	Marinoa	Notau	Ngatotiu	.
	6	Tavi	Samoa	Maniva	.
	7	Torokinga	.	Siku	.
	8	.	.	Fasi	.

Two possible patterns of expectations at once come to mind. One is the pattern of direct priority reflection—the chiefly lineages rank higher than the commoner lineages, therefore the origin tales of the community will state that they were first in the land, and the others came later, and so took secondary position. The other obvious possible pattern is that common in African conquest communities, as where there are pastoral Hima rulers and agricultural Iru commoners. Here the origin tales may be in exact reverse to the social status; the commoners were in the land first, then came their conquerors and assumed control. What is the Tikopia position?

In Table 2 I have set out the results. I have graded the type of origins described in the lineage tales, in a series roughly in accord with Tikopia estimation, which rates autochthonous origin as the most worthy and immigrant origin as the lowest. Then I have distributed the lineages, each set down by its clan status number, according to the rating ascribed to its traditional tale of origins. It will be seen at once that there is no close coincidence between the status rating of the lineages—or their elders—in modern socio-ritual terms, and the status-rating of the origins with which they are credited. In Tikopia theory, priority of origins gives status and power, but the existing social structure is not closely reflected in those terms. It is true, and perhaps a little surprising to find that there is some grading of the chiefly lineages according to their religious ranking. This is noteworthy, since in the socio-political field the chiefs are all broadly of equal status, and their traditional validation might have borne this out instead of their ritual differentiation. But it is equally noteworthy to see how the undisputed ritual leader (in the pagan field), the Ariki Kafika, is not the undisputed leader in the field of traditional origins, and that no chiefly lineage has the most respected traditional rating.

TABLE 2
Major Lineages Ranked by Relative Status in Terms
of Traditions of Origin

	Clan Lineage			
Traditional origin	A	B	C	D
Autochthonous: agreed	3	.	.	.
Autochthonous: disputed	1, 2, 4	1	.	.
Autochthonous: agreed lost and re-constituted	.	3	1	.
Autochthonous: but residuum of conquest	7	.	7, 8	1
Segment-offshoot of chiefly lineage	6	2	2, 3, 6	2
Immigrant *ab initio*	5	4, 5, 6	4, 5	.

From this two inferences could receive support. One is that the more firmly established aspects of the social structure may not have, and may not need a reflection and legitimization in traditional tales. But another inference, which I think is more clear, is that *traditional tales may be not so much a reflection of the social structure itself as of organizational pressures within the social structure.* As such also, they allow of attribution to ancestors and superhuman beings of some of the kinds of response to strains and tensions in the society which the tellers of the tales themselves would perhaps like to make.

Here a distinction must be drawn between the *claim* to a traditional origin and a general *acceptance* of it. In Tikopia there is only one lineage whose claim to autochthonous origin is generally accepted. This is a lineage in the clan whose chief ranks first in the ritual hierarchy; but the head of the lineage is neither a chief nor the first in the ranking of the commoner lineage heads. Part of the traditional material in fact goes to explain just why he is not in this position, and to this extent the traditions offer him some form of social compensation. The chiefly lineage of Kafika, and its closely associated commoner lineages of Rarovi and Porima, have all put forward claims to autochthonous origin, but these claims have been specifically denied by other members of the Tikopia community, and one, that of Rarovi, had been withdrawn during the generation between my visits. The making of these claims gave a private status increment to the leaders of the groups concerned, and to the extent that they could get these claims agreed to by others in their immediate circle or beyond, so their status could be regarded as increased. So also with Tafua. Various other lineages could claim autochthonous origin for their unit, though not for its modern representatives, or autochthonous status and later supersession. This type of retrospective claim was itself a current claim also, using past glory as a present social counter. In one way or another, then, half the lineages of Tikopia in 1929 had some kind of claim to be aboriginal; taking into account also those lineages which were offshoots from the chiefly ones, there were only half-a-dozen lineages in all Tikopia which did not link themselves in some way with the beginnings of things in the land. These other lineage heads did not seem to manifest any particular sense of deprivation in this regard, but concentrated on demonstrating their status by special reference to the power of the gods their immigrant ancestors brought with them.

Empirically, as regards claims, one finds at times not only inconsistent origin stories as between representatives of different groups, but also even told by the same person at different times. Sociologically, it seems to me that the most valid interpretation of this is that the inconsistency is a function of the particular context of situation. As in the case of the Ariki Tafua and his discrepant stories of Pu Ma, the personal account of origins may vary as the narrator wishes to stress one or the other aspect of his status and role. The story of the origin of Pu Ma from Tangata-katoa, in the Sacred Tale, is a part of a whole set of traditions that the pagan Tikopia generally admitted as correct, and which I do not remember ever to have heard directly denied. But the contrary affirmations, that Pu Ma came from abroad, seemed to be partisan statements made when the informant was considering not the tale as such but relative status in terms of priority. Such an interpretation rests upon an assumption that such partisanship has a meaning, not as a simple personal idiosyncracy, but against a structural framework of social relationships. The structure has some marginal areas of alternative interpretation, and the traditions are used as instruments to take advantage of this.

Now let us look at the tales about the deified Kafika culture-hero from this sociological point of view. These tales of the Atua i Kafika have a threefold general function. They provide an explanation for the general establishment of order in natural phenomena; they give a charter also for the establishment of many of the most important Tikopia ritual institutions (particularly the Work of the Gods); and they give a kind of ideal standard of achievement which serves to emphasise the limits of ordinary human accomplishment, but illustrates what is possible with superhuman power. Moreover, they have a specific group function: they provide the people of Kafika with an opportunity for boasting and self-aggrandisement at the expense of others, who can only protect themselves and compensate by correction on a few points. Why tradition should give Kafika people this opportunity it is impossible to say with certainty. One can of course put forward the hypothesis that the Atua i Kafika was actually a chief of great organising power and personality. But it is also possible that these traditions are really a fictional reflection of the present ritual primacy of the Ariki Kafika attained in some other historical manner. There are several difficulties in the acceptance of the theory that the Atua i Kafika was in history a chief of outstanding powers of organisation. In the first place it is merely dogmatically affirmed that he set up the Work of the Gods but no details at all are given of how he did it, or any reorganisation of the society contingent upon this. Moreover, the traditions of Tafua and other groups imply that their roles in the ritual scheme were antecedent to the period at which the Atua i Kafika is represented as having instituted it. Again if the Atua i Kafika were this supreme organising genius who induced both Nga Faea and Nga Ravenga as well as the other two chiefs to combine in this complicated ritual scheme, it is difficult to believe that his group with this primacy should have remained cooped up for several generations more in one small corner of the island. Finally, the real ritual reorganisation or reintegration of the society may have been consequent upon the disappearance of Nga

Faea and Nga Ravenga. The placing of the ritual reorganisation at an earlier time is quite possibly an attempt to give an added sanction—of purported creation at the time when man himself was first definitely established as a human social entity.

In general then, taking these origin tales in Tikopia as an example, it may be said that traditional tales, sociologically viewed, are instruments, and flexible. Belief in them is not random, but uses certain themes with vigour. They are linked to the social structure, but not in a simple relationship. To conclude—the material the anthropologist collects is from the native point of view an account of past happenings, but this account is necessarily moulded into forms that are dependent upon existing social relationships and therefore must be largely a projection of the present into the past. Descriptions of a former state of society in which a different arrangement of groups or institutions existed can only be visualised by the narrator of the tale from the point of view of the social arrangements which he himself knows and in which he is an active participant. Merely to prune the tales of obvious impossibilities and imaginative embroidery and accept the rest as a historical record is therefore inadequate. But this does not mean that the anthropologist can ignore the factor of continuity. He must assume that the social structure he has under observation stretches back into the past if only into the period immediately before his appearance on the scene. He must assume also that there is some validity in the memory of his informants so that many things which they relate as having come under their own observation may be regarded as substantially correct. Some validity must also be attached to the accuracy of the traditional tales as far as their oral reproduction through the generations is concerned. The position usually taken up by Polynesian scholars has been that the lack of correspondence which is reasonably inferred in the relation of present traditional tale to past event is due to defects in memory and the occasional embroidery of imagination. But a more fundamental point is that in each generation quite apart from any lapse of memory the tale becomes remoulded to some extent by the social situation of the narrator. The difficulty of calculating past history from present traditional narratives lies not so much in the characteristics of the memory process by which the tales are transmitted as in the nature of the social process which conditions and impells their transmission.

A sociological theory of traditional tales does not imply that they are a simple product of free association in the teller. It is practically impossible for the narrator or a set of narrators to invent a complete mythical system with the coherence which the material reveals. Continuity with the past must have been maintained. But with this has gone constant reformulation. In the process of reformulation certain elements of the tales – those which describe the physically impossible – are obvious inventions; but in addition descriptions of the physically possible may also be inventions, and many of them in fact must be so. Any attempt at historical reconstruction must therefore rest on the interpretation of probabilities and is arbitrary even where the accounts considered are within the sphere of physical possibility. Even where it is plausible that there was in the past an event substantially as described, the record of it obtained by the anthropologist from the present day informant is essentially the perpetuation of a social situation rather than of a crude objective item of history.

All this points again to the arbitrary nature of any attempt to distinguish clearly myth, legend, and history in the field material. The anthropologist is confronted empirically by a set of tales of varying social context all of which have been subjected to the same process of remoulding, if in varying degree.

This analysis has been of a very different kind from those which examine the material of oral tradition from the point of view of its style, its frequency of content-themes, its comparative interest, or the light it throws on personality types. Its treatment has been specifically sociological, to try and relate the traditional stories to the structure and operations of the society which was "present-day" at the time the material was collected. The context of the stories has been regarded as essential to their interpretation, but this context has been seen more in terms of individual and group status interest, ritual functions and other social elements than in terms of individual mental associations. This is an emphasis which is probably to be expected when it is remembered that these stories were told by people who were pursuing an active collective social life, and for whom the stories were part of the living reality of this life. From this analysis it can be affirmed that the truth of Tikopia tradition does not consist simply in a recreational filling in of leisure time, in the simple promotion of harmony and unity between members of the society, in a symbolic expression of their ritual, or in a dramatic exposition of the basic principles of their social and natural order. Any or all of these may be operative at a given time. But tradition also offers a personal and small-group resource, a manipulative instrument for defending and enhancing social status. As such it is a very significant part of the organisational mechanisms of the society. This assumes, of course that status involvement, and the possibility of status enhancement, are important elements—though not necessarily the most important—in man's social behaviour. In the sense not of specific ratings and gradings, but of much more generalised notions of the integrity of the self, which is affected by the affirmatory or aggressive acts of others, I believe that this assumption can be validated, though this is not the place in which to examine the question.

This analysis may be of interest apart from its presentation and clarification of material from Tikopia. It may be of comparative use to other social anthropologists working on the traditional material from other communities. It may strengthen the approach of scholars seeking a more realistic appraisal of Polynesian traditions in sociological terms. And it may help to sound a note of caution to those historians who would like to be able to incorporate conclusions derived from a study of oral tradition into their interpretations.

Myth as a Justification for Faction

and Social Change*[1]

EDMUND LEACH

IN Chapter I, I argued that in the language employed in this book, myth and ritual are essentially one and the same. Both are modes of making statements about structural relationships. In Chapter V, where I describe a number of the leading concepts which occur in *gumsa* Kachin ideology,[2] I have elaborated this theme. What I describe are culturally defined objects, actions and ideas; what I am interested in is their implication for the formal relationships that exist between social persons. So far I have tried to keep the emphasis

---

*Reprinted from *Political Systems of Highland Burma* (reprint edition, London, 1964), Chapter IX, pp. 264-78, by permission of the author, the London School of Economics and Political Science in the University of London, G. Bell and Sons, Ltd., and the Beacon Press.

[1] Ed. note: The opening paragraph of Chapter IX of *Political Systems of Highland Burma*, which consists of a single transitional sentence, has been omitted from this reprinted version.

[2] Ed. note: A number of terms used throughout this excerpt warrant brief explanations. The populations studied by Leach are the *Shan* and *Kachin* peoples who inhabit the Kachin Hills Area of Northeast Burma. Leach describes the Shan as valley dwellers and cultivators of wet-rice who are Buddhists and who speak (with the exception of some low-caste commoners) some dialect of Tai. There is class stratification into aristocrats, commoners, and low caste; and the Shan people are organized politically into states *(möng),* some of which are autonomous and others of which constitute units or subunits of a larger *möng.* The term *Kachin* is used to refer to all peoples of the Kachin Hills Area who are not Buddhists. The Kachin people speak a variety of dialects and have diverse political systems which can be considered variations of two polar types, the *gumlao* and the *gumsa.* The *gumlao,* according to Leach (p. 57 of *Political Systems of Highland Burma*), is "a 'democratic' species of organisation in which the political entity is a single village and there is no class difference between aristocrats and commoners"; the *gumsa,* on the other hand, is "an 'aristocratic' species of organisation," its political entity being a territory (a *mung*) "which has at its head a prince of aristocratic blood called a *duwa* who assumes the title *Zau.*" The Kachins and Shans, Leach notes (p. 2), "are almost everywhere close neighbours and in the ordinary affairs of life they are much mixed up together."

on ritual rather than on myth—that is on actions rather than on verbal statements which are counterparts to the action, but already in a number of instances, particularly when attempting to explain the conceptual difference between *gumsa* and *gumlao,* I have had to explain by means of myth.

This raises issues of theoretical importance, the most important of which is "How can mythology be held to justify change, in the social structure?" Isn't it almost a contradiction in terms to suggest such a possibility?

Within the general Kachin-Shan complex we have, I claim, a number of unstable sub-systems. Particular communities are capable of changing from one sub-system into another. Let us assume for the moment that this analysis is correct from the sociological point of view. We must then ask ourselves how do such changes and alternative forms of organisation present themselves to the participant Kachins and Shans?

I have asserted that the social structure is "represented" in ritual. But if the social structures with which we are here dealing are unstable, this instability must also be "represented" in the ritual system. Yet ritual, being backed by tradition, is surely always the most rigid and conservative element in social organisation?

I think it is fair to say that most British social anthropologists commonly look upon myth from much the same point of view as that adopted by Malinowski in his well-known essay *Myth in Primitive Psychology.*[3] According to this view myth and tradition are to be thought of primarily as a sanction or charter for ritual action. Ritual action reflects the social structure, but it is also a dramatic recapitulation of the myth. Myth and ritual are thus complementary and serve to perpetuate one another. It is no part of this doctrine that the myths of any one culture should be mutually consistent, but adherence to the rest of Malinowski's functionalist theory leads to the assumption that they must be. In the Malinowskian scheme the various aspects of a culture are necessarily integrated to form a coherent whole; hence the myths of a people must be mutually consistent—for any one group of people there is only one culture, one structural system, one mutually consistent set of myths.

Now in my view it is unnecessary to postulate this kind of consistency. I think social anthropologists only tend to think of myth

---

[3] [London,] 1926.

systems as internally consistent because they retain something of the ethnologist's notion that myth is a kind of history. Because of this prejudice they come to be selective in their analysis of myth and tend to discriminate between "correct" and "incorrect" versions of the same tale.

In the case of Kachin mythology there can be no possibility of eliminating the contradictions and inconsistencies. They are fundamental. Where there are rival versions of the same story, no one version is "more correct" than any other. On the contrary, I hold that the contradictions are more significant than the uniformities.

Kachins recount their traditions on set occasions, to justify a quarrel, to validate a social custom, to accompany a religious performance. The story-telling therefore has a purpose; it serves to validate the status of the individual who tells the story, or rather of the individual who hires a bard to tell the story, for among Kachins the telling of traditional tales is a professional occupation carried out by priests and bards of various grades *(jaiwa, dumsa, laika).*[4] But if the status of one individual is validated, that almost always means that the status of someone else is denigrated. One might then infer almost from first principles that every traditional tale will occur in several different versions, each tending to uphold the claims of a different vested interest.

And that is the case.'There is no "authentic version" of Kachin tradition to which all Kachins would agree, there are merely a number of stories which concern more or less the same set of mythological characters and which make use of the same kinds of structural symbolism (e.g. the marriage of a man with the daughter of a nat), but which differ from one another in crucial details according to who is telling the tale.

A good example of this kind of adaptation is to be seen in the two published versions of the story of the origin of the Nsu nat—the spirit of jealousy—to which reference has already been made. The Kachin stereotype of a jealousy situation is the relation between

---

[4] Ed. note: By using the words "various grades" here, Leach is apparently referring to what might be termed the social status and principal responsibility of classes of storytellers. A *jaiwa,* for instance, is a priest (a *dumsa*) who can recite traditional sagas which last for eight to ten hours at a stretch and which may even continue from day to day. Leach indicates (pp. 190-91) that to employ a *jaiwa* in 1940 (at the time that he was conducting his fieldwork) would have required a substantial fee, for such reciters were very few in number. This suggests that such sagatellers would have enjoyed high social status and commanded considerable respect as a result of their special skill.

elder and younger brother. Two Kachin ethnographers, Hanson and Gilhodes, recount very nearly the same myth but the one is the reverse of the other.[5] In Gilhodes' story the eldest brother is jealous of the younger brother, who is favoured by the nats. In the end the elder brother is drowned in a coffin he has prepared for the younger brother and the younger brother lives on to become a rich chief. In Hanson's story the roles are reversed and the younger brother, having long defrauded the elder, is finally drowned in the coffin he has prepared for his elder brother.

Neither of these versions can be said to be more correct than the other. It is simply that where bad blood exists between an elder and a younger brother either party may suspect the other of bringing on misfortune by jealous thoughts; either party may then make an offering to the Nsu nat. If the younger brother makes the offering, Gilhodes' version will figure as the mythical sanction; if the elder brother makes the offering Hanson's version will serve the same purpose. The bard-priest *(dumsa)* will adapt his stories to suit the audience which hires him.

Now, in the past, Kachin ethnographers have never appreciated this point. They have regarded tradition as a species of badly recorded history. Where they have found inconsistencies in the record, they have felt justified in selecting that version which seemed most likely to be "true" or even in inventing parts of the story which appeared to be missing.

Such an approach to the data makes it possible to represent the basic structure of Kachin society as very simple. Confusions of practice are regarded as due to the fact that the stupid Kachins fail to understand their own society or to obey their own rules. Enriquez, for example, has reduced the whole structural system to a couple of paragraphs.

There is a common misconception amongst Europeans with regard to the existence of Kachin tribes. There is, as a matter of fact, hardly any tribal feeling amongst the Kachins, except in connection with property and boundaries, and the reason for this is that they consider themselves divided into families rather than into tribes. The so-called five main tribes (Marip, Lahtaw, Lahpai, N'Hkum and Maran) are really five aristocratic families descended from the five eldest

---

[5] C. Gilhodes, *The Kachins: Religion and Customs* (Calcutta, 1922), pp. 52-54; and O. Hanson, *The Kachins: Their Customs and Traditions* (Rangoon, 1913), pp. 126-28. The whole story is a long one. All the incidents in Hanson's version occur (reversed) in Gilhodes' version, but the latter has some features missing in the former.

sons of Wahkyet Wa, the reputed father of the Kachin race. Their order of precedence is as given above, the Marips being the senior family. Any man with one or other of these names may be regarded as well born; and *Duwas* or "chiefs" always belong to these families. Other clans are subsections of the five main ones, or are in some degree related to them. A man may not marry into a family bearing the same family name.

Every Kachin family knows exactly with what families it may intermarry. Amongst the five aristocratic families Marips take their brides from Marans, Marans from N'Hkums, N'Hkums from Lahpais, Lahpais from Lahtaws, and Lahtaws from Marips. This, however, is only a very broad statement. The sub-sections of nearly every clan have modifications of the marriage rules peculiar to themselves. No European, as far as I know, has ever understood them, and certainly no Kachin does. A discussion of marriage laws usually becomes heated. In the case of *Duwas* the rule is further modified, because there are no longer any Marip *Duwas;*[6] and with commoners there are many minor exceptions amongst individual families. The rules are, however, not as rigidly enforced now as they used to be.[7]

If mythological inconsistencies are eliminated on the grounds that there could after all be only one set of historical facts, inconsistencies in traditional law and custom are also necessarily eliminated and the whole scheme becomes rigid and simple. If, however, we regard Kachin mythology as expressing a system of *ideas* instead of a system of *rules* or a set of historical events, the need for internal consistency in the various traditions disappears. The contradictions between rival versions of the same story then take on a new significance.

My argument here can be well illustrated by a comparison between the various published versions of the Kachin stories concerning the relationship between the first men and the nats, and the relationship between the ancestors of the principal aristocratic clans.

The saga-teller's *(jaiwa)* account of a Kachin chief's genealogy "from the beginning" *(ahtik labau gawn)* normally falls into several sections corresponding to the system of "branches" or segments in terms of which the family tree is conceived. The first section takes the tale from the creation to the birth of Shapawng Yawng—the first Kachin; the second section proceeds from Shapawng Yawng to the sons of Wahkyet Wa—who, as noted by Enriquez, are regarded as clan founders; the story then splits up and pursues the fortunes of each clan independently, noting the various points of segmentation.

---

[6] This is not true, although it is generally believed to be the case among Kachins in the Bhamo area.

[7] C. M. Enriquez, *A Burmese Arcady* (London, 1923), pp. 26-27.

Only one authority (Kawlu Ma Nawng) has provided us with extensive material of the third type, but for the first two sections of the story we have rival versions from George, Wehrli, Hertz, Gilhodes, Hanson, Carrapiett, Kawlu Ma Nawng. Although in some respects these rival authorities are derivative from one another, their mutual contradictions are sufficient to illustrate my argument.

The first section of the story is really concerned only with establishing the fact that the Shadip nat is the Supreme Being and that the first humans were *dama* to the sky nats *(mu nat)* and that the chiefs alone are *dama* to Madai nat.[8] The rival versions differ from one another only in the degree of condensation, i.e. in the number of generations intervening between two events. That part of the story which concerns us here can be reduced to the following precis (Fig. 6):

In the beginning there was a female-male creator spirit which gave birth to the various elements of the universe. This being, Chyanun-Woishun, a sort of personification of earth and sky is now worshipped in the form of Shadip (Ga Nat)—the Earth Spirit of the chiefs.

From Chyanun-Woishun are descended:

a. Ninggawn Wa, a half-human half-divine creator who "forges" the Earth. He later assumes a more human form and is known as the Ka-ang Duwa, chief of the *middle* land, a title with a strongly Chinese flavour.

The Ka-ang Duwa marries an alligator *(baren)* and has six sons who are the progenitors of the Nungs, Chinese, Shans, Maru, Nagas *(Kang),* and Jinghpaw.

It is the youngest of these sons Shapawng Yawng who is first parent to the Jinghpaw.

b. The Mu Nat—the sky nats who control general prosperity and wealth. The principal Mu Nat are a series of 7, 8 or 9 brothers. Although there is agreement about the names of most of them, there is a significant disagreement about their order of birth. The chief of the Mu Nat is La N'Roi Madai and it is this Madai Nat which can only be approached by chiefs. The Madai Nat is the youngest of the Mu Nat.

c. The Maraw—these beings have been described on p. 177 f.[9]

---

[8] Ed. note: The word *nat* is an anglicization of a native word meaning "a spirit, a supernatural being." The word *dama,* which literally means "the permanent children," refers to the lineages into which females of Ego's lineage have recently married. The *dama* lineages are subordinate to the *mayu* lineages, those from which males of Ego's lineage have recently taken brides.

[9] Ed. note: Leach provides the following explanation of the concept of the Maraw (p. 177): "The basic notion of the Maraw as nats [i.e., spirits, supernatural beings] is that they are beings who, despite their very lowly origin, have the power of cancelling even the gifts of the highest gods. They function therefore as a defence mechanism for the system of diagnosis practised by the priests and diviners. If, in the last resort, things do not turn out as was predicted, it must be the fault of the Maraw. Consequently sacrifices to the ordinary nats are always supplemented by an additional sacrifice to the Maraw."

FIGURE 6
The Relationship of Humans to Gods

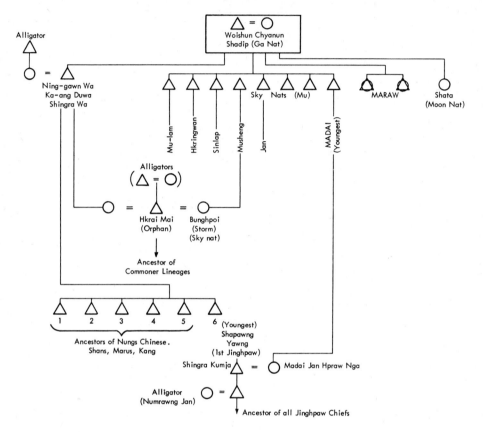

Shapawng Yawng, the first Jinghpaw, founds a lineage called Shingra who are lords of Shingra Ga (original land). A scion of this house marries a daughter of the Madai Nat named Madai Hpraw Nga (Madai White Buffalo). Other descendants continue to marry alligators *(baren numraw)*. Madai Hpraw Nga's marriage constituted the first *manau*. All aristocratic Jinghpaw are descended from Madai Hpraw Nga.

Nearly all lineages in *gumsa* society can make out a case for claiming that they have aristocratic connections, but it is maintained by present day aristocrats that commoners are wholly and innately inferior. There are consequently a variety of stories which trace the descent of commoners from orphans *(hkrai)*. The descendants of these orphans (who are again sometimes the children of alligators) are given a status *vis-à-vis* the minor sky nats, similar to that of the chiefs *vis-à-vis* the chief of the sky nats, Madai.

In one account Hkrai Mai, the orphan, marries Bunghpoi, the daughter of Musheng, in another he marries a daughter of the Ka-ang Duwa. The commoners are thus *dama* to the sky nat Musheng but not to Madai; they are also *dama* to the line of chiefs descended from the Ka-ang Duwa.

I have, in a previous chapter, pointed out that the affinal status of the commoners in relation to the chiefs is a kind of paradox in the *gumsa* structure.[10] It is symptomatic of this that alongside stories which make the commoners *dama* to the chiefs and/or the minor sky nats we find other stories which make the commoners descend from a pair of orphans who are sole survivors of the Flood and who have no connection with the chiefs or the nats.[11]

The story now enters its second section. Here the discrepancies between different versions become more serious. The skeleton of the story is given above in the quotation from Enriquez. Shapawng Yawng has a descendant, Wahkyet Wa, whose sons are the founders of major clans. The birth order of these sons should, as Enriquez perceives, affect the rank order of the clans, but the different clans have very different ideas about what this rank order is. Without seriously altering the structure of the mythological story each of the five clans named—as well as several others—can put forward a case to be regarded as the senior group. First as to the agreed part of the story. This is represented in diagram form in Fig. 7.

There is agreement that the male line of descent from Shingra Kumja and Madai Jan Hpraw Nga leads eventually to Wahkyet Wa Ma Gam who is father to a series of sons. There is agreement that the first three sons are respectively the ancestors of Marip, Lahtaw and

---

10 Ed. note: This is discussed in Chapter VII, pp. 213-26, of *Political Systems of Highland Burma*.

11 My account is based mainly on the following sources: W. J. S. Carrapiett, *The Kachin Tribes of Burma* (Rangoon, 1929), pp. 12, 75, 76, 79; Gilhodes [see n. 5 above], pp. 9, 10, 13, 44, 51, 70-75, 79-83, 126; E. C. T. George, "Memorandum on the Enumeration of the Tribes Inhabiting the Kachin Hills"; "Memorandum on the Kachins of Our Frontier," *Census*, IX (1891); Hanson [see n. 5 above], pp. 110, 121, 165; H. F. Hertz, *A Practical Handbook of the Kachin or Chingpaw Language* (Calcutta, 1943), pp. 135, 156; J. Anderson, *Mandalay to Momien* (London, 1876), Appendix; Kawlu Ma Nawng, *The History of the Kachins of the Hukawng Valley,* trans. J. L. Leyden (Bombay, 1942), pp. 1 f.; and G. T. Bayfield, "Narrative of a Journey from Ava to the Frontiers of Assam and Back, Performed Between December 1836 and May 1837 under the Orders of Col. Burney," *Selection of Papers Regarding the Hill Tracts between Assam and Burma and on the Upper Brahmaputra* (Calcutta, 1873), p. 223. There is greater consistency between the various versions than might at first appear. For instance, while the alligators *(baren)* are missing in some, they are replaced by females of the Numrang or Numrawng lineage. But allegators [sic] are often described as *baren numraw(ng)* —"monstrous alligator"— so the stories are really the same. As has been pointed out on p. 178 n. the mythological concepts of *baren numraw* and *maraw* are closely associated. Also, as noted before, the notion of *baren* resembles the Chinese notion of "dragon" *(lung)*.

FIGURE 7
The Rank Order of Clan Ancestors

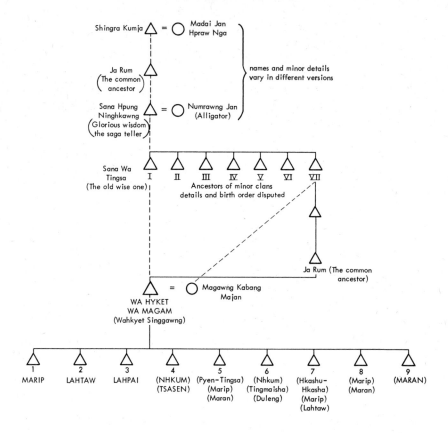

The nine sons of Wahkyet Wa Ma Gam in the bottom line of the genealogy are the ancestors of the major clans. Only the clan affiliation of the first three sons is generally agreed. For the rest both the number of sons and the order of birth is disputed. Hkashu-Hkasha (7) ("the descendants") is a fictitious clan but it is mythologically important since it is usually regarded as the youngest line and hence *uma*.

Lahpai. Other clans are said to be descended either from the younger brothers of these three or else from an ancestor of Wahkyet Wa by a collateral line. Wahkyet Wa is usually in the "youngest son" line of descent. Kawlu Ma Nawng's version, which makes him a member of an eldest son branch, makes his principal wife Magawn Kabang Jan, a member of the "youngest son" lineage.

Now for the variations put forward by different clans.

Clan Marip: Wahkyet Wa had seven sons. The eldest was Marip Wa Kumja, ancestor of the royal Marip. The youngest and *uma* was La N'Hka Hkashu Hkasha. But apart from a few elements who have become absorbed into the Marip, the Hkashu Hkasha have died out. Therefore the Marip are the senior clan.[12]

Clan Lahtaw: Wahkyet Wa had seven sons. The second son was ancestor of the Lahtaw. The youngest and *uma* was La N'Hka Hkashu Hkasha. The latter have largely died out but have become absorbed with the main branch of the Lahtaw. Apart from this a descendant of the Lahtaw Wa (second son of Wahkyet Wa) named Ngaw Wa married a daughter of the sky nat Musheng. Furthermore the claims of the Marip chiefs are bogus as all the "true" Marips died out long ago and modern Marip chiefs are mere pretenders.[13]

Clan Lahpai: Wahkyet Wa had numerous sons of whom the third was ancestor of the Lahpai. Wahkyet Wa had numerous wives but only the first three sons were born to his chief wife Magawng Kabang. Therefore the third son was the true *uma* and the Lahpai are the senior clan. (There is no printed version of this; it was the first version which I recorded myself).

Clan Nhkum: Most people say that the Nhkum are descended from one of the younger sons of Wahkyet Wa—the fourth or the sixth. This is incorrect. The first Nhkum was Mahtum Hkum, identified as II in Fig. 7. He married Madai Jan, a daughter of the Madai nat and had a son Tsinghkum Tu (Matsaw Wa Tsinghkum) who married a daughter of the sun nat (Jan Jan). The Nhkum thus have better connections with the nat world than any of the descendants of Wahkyet Wa.[14]

Clan Maran: Wahkyet Wa had eight or nine sons not seven. The youngest was La N'Kying Maran Wa Kying Nang and the *uma*. The Maran are therefore the senior clan. Alternatively in areas where the Lahpai maintain that only a few of Wahkyet Wa's sons were the offspring of his first wife, the argument becomes: Wahkyet Wa had five sons by his first wife, of these the youngest, an *uma,* was La N'Tang Maran Wa Ning Shawng.[15]

Clan Kareng-Hpauwi: Some allege that the Kareng are not of royal blood at all. This is most insulting. The Kareng are descended from III in Fig. 7. Their claims are then similar to those of the Nhkum.[16]

And so on.

The above variants all represent claims to seniority by different major *gumsa* clans. The same kind of rivalry and conflicting interpre-

---

[12] Kawlu Ma Nawng, pp. 2, 3, 7.
[13] Enriquez, p. 27; Carrapiett, p. 80; Gilhodes, p. 84; Hanson, p. 14.
[14] Kawlu Ma Nawng, pp. 1-6; cf. Hanson, p. 14.
[15] Kawlu Ma Nawng, pp. 2-3; Hanson, p. 14; Gilhodes, p. 84.
[16] Carrapiett, p. 2; Kawlu Ma Nawng, p. 1; Enriquez, p. 27.

tation of myth is also noticeable at lower levels of clan segmentation, as between different lineages of the same clan. For example:

Aura branch of Shadan lineage of Lahpai clan.   The Lahpai chiefs of the Gauri and Atsi all consider themselves Lahpai-Shadan-Aura. The Aura are further divided into various minor segments.

The 19th-century feud between the Gauri chiefs of the Mahtang area and their neighbours of the Sinlum-Lawdan group of villages has already been mentioned.[17] The latter group are now in the ascendancy; they are mainly Baptists while most of their rivals are Catholics. It is the Sinlum version which the Baptist missionary Hanson thus reports:

"The division of the Gauri territory into two sections took place after a feast of a certain Jauhpa Hkun Wa[18] who made a double dance *(hting htang manau)* for his twin sons, the last-born of which was an *uma;* the first-born of the two sought a country of his own, that is he went to 'another country' *(mung kaga)* and therefore called his territory Mung Ga, while the country of the younger twin was called Uma Ga."[19] This account needs to be compared with the historical evidence which I have cited. . . .[20]

The story is nicely designed to denigrate the undoubted high status of the former chiefs of Mung Ga (Möng Hka). In this connection it has to be remembered when reading Kawlu Ma Nawng's usually excellent account that his own lineage (Kawlu) is commonly considered a subordinate branch of this same Aura lineage. In Kawlu Ma Nawng's story a crucial Lahpai ancestor is Numtin La Jawng who has five wives and a large number of sons who are specified as ancestors of different Lahpai lineages. Aura are given as the *uma* line—the offspring of the fifth son of the first wife.

Here is another example in which rival parties cite different myths to justify the same facts. In the Duleng country south of Putao the empirical situation is that the Duleng are now *gumlao*. Their immediate neighbours to the south are *gumsa*.

The first version is one recorded by myself from Duleng *gumlao* elders:

---

[17] Ed. note: This is discussed in Chapter VII, pp. 213-26, of *Political Systems of Highland Burma.*

[18] Jauhpa Hkun Wa (Saohpa Hkun) is a particularly blatant Shan title. . . .

[19] See O. Hanson, *A Dictionary of the Kachin Language* (Rangoon, 1906), p. 46. Cf. also the myth which links up the Gauri chiefs (Lahpai-Aura) with the Atsi chiefs and the Hpunggan chiefs (J. G. Scott and J. P. Hardiman, *Gazetteer of Upper Burma and the Shan States,* Part I, Vol. I, 1901, 378). This also exists in several rival versions.

[20] Ed. note: The "historical evidence" to which Leach refers (on p. 225 of *Political Systems of Highland Burma)* indicates that the territorial division resulted from economic conflicts of interest.

The Duleng claim that they are all descendants of one Duleng Hkawp Gumwa, the eldest son of Duleng Yawng Nang, sixth son of Wahkyet Wa. This Duleng Hkawp Gumwa had a younger brother Duleng Nawng Dungmai who was driven out of the Duleng country and went to live in the Hukawng Valley. The descendants of Duleng Hkawp Gumwa (unlawfully) assumed the chieftainship. At a time when there were two chiefs with the ominous names Maju Kinji and Hpyi, the chiefs were driven out. Since then the Duleng country has been governed on the *gumlao* system without chiefs.

The second version is that given by Kawlu Ma Nawng and clearly derived from *gumsa* sources:

The sixth son of Wahkyet Wa (the ancestor of the Duleng) was Tingmaisha Dawng Yawng (N'Dawng Wa). From him are descended the Tingmaisha or N'Dawng clan, which includes the Duleng.

At the great *manau* at which the precedence of the clans was decided and at which the Hkashu Hkasha were recognized as the senior line, the N'Dawng arrived late after all the feasting was over. "They knew that they had arrived too late for meat so they decided to collect the scattered bamboos in which meat had been cooked and lick out the insides." The N'Dawng are thus classed by the *gumsa* as of the status of pariah dogs. "To this day people quarrelling with the N'Dawngs can insult and annoy them by saying, 'You N'Dawngs who licked bamboos at the head waters of the Punghkang.'" [21]

In all the foregoing examples the rivals for precedence all agree as to what the principles of seniority are, they merely disagree about the crucial mythological incidents which are supposed to sanction present day status. A slightly different kind of conflict arises when the rival parties disagree about the "ethic" of the myth itself, as for instance in the rivalry between the *gumsa* and *gumlao* sections of the Tsasen clan reported by Kawlu Ma Nawng.

The principal features of the relevant myth have already been given in Chapter VI.[22] It will be seen that in this case the facts of the myth are equally acceptable to both sides, but there is disagreement about the formally correct structural rules. The *gumsa* claim that the children of a "collected widow" are *ipso facto* of lower ranking status than their half siblings, so that the descendants of the former can be treated as commoners by the descendants of the latter. The *gumlao* on the other hand repudiate this notion of rank and claim that siblings or half siblings and all their patrilineal descendants should

---

[21] Kawlu Ma Nawng, pp. 2, 7. The names Maju Kinji and Hpyi mean "unlucky priest's wand" and "witch" respectively.

[22] Ed. note: Printed on pp. 201-2 of *Political Systems of Highland Burma*.

rank equally as clan brothers. The very essence of the *gumsa-gumlao* opposition is that while the latter repudiate hereditary class distinctions, the former glory in them. Since *gumsa* validate class difference by reference to such features as levirate marriage and the inferior status of secondary wives, it is appropriate that the *gumlao* should validate their own principles by reference to a myth which challenges the *gumsa* on this very point.

The following example is similar. Here again the *gumlao* do not dispute the facts of the myth but challenge the ethical deductions made from it by the *gumsa,* and thereby again deny the principle of hereditary class inferiority.

Pyen Tingsa Marip: Most versions say that the descendants of the fifth son of Wahkyet Wa are either Marip or Pyen Tingsa. The *gumsa* version is that the oldest son of Wahkyet Wa, Marip Wa Gumja, was married to Woigawng Sumpyi. Marip Wa Gumja went on a long journey leaving his wife at home. While he was away Woigawng Sumpyi had four children by Pyen Tingsa Tang, fifth son of Wahkyet Wa and younger brother of Marip Wa Gumja. As punishment for this offence the descendants of Woigawng Sumpyi and Pyen Tingsa Tang, though classed as Marip, are for ever commoners and hereditary serfs of the descendants of Woigawng Sumpyi and Marip Wa Gumja the true aristocratic Marip.

The *gumlao* accept most of the above story but say that it was Marip Wa Gumja's own fault if his wife was unfaithful, he should not have left her alone so long. In any case many Kachins hold that if a husband is away for a long time, it is quite proper for the wife to sleep with the husband's brother. The ancestors of the Pyen Tingsa sub-clan therefore rightly refused to accept a status of inferiority and joined the *gumlao* movement.[23]

This particular story appears to serve as a banner for several different kinds of faction. It is commonly held that the modern representatives of the Pyen Tingsa sub-clan are the N'Ding major lineage of which there are a large number of branches. Some of these are *gumlao,* others include chiefs of great influence. The story cited above can therefore be used not only to point out the opposition between *gumsa* and *gumlao* Marips but also to justify factions between rival *gumsa* sections of the Marip clan—the N'Ding on the one hand and the Um, Ningrang, Rureng on the other.[24]

It will be agreed, I think, that all the examples of tradition which I have cited in this chapter are unquestionably myth in an orthodox

[23] Kawlu Ma Nawng, pp. 4, 5, 13.
[24] Cf. Kawlu Ma Nawng, pp. 6, 8.

classical sense. Yet in every case the structural implications of the myth are wholly ambiguous and vary according to the vested interests of the individual who is citing the story.

In Chapter IV, when describing the feuds and factions of Hpalang, I showed how traditions about the fairly recent past are used to make argumentative assertions about the relative status of living individuals. I referred to these Hpalang stories as "myth," though I pointed out that they do not fall into the ordinary definition of myth, since the events purport to be recent and the characters ordinary humans. The tales I have now given are myths in a classical sense; they concern gods and demi-gods and ancestors of semi-divine status and most of them are very widely shared among all Jinghpaw-speaking peoples. I don't think that it is going too far to say that any Jinghpaw saga-teller *(jaiwa)* in the Kachin Hills, if suitably questioned, would give a version of the creation and of the beginning of mankind which could readily be seen to be the "same story" as that given in Figs. 6 and 7. But it would be the same story only in general framework, the minor details would vary in such a way as to enhance (by implication) the personal status of the story-teller. In other words, what the evidence of this chapter has shown is that myth of the orthodox kind varies in the same way and for the same reasons as myth of the unorthodox kind which I cited for Hpalang.

My conclusion is that the ordinary anthropological definition of myth is an inappropriate category as far as the Kachins are concerned. Sacred tales—that is to say tales about divine beings which are widely known—have no special characteristics which make them any different from tales about local happenings 20 years ago. Both kinds of tale have the same function—the telling of them is a ritual act (in my sense of the term) which justifies the particular attitude adopted by the teller at the moment of the telling.

I am led therefore to the conclusion that the existence of an agreed framework is in no sense an index of social solidarity or equilibrium. This view conflicts with what most anthropologists have held—at any rate until very recently. Since Malinowski's day it has been a commonplace that myth serves to sanction social behaviour and to validate the rights of particular individuals and groups within a particular social system. Since any social system, however stable and balanced it may be, contains opposing factions, there are bound to be different myths to validate the particular rights of different groups of people. Malinowski himself saw this and the point has been force-fully made by others—notably Fortes[25] and Firth.[26] But the argument of these writers, if I understand them correctly, is that whatever may be the local tensions and oppositions within a social system, the overall structure is somehow in equilibrium, the claims of one group balancing out against the claims of another. In Fortes' analysis, for example, the very fact that the rival Namoos and Talis in Tallensi society use a common language of ritual expression seems to be taken as evidence for the overall stability of the total system.[27]

What I am suggesting is exactly the opposite to this. Myth and ritual is a language of signs in terms of which claims to rights and status are expressed, but it is a language of argument, not a chorus of harmony. If ritual is sometimes a mechanism of integration, one could as well argue that it is often a mechanism of disintegration. A proper assimilation of this point of view requires, I would maintain, a fundamental change in the current anthropological concept of social structure.

---

[25] M. Fortes, *The Dynamics of Clanship among the Tallensi* (London, 1945).

[26] R. Firth, "Totemism in Polynesia," *Oceania*, I (1932).

[27] Fortes, especially pp. 24 ff.

Overture to *Le Cru et le Cuit**[1]

CLAUDE LÉVI-STRAUSS

THE aim of this book is to show how certain categorical opposites drawn from everyday experience with the most basic sorts of things—e.g. "raw" and "cooked," "fresh" and "rotten," "moist" and "parched," and others—can serve a people as conceptual tools for the formation of abstract notions and for combining these into propositions. (The values of such categorical terms can be defined with any necessary degree of precision, and of course always from the point of view of a particular culture, by means of quite simple acts of ethnographic observation.)

The form of this hypothesis requires one's starting point to be at the level of the most concrete; that is to say, one must proceed from some particular social group, or from a cluster of such groups as are reasonably close to one another in habitat, history, and culture. This is a precaution of methodology, necessary to be sure, but one that need neither conceal nor restrict the goals of our project. By means of a small number of myths taken from certain aboriginal societies which will serve as our laboratory we hope to construct an experiment whose significance, if we succeed, will be of a general order; for we anticipate that it will demonstrate the existence of a logic of perceived attributes: one that occurs over and over again, and that reveals its own inherent laws.

---

* "Overture to *Le Cru et le Cuit*" by Claude Lévi-Strauss, translated by Joseph H. McMahon, in *Yale French Studies.* Copyright © 1966 by Yale French Studies. Reprinted by permission of Harper & Row, Publishers, who will publish a complete English translation in January, 1969, under the title of *The Raw and the Cooked,* translated by John Weightman.

[1] Ed. note: This excerpt is taken from the opening section of *Le Cru et le Cuit* (Paris, 1964). The English translation was prepared by Joseph H. McMahon for publication in *Yale French Studies,* from which it is reprinted.

We take off from a single myth, one deriving from a single society, and we analyze it by having recourse first to its ethnographic context, and then to other myths from the same society. Our area of interest widens as we move along; once we have placed them in their appropriate ethnographic context, we will move on to study the primitive myths of neighboring societies. Gradually, we reach even more distant societies. But one basic condition remains: between these societies there must either be genuine historical or geographical connections or else such connections can be reasonably postulated. This work describes only the first steps of a long excursion through the myths native to the New World. The excursion begins in the heart of tropical America and will probably carry us to the northern regions of North America. From start to finish, the guiding line is furnished by the myth of the Bororo Indians of Central Brazil. This choice has been made, not because the myth is more archaic than others we will subsequently study, nor because it is an easier or more complete one. The causes which brought it to our attention are in large measure contingent. Our hope has been to present a systematic account which will reproduce as thoroughly as possible the analytic procedure used. In so doing, it is possible to show the close tie between the empirical and systematic aspects which is found in such materials. If the method chosen to demonstrate this tie embodies that kind of connection the demonstration will be all the more effective.

As we shall try to show, the Bororo myth—which we will henceforth refer to as the *reference myth*—is a more or less extended transformation of other myths which have originated either in the same society or in other near and distant societies. Because of this, it would have been quite possible to take our point of departure from any single representative of the group. What is of interest in the reference myth does not depend on its typical character; rather it depends on its irregular position within the group. And, because of the problems in interpretation which it brings up, the myth is especially thought-provoking.

Despite these cautionary statements, we can reasonably fear that this undertaking will knock up against prejudicial objections from mythographers and specialists of tropical America. And it is unquestionably true that this undertaking does not respect territorial limits

or even the contexts of a single classification. From whatever viewpoint we look at it, it is seen to develop nebulously. Like a nebula it
never brings together in a durable or systematic way the sum total
of the elements from which it blindly derives its substance. Yet we
are firmly convinced that the real serves as its guide and indicates a
surer path than any the book might have plotted out synthetically.
We begin, then, with a myth which has not been chosen arbitrarily;
rather it has been selected because of an intuitive feeling that it is
promising and productive. We analyze it according to rules we have
set forth in earlier works,[2] and establish for each sequence the group
of its transformations either as they are manifested within the myth
itself or as they are elucidated in isomorphic elements of sequences
taken from a number of myths belonging to the same population.
From the consideration of particular myths, we move, therefore, to
the consideration of certain major diagrams which are ordered about
a common axis. At each point on this axis where a schema is indicated, we subsequently trace out the other axes which are produced
by a similar operation. The operation, however, is no longer the
result of a single population's myths—myths which had all seemed
different. Rather the operation results from a realization that the
myths, though they come from neighboring populations, offer certain analogies to the first. Because of this, the leading schemas are
simplified, enriched, or transformed. Each becomes a source of new
axes which are perpendicular to those on the other planes. There, by
a movement which is both prospective and retrospective, we see
outlined sequences which have been extracted from myths belonging
to more distant populations or myths which have been neglected in
the past because they seemed of no use or were impossible to interpret despite the fact that they belonged to a people who had already
been studied. As our nebula spreads out, its nucleus condenses and
becomes organized. Sparse filaments are soldered; lacunae are filled;
connections are established; something resembling order is visible
behind the chaos. As though clustering around a germinal molecule,
the sequences which have been ranked in transformation groups are
incorporated into the initial group and reproduce its structure and

---

[2] Claude Lévi-Strauss, *Anthropologie structurale* (Paris, 1958); "Le Geste d'Asdiwal,"
Ecole Pratique des Hautes Etudes, Section des Sciences Religieuses, Annuaire 1958-1959
(Paris, 1958); *Leçon Inaugurale,* delivered Tuesday, January 5, 1960, on assuming the Chair
of Social Anthropology in the Collège de France, Paris, 1960; *La Pensée sauvage* (Paris,
1962).

determinations. A multi-dimensional body is born whose central parts reveal a pattern or organization, though uncertainty and confusion continue to rule on the periphery.

We do not anticipate a point where the mythical material, having been dissolved by analysis, will crystallize into a mass and offer in all respects the image of a stable and well-determined structure. We must recognize that the science of myths is still in its infancy and should be satisfied with the sketchiest of results. But beyond that we must also recognize that the final step will never be taken simply because no population or population group now exists or will exist whose myths and ethnography—and without these there can be no study of myths—can be the object of exhaustive knowledge. There would be no point to holding such ambitions anyway. We are dealing with a reality in process, a reality which is perpetually under the attack from a past which ruins it and a future which changes it. Each case in the literature illustrates how distant such a goal is and we must content ourselves with samples and remains. We have shown that the starting point of the analysis must inevitably be chosen haphazardly because the organizing principles of the mythic material are in the material and will only be revealed progressively. It is inevitable that the finishing point will also impose itself in an equally unexpected way. That will come when the undertaking arrives at the point where its ideal object has acquired adequate form and consistency. There will then be no possibility of doubting its existence as an object properly considered as such nor of certain of its latent properties. Here, as with the optical microscope which cannot reveal matter's ultimate structure to the observer, our only choice is between certain enlargements; each manifests a level of organization whose truth is relative; each, while in use, excludes the perception of other levels.

To some extent these remarks explain the characteristics of a book which otherwise might seem paradoxical. It is a complete work, which presents conclusions designed to answer the questions raised at the outset; yet it makes frequent references to a second work in whose shadows a third work is probably beginning to take shape. If they ever come to fruition, these other volumes will not be a continuation of this one; rather they will pick up the same materials and will offer a different attack on the same problems in the hope of accentuating properties which have remained confused or have not been perceived. They will do this by resorting to new ways of seeing or by coloring historical cross-sections in another manner. If the inquiry proceeds according to these hopes, it will not develop along a linear axis but rather as a spiral: it will return regularly to the earlier results; it will embrace new objects only when knowledge of them will make it possible to understand better the fragmentary knowledge previously acquired.

The reader should not be astonished that this book, which by its own statement of purpose is devoted to mythology, reaches into tales, legends, and pseudo-historical traditions, nor that it calls on a wide variety of ceremonies and rites. We reject all hasty judgment about what is properly considered mythic and claim, as appropriate to our interest, every manifestation of social and mental activity which can be discerned among the populations under study. As the movement of our analysis will show, this allows us to round off the myth or clarify it even in those instances where such manifestations do not amount to what musicians call an obligato.[3] Even though the research has been centered on the myths of tropical America from which the greater number of examples has been drawn, the progressive demands of the analysis have made it inevitable that we should use contributions culled from more distant regions. The process is very much like that of those primitive organisms which, although they are already enclosed in a membrane, maintain a capacity to move their protoplasm within this envelope and to distend it extraordinarily in order to emit pseudopodia. Such behavior is a good bit less strange once we have verified that its object is to capture or to assimilate foreign bodies. Finally, we have avoided all preconceived classifications about cosmological, seasonal, divine, technological, and other sorts of myths. Once again it is the myth itself, subjected to analysis, which we are allowing to reveal its own nature and to find its own place within a type. To the extent that he bases his work on external and arbitrarily isolated marks, such a goal remains beyond the mythographer.

The concern of this book, then, is to have no subject. Since it begins by limiting itself to the study of a single myth, it must, if it wishes to be complete, assimilate the material of two hundred myths. While the study does indeed block out a clearly delimited cultural and geographical region, the possibility of its resembling from time to time a general treatise on mythology is not excluded. It has no real beginning; it could as easily have begun in a different fashion.

---

[3] Cf. Lévi-Strauss, *Anthropologie structurale,* Chapter XII.

Had it, it would none the less have developed in an analogous way. It has no end either; numerous problems are treated only in summary fashion here and others are given the sparsest space. They await a better fate. In setting up our map, we have been obliged to place complex contours in relief. Using the tools of ethnography and utilizing other myths, we create the semantic field of a myth. The same operation is repeated for each of them with the result that the central zone, chosen arbitrarily, can be crisscrossed by numerous lines; still, the frequency of the overlappings is reduced in proportion as one is further separated from it. In order to obtain at all points an equally dense scanning, the procedure would have to be renewed several times by tracing new circles at points situated on the periphery. In the process, the primitive territory would of course be enlarged. Mythical analysis is very much like Penelope's task. Each step forward offers a new hope which hangs on the solution of a new difficulty. The books are never closed.

Far from alarming us, the odd conception of this book has special significance for us; it indicates that we have perhaps managed to capture certain of the fundamental properties of our object. The discovery is the result of a plan and method which have been imposed on us rather than selected by us. Of the study of myths, Durkheim has written: "It is a difficult subject which must be treated in itself, for itself, and by following a method special to it."[4] He also suggested the reason for this state of things when, further on (p. 190), he mentioned totemic myths "which, beyond any doubt, explain nothing and serve only to displace the difficulty; yet, in displacing it, they appear at least to attenuate their logical scandal." This profound definition could, we believe, be extended to the whole field of mythic thinking by giving it fuller meaning than its author would have admitted.

The study of myths poses a methodological problem if only because such study cannot follow the Cartesian principle of breaking the difficulty down into as many parts as are required for its solution. No term proper to mythic analysis exists; nor is there any secret unity which one can seize hold of at the end of the analysis. The themes can be subdivided endlessly. When we think we have unraveled one from the other and can maintain them separately, we

---

[4] Émile Durkheim, *Les Formes élémentaires de la vie religieuse* (2d ed.; Paris, 1925), p. 142.

soon find that they are blending together as though under the pressure of affinities we had not foreseen. Consequently, the myth's unity is tendentious and projective; it never really reflects a state or a fixed moment of the myth. It is no more than an imaginary phenomenon implicit in the effort of interpretation. As such its role is to give synthetic form to the myth, to keep it from being dissolved in the war of contraries. We can therefore say that the science of myths amounts to an *anaclasis,* taking this term in the broad sense permitted by its etymology; by definition, it permits us to study reflected rays along with refracted rays. But, in contradistinction to philosophic reflection, which claims it goes directly back to the source, the reflections with which we are here concerned can claim only a virtual source. The diversity of sequences and themes is a fundamental attribute of mythic thought. Such thought manifests itself in a burst of rays; it is only by measuring directions and calculating angles that we arrive at the possibility of a common origin, an ideal point where all the rays reflected elsewhere by the myth's structure would be rejoined. But this does not ever really happen; the rays may very well have come from elsewhere and they have not remained parallel throughout the entire length of their history. As the conclusion of this book shows, there is something quite essential in this multiplicity, for it has to do with the double character of mythic thought: it coincides with its object of which it is an homologous image, but it does this without ever being absorbed into the object since the myth, as image, evolves on another level. The recurrence of themes translates this mixture of impotency and tenacity. Unconcerned with neat beginnings and clear goals, mythic thought does not effect complete courses; it always has something more to achieve. Like rites, myths are *in-terminable.* Our undertaking—which is at once too long and too short—will try to imitate the spontaneous movement of mythic thought; to do so, we have had to bow to mythic thought's demands and respect its rhythm. As a result this book about myths is, in its own way, a myth. Whatever unity might be claimed for it will appear hidden in the recesses of the text and perhaps even beyond it. In the best of circumstances, that unity will only be worked out in the reader's mind.

We shall most probably hear the greatest number of criticisms from ethnographers. Despite our concern with sources of information, some, which were not inaccessible, have been neglected.[5] Those of which we have made use are not always cited in this final version. In order not to needlessly overburden the account, we have had to sort out myths, choose certain versions, prune the motifs of their variations. Some will accuse us of shaping the material used to fit the needs of our project. But if, from the vast mass of myths, we had retained only those most favorable to our intentions much of the force of this book would have been lost. Yet surely the converse is not true: that in order to touch on a comparison of myths one must work with and mix together the totality of known myths derived from tropical America.

This particular objection is especially pertinent in light of the circumstances which have delayed the appearance of this book. It was almost completed when the publication of the first volume of the *Encyclopédie Bororo* was announced. We waited until the book had arrived in France and inspected it before putting the finishing touches to this text. Yet couldn't this sort of practice be pushed even further, and shouldn't we be obliged to await the publication two or three years hence of the second volume of the *Encyclopédie* which will be devoted to the myths? And, after that, for a third volume which will treat proper names? Oddly, and despite its many riches, the study of the first volume taught quite another lesson. For the Salesians, whose changes of mind are recorded with great placidity when they are not passed over in silence, are quite willfully acerbic when they come across a study prepared by hands other than theirs and which does not coincide with their own most recent work. When one study contradicts another, we have a problem but not a solution. We have a good bit more respect for sources, whether they be ours or those used by the missionaries. Their evidence possesses a special value. The Salesians' merits are so outstanding as to allow one to reproach them, without denying any of the recognition due them, for one slight practice: they have an unfortunate tendency to believe that the most recent inquiry cancels out all others.

---

[5] Because of their recent publication certain works like *Die Tacana* by Hissinck and Hahn (Stuttgart, 1961) have been looked at only superficially; others which arrived in France after this book had been completed have not been consulted at all. This has been the case with: J. Wilbert, *Indios de la región Orinoco-Ventuari* (Caracas, 1963), *Warao Oral Literature* (Caracas, 1964), and N. Fock, *Waiwai, Religion and Society of an Amazonian Tribe* (Copenhagen, 1963). In the last book, we came across a sargus myth which verifies our analyses in the third and fourth parts of this book. We will profit from these new materials in a future volume.

Study of other documents which have already appeared and of those which will appear in the future will always influence our interpretation. Those put forward with care will perhaps be confirmed; others will have to be abandoned or modified. But these are not really obstacles. In a discipline like ours scientific knowledge advances with hesitant steps, driven along under the whips of contention and doubt. It leaves to metaphysics the impatience for all-or-nothing solutions. In order for our understanding to be valid, it is not necessary to have the guarantee that, over the years, we can be assured of the truth of every detail of our work. It will be quite enough if we can have the more modest assurance of having left difficult problems in a less bad state than they inhabited when we began working with them. Nor should we ever forget that in science established truths do not exist. The scientist does not supply true answers; rather he asks true questions.

We can be even more firm about this. Critics who may reproach us for not having made an exhaustive inventory of South American myths before proceeding to our analysis of them will be seriously misconstruing the nature and role of the document in question. The ensemble of a population's myths belongs to the realm of discourse. Unless the population is morally or physically extinct the ensemble is never fully rounded off. We do not think of criticising a linguist when he writes the grammar of a language without having included the totality of all the words used since the language's beginning and without knowing the verbal exchanges which will take place so long as the language remains in existence. We know from experience that even a ridiculously small number of phrases, only a sampling of those he might theoretically have had at his disposal, permit the linguist to work out a grammar of the language he is studying. (And we need not tarry over the problem of words he cannot know either because they were not at his disposal or because they have not yet entered the language.) Even a partial grammar, or the sketch of a grammar, represents a valuable acquisition where an unfamiliar language is concerned. We do not have to wait for a tally of a theoretically limitless series of events in order to see syntactical processes at work, especially since syntax consists of the body of rules which governs the engendering of those events. The sketch we have tried to make is of the same ilk; it is a syntax of South American mythology. When and if new texts come to enrich mythic discourse, there will be occasion to check or to modify the manner in which certain grammatical laws have been formulated. Some will be given up; others will be discovered. But in no case can the argument of the need to possess a total mythic discourse have any relevance to this undertaking. As we have just seen, such a demand makes no sense.

Another possible objection is more serious. Our right to choose our myths here and there and to illuminate a Chaco myth by a Guyanian variant, or a Ge myth by its Colombian analogue might be contested. Yet, though it is respectful of history and anxious to profit from its lessons, structural analysis refuses to be enclosed in the already circumscribed perimeters of historical investigation. On the contrary, by demonstrating that myths of very diverse origins objectively form a group, structural analysis raises a problem for history; it invites history to go looking for a solution. We have constructed a group, and we hope to have supplied proof that such a group is indeed real. It is incumbent on ethnographers, historians, and archeologists to show how and why this is the case.

They can be reassured. In order to explain the group character of the myths drawn together in our enquiry — and drawn together for this reason alone — we are not counting on historical criticism to restore one day a system of logical affinities to the enumeration of a multitude of successive or simultaneous borrowings that contemporary or ancient populations have made from one another across distances and lapses of time which are sometimes so considerable as to make all such interpretation highly implausible. In any case, such interpretation could not be verified. We begin simply by inviting the historian to look on Indian America as a phenomenon whose Middle Ages had no Rome: it is a confused mass, issuing from an older syncretism of unquestionably loose texture; at its center and over a period of centuries there subsist centers both of high civilization and barbarous people, both centralizing tendencies and disruptive forces. Although the latter finally carried the day because of the play of internal causes and because of the arrival of the European conquerors, it is none the less certain that a group—much like the one we are investigating—owes its character to the fact that it was crystallized in an already organized semantic milieu whose elements had served for all kinds of combinations. Without doubt this was less the result of any concern with imitation than it was of a desire to allow smaller, less populous societies to affirm their respective originality by exploiting the resources of a dialectic of oppositions and correlations within the framework of a common conception of the world.

Such an interpretation, which we present in sketchy fashion, clearly rests on some historical conjectures: the great antiquity of tropical American settlements, repeated displacements of numerous tribes in many directions, demographic fluidity, and phenomena of fusion. The last created the conditions of a very ancient syncretism from which the differences observable among the groups were created. These reflect nothing, or practically nothing of the archaic conditions which most often are secondary or derived. Despite the formal perspective it adopts, structural analysis validates the ethnographical and historical interpretations we advanced twenty years ago. Though they were considered adventurous then, they have continued to gain ground.[6] If an ethnographic conclusion emerges clearly from this book, that is because the Ge, far from being those "marginal people" they were imagined to be in 1942 when the first volume of the *Handbook of the South American Indians*—we objected to the suggestion at that time—actually represented a pivotal element in South America. Their role is comparable to that played in North America by the very old cultures whose survivors were established at the basins of the Fraser and Columbia rivers. When our inquiry gets to the southern regions of North America the bases of this rapprochement will be more evident.

It has been necessary to cite these concrete results of structural analysis—others, limited to the cultures of tropical America, will be pointed out in the course of the book—in order to put the reader on his guard against the reproach of formalism, indeed of idealism, which we sometimes hear. Does not this present work, even more than its predecessors, push ethnographical research into the realms of psychology, logic, and philosophy—paths which should be forbidden to it? Are we not then distracting ethnography, in part at least, from its genuine tasks: the study of concrete societies and of the problems raised in those societies by the social, political, and economic conditions which governed the relations between individuals and groups? These oft-expressed worries strike us as resulting from a complete misunderstanding of the task we have taken on. But—and this is much more serious—they cast doubt on the continuity of the program followed methodically since *Les Structures*

---

[6] Cf. Lévi-Strauss, *Anthropologie structurale,* p. 118 ff., and all of Chapter VI.

élémentaires de la parenté.[7] Certainly no such criticisms can be reasonably directed against that work.

While *La Pensée sauvage* does represent a pause in our attempt, the pause was needed in order to catch breath between two efforts. There was no doubt about the profit derived from looking closely at the panorama spread before us or of seizing that occasion to measure the distance which had been covered, to take bearings on the remainder of the itinerary, and to get some idea of the unfamiliar countries still to be traversed. We were determined none the less never to stray long from our route and, except for some minor poaching, never to go adventuring into the securely guarded grounds of philosophy. *La Pensée sauvage,* though some thought it was a terminus, was only a stop. It was meant to be no more than a temporary halt between the first step ventured in *Les Structures* and the second which this book is undertaking.

Most important of all, the destination has not changed. From the very beginning of the ethnographic experience, it has always been a question of setting up an inventory of mental enclosures, of reducing apparently arbitrary data to order, of reaching a level where necessity reveals itself as immanent in the illusions of freedom. In *Les Structures* we had disentangled a small number of simple principles from the apparently superficial contingency and incoherent diversity of the rules of marriage. Because of those principles a very complex ensemble of usages and customs was drawn together into a meaningful system, though at first they seemed absurd and had generally been so judged. There was nothing meanwhile to guarantee that these constraints were of internal origin. It was quite possible that they only reflected, within the minds of men, certain demands of social life which had been objectivized in institutions. Their reverberations on the psychic level would then have been the effect of mechanisms whose mode of operation alone remained to be discovered.

The experiment in mythology which we are now undertaking will be even more decisive. Mythology has no evident practical function; unlike the phenomena previously examined, mythology is not in direct contact with a different reality, endowed with an objectivity higher than its own whose orders it transmits to a mind which seems perfectly free to abandon itself to creative spontaneity. If, as a result,

---

[7] Ed. note: Lévi-Strauss refers here to his study, published in 1949, which deals principally with cross-cousin marriage systems.

we were able to demonstrate that, here too, the arbitrary appearance, the apparently free outsurge, and a seemingly unbridled inventiveness presuppose laws which operate at a deeper level, we could posit as ineluctable the conclusion that the mind, freed for conversation with itself and rescued from the obligation of dealing with objects, finds itself reduced in some way to imitating itself as an object. Since the laws of its operations are no longer fundamentally different from those it manifests in its other functions, it avers its nature as a thing among things. Without pushing this line of reasoning too far, we need only to have acquired the conviction that the human mind appears as determined even in its myths; if that is so, then a fortiori it must be determined in all its manifestations.[8]

Since what we are positing is a process which would allow itself to be guided by a search for mental constraints, we see that it is not unlike Kantianism, though we are indeed making our way along other roads which do not lead to the same kind of conclusions. Unlike the philosopher, the ethnologist does not feel obliged to accept as the basis for his reflections the working conditions of his own thought or of a science which belongs to his society or his times in order to extend his particular statements to a judgment whose universality would be only hypothetical and virtual. Preoccupied with the same problems, he adopts a doubly inverted procedure. Rather than the hypothesis of universal judgment, he prefers the empirical observations of collective judgments. Their properties, solidified in some way, are manifested to him by innumerable concrete systems of representation. Since he is a man of one social milieu, of one culture, one region, and one period of history, these systems represent the whole gamut of possible variations within a genus; he chooses those whose divergencies strike him as most noticeable. His hope is that the methodological rules which will be imposed on him will translate these systems in terms of his own and, reciprocally, will bare a network of fundamental and common constraints. This is a very high form of gymnastics indeed since it pushes the exercise of reflection to its objective limits—and the limits have initially been marked and inventoried by the ethnographic inquiry itself—flexes each muscle, and reveals all the skeleton's joints, thereby exposing the lineaments of the general anatomical structure.

---

8 ". . . if there are laws in some areas, there must be laws everywhere." This was the conclusion of one of Tylor's passages which, seventeen years ago, we used as the epigraph for *Les Structures élémentaires de la parenté.*

What we are attempting to do is well described in Paul Ricoeur's qualification of our effort as "Kantianism without a transcendental subject."[9] We see no indication of a lacuna in this restriction; instead we see the inevitable consequence, on the philosophical level, of the ethnographic perspective we have chosen. By pursuing conditions where systems of truth become mutually convertible and can therefore be simultaneously admissible for several subjects, the ensemble of these conditions acquires the character of an object endowed by a reality proper to itself and independent of any subject.

More than any other phenomenon, mythology allows us to illustrate this objectified thought and to demonstrate its reality empirically. We do not exclude the possibility that the speaking subjects, who produce and transmit the myths, may be conscious of their structure and their mode of operation; such an occurrence, however, is more partial and intermittent than it is routine. The situation with myths is very much the situation we find with language. Any speaker who consciously applies phonological and grammatical laws in his speech—and we are presupposing, of course, that he has the requisite knowledge and virtuosity—would not be able to pursue the line of his argument very long. In the same way, the exercise and practice of mythic thought demands that its properties remain hidden; if they are not, one would find himself in the position of the mythologist who cannot believe in myths because he spends his time expounding about them. Mythic analysis does not and cannot have as its object to show how men think. In the special case with which we are concerned here, it is at least doubtful that the natives of Brazil go beyond the delight with which they listen to narratives and conceive openly the systems of relations to which we are reducing these myths. When, using these myths, we validate certain archaic or highly imaged turns of phrase found in our own popular language, the same observation imposes itself: we make these discoveries under the influence of a foreign mythology; our discovery is the result of an

---

[9] Paul Ricoeur, "Symbole et temporalité," in *Archivio di Filosofia*, Nos. 1-2 (Rome, 1963), p. 24. See also p. 9: "More a Kantian unconscious than a Freudian one; a categorical, unifying unconscious . . ." and on p. 10: ". . . a categorical system without reference to a thinking subject . . . homologous to nature; it might even be nature. . . ."

With his usual finesse and perspicuity, Roger Bastide ("La Nature humaine: le point de vue du sociologue et de l'ethnologue," in *La Nature humaine*, Acts of the XIth Congress of the *Sociétés de Philosophie de langue française*, Montpellier, September 4-6, 1961, Paris, 1961) anticipates the preceding argument. This coincidence is all the more indicative of his clear thinking since I had no knowledge of his text until he kindly sent it to me while I was correcting the proofs of this book.

awareness which works retroactively. We are not, therefore, claiming to show how men think the myths, but rather how the myths think themselves out in men and without men's knowledge.

We have already suggested that it may be appropriate to go even further and, setting aside consideration of the subject's role, weigh the possibility that, in a certain way, the myths think themselves out among themselves.[10] This is not so much a question of extricating what is within the myths without necessarily being held in the consciousness of men; rather it is a question of extricating the system of axioms and postulates which define the best possible code, a code capable of giving a common sense to the unconscious elaborations which are the actuality of minds, societies, and cultures which, set off one against the other, offer the greatest separation. Since the myths themselves depend on codes of the second order—codes of the first order are those of language—this book is offering the sketch of a code which would belong to a third order, an order designed to assure the reciprocal translatability of several myths. For this reason, a reader would not be wrong if he took the book itself as a myth: the myth of mythology.

But, in common with the other two, this third code has neither been invented nor hunted for elsewhere. It is immanent in the mythology itself; we only discover it. An ethnographer working in South America was astonished by the way in which the myths came to him: "Practically every narrator told the stories in his way. Even in important details, the margin of variations is enormous. . . ." Still, the natives seem not to be bothered by this state of things: "A Caraja who accompanied me from village to village heard a great number of these kinds of variations and greeted them all with an almost identical trust. It wasn't that he didn't perceive the contradictions. But they had no interest whatever for him."[11] A naive commentator, one who came from another planet, might have a better right to be astonished—since he would be dealing with history and not with myth—by the mass of works devoted to the French Revolution. In them, authors do not always make use of the same incidents; when they do, the incidents are revealed under quite different lights. And yet these are variations which have to do with the same country, the

---

[10] The Ojibwa Indians consider myths as "being endowed with consciousness, capable of thought and action." W. Jones, "Ojibwa Texts," in *Publications of the American Ethnological Society,* Vol. 3, Part 2 (New York, 1919), p. 574, n. 1.

[11] W. Lipkind, "Caraja Cosmography," *Journal of American Folklore,* Vol. 53 (1940), 251.

same period, and the same events—events whose reality is scattered across every level of a multi-layered structure. The criterion of validity clearly does not depend on the elements of history. Pursued in isolation, each element would show itself to be beyond grasp. But certain of them derive consistency from the fact that they can be integrated into a system whose terms are more or less credible when set off against the overall coherence of the series.

In spite of worthy and indispensable efforts to bring another moment in history alive and to possess it, a clairvoyant history should admit that it never completely escapes from the nature of myth. Mythic schemes offer in the highest degree the character of absolute objects; if they were not subject to external influences they would neither lose nor acquire other elements. The result is that when a schema undergoes a transformation the transformation affects the myth in every aspect. Whenever some aspect of a myth appears unintelligible, we are justified in treating it, in a hypothetical and preliminary way, as a transformation of the homologous aspect of another myth which has been attached to the same group because it lends itself better to interpretation. We have done this several times. For example, in resolving the episode of the covered jaw of the jaguar in M_7 by using the universe episode of the open jaw in M_{55}, or that of the real obligingness of the carrion vultures in M_1 by looking at the manifestations of their deceptive obligingness in M_{65}.[12] Contrary to what one might believe, the method does not fall into a vicious circle. It implies only that each myth, considered by itself, exists as a restrained application of a scheme which can be progressively extricated with the aid of those relations of reciprocal intelligibility which are perceived among several myths.

We shall probably be accused of over-interpreting and over-simplifying in the use we make of the method. By way of reply, we can only point out once again that we have never claimed that all the solutions suggested have an equal value; to this we can add that we have at times pointed out the precarious value of some of them. Still, such a reply would be a hypocritical evasion of a declaration of the full weight of our thinking. To such eventual critics, we offer an immediate answer: what difference does it make? If the final goal of anthropology is to contribute to a better knowledge of objectivized thought and its mechanisms, then in the end it does not make much

---

[12] Ed. note: Symbols such as M_7 and M_{55} refer to a list of myth texts which is appended to *Le Cru et le Cuit* (pp. 367-71).

difference whether the thought of Latin American natives finds its form in the operation of my thought or if mine finds its in the operation of theirs. What does matter is that the human mind, unconcerned with the identity of its occasional bearers, manifests in that operation a structure which becomes more and more intelligible to the degree that the doubly reflexive movement of two thoughts, working on one another, makes progress. It is a process in which now one, now the other can be the wick to a glimmer of rapprochement from which their common illumination will spring forth. If a treasure is uncovered in the process, we will have no need of an arbiter in order to move on to the division of the riches; from the very start we have recognized that the inheritance is inalienable and that it must remain undivided.[13]

At the outset we said that we were seeking to transcend the opposition of the perceptible and the intelligible by straightaway placing ourselves on the level of signs. Through signs the one is conveyed by means of the other. Yet, even when restricted in number, they lend themselves to rigorously grouped combinations which can translate, in their most discrete nuances, the whole diversity of perceptible experience. Our hope is to attain a level where logical properties will be manifested as attributes of things quite as directly as savors and perfumes. Their special nature, excluding all error, can still evoke a combination of elements which, were they selected or disposed in other ways, would evoke awareness of another perfume. Because we have the notion of the sign, our task is that of bringing secondary qualities to the business of truth at the level of the intelligible; we are no longer exclusively limited to the perceptible.

This search for a middle way between the exercise of logical thought and esthetic perception should naturally be inspired by the example of music which has always followed the middle way. Something more than a general point of view suggests the rapprochement. Almost as soon as work on this book had started, it was evident that it would be impossible to arrange its materials according to any plan which respected traditional norms. Chapter divisions would not only have done violence to the movement of its thought but would have brought impoverishment and mutilation; all the bite would have been gone. If the presentation was to appear decisive, then, paradoxically, more freedom and suppleness would have to be conceded to it. We

---

[13] Lévi-Strauss, *La Pensée sauvage*.

noticed, too, that the order chosen for the presentation of documents, could not be linear; the sentences in the commentary could not be connected by a simple before and after relationship. If the reader were to have from time to time a sense of simultaneity, then artifices in composition would be essential. His sense of simultaneity would, of course, be illusory, for he would still be tied down by the order of the narrative. Yet a close equivalent could be hinted at through alternation of a lengthy discourse with a diffuse one, by speeding up rhythms which had been slowed down, by heaping up examples at some points and, at others, by keeping them separated. We noticed thus that our analyses were situated on several axes. One was the axis of succession; but there was also the axis of relative density which demanded that we have recourse to those evocative musical forms, the *solo* and the *tutti*. Furthermore, there were the axes of expressive tensions and replacement codes which produced, as the book was being written, oppositions comparable to those between song and recitative, between the instrumental ensemble and the aria.

In choosing this free recourse to a multi-dimensional approach which would best display our themes, we had to give up something. The usual division of a book into isometric chapters had to give way to a division into less numerous parts. These, as a result, are more voluminous and complex; they are also unequal in length. But each forms a whole by virtue of its internal organization which is the outflow of a certain unity in inspiration. For the same reason these parts could not be poured into a single mold; rather each has had to obey the rules of tone, genre, and style required by the nature of the materials being used and by the nature of the technical means employed for each case. The result was that musical forms once again offered the resources and diversity already gauged by experience. Comparisons with the sonata, the symphony, the prelude, the fugue, and other forms permitted easy verification of the fact that problems of construction analogous to those posed in the analysis of myth had already cropped up in music where solutions had already been invented for them.

At the same time there was no way of eluding another problem: what deep causes were behind this at first surprising affinity between music and myths? (Structural analysis limits itself to pointing out their value, simply taking them into account and transporting them to another level.) Certainly a major step towards an answer had already been taken once we could evoke a constant element in our personal history which no sudden event could shake. We speak of the service we had rendered since childhood at the altars of the "god Richard Wagner," a devotion in no way shaken either by hearing *Pelléas* as an adolescent or, later, *Les Noces.* If one must see in Wagner the unimpeachable father of the structural analysis of myths (and, in the case of *Meistersinger,* of tales), then it is highly revealing to note that such analysis was first made *in music.*[14] In suggesting that the analysis of myth was comparable to the perusal of a great score, we were only drawing the logical consequence of the Wagnerian discovery: the structure of myths is revealed through means of a score.

This prefatory homage does more to confirm the existence of the problem than to resolve it. The true answer is found, we believe, in the character common to the myth and the musical work: each after its fashion is a language which transcends the level of articulated language; each requires at every instance a temporal dimension in order to become manifest; the same is true with language but is not true with painting. This relationship to time is of a very special nature: everything takes place as though music and mythology needed time only in order to deny its place. Both, in effect, are mechanisms designed to do away with time. Underneath the sounds and rhythms, music operates on a rough terrain which is the physiological time of the listener; that time is irremediably diachronic because it is irreversible; music none the less transmutes the segment of that time which is devoted to listening into a totality which is synchronic and enclosed in itself. The act of listening to the musical work has immobilized the passage of time because of the work's internal organization; like a cloth billowing in the wind, it has caught up and infolded it. In listening to music—and while we are listening—we have achieved a kind of immortality.

It is clear now in what way music resembles myth; myth, too, overcomes the antinomy of historical and elapsed time; it has also overcome the limitations of a permanent structure. In order to justify the comparison fully, it must be pushed further than in one of

---

[14]While acknowledging this paternity we would be guilty of ingratitude if we did not admit our debts: first of all to the work of Marcel Granet, which glitters with brilliant intuitions; then—and if last, not least—to the work of Georges Dumézil and to the *Asklēplos Apollon Smintheus et Rudra* of Henri Grégoire *(Mémories de l'Académie Royale de Belgique, classe des Lettres,* XLV, fascicle 1, 1949).

our earlier works.[15] Like the musical work, the myth operates with a double continuum as its starting point: One is external; in one case its matter is made up of occurrences which are either historical or believed to be historical; these form a theoretically unlimited series from which each society extracts a restricted number of pertinent events in order to elaborate its myths. In the other case, it is made up of an equally unlimited series of physically possible sounds from which each musical system appropriates its scale. The second continuum is of an internal order. It has its seat in the psycho-physiological time of the listener whose factors are very complex: the periodicity of the cerebral waves and the organic rhythms, the capacity of memory, and the power of attention. These are neuro-psychical aspects which mythology especially challenges by the length of the narration, by the recurrence of the themes, and by the other forms of recurrence and parallelism. In order to be properly taken in, mythology demands that the mind of this listener sweep thoroughly back and forth across the field of the narrative as it spreads out before him. This applies equally to music. But, aside from psychological time, music addresses itself to physiological and even visceral time. Mythology does this, too; we do not hesitate to say that a told story has been "breathtaking." But in mythology it does not play the same essential role as in music: all counterpoint contains a mute part to be filled in by the cardiac and respiratory systems.

In order to simplify this line of reasoning, we shall limit our discussion to visceral time. We will say that music operates through two grids. One is physiological and therefore natural; its existence is connected to the fact that music exploits organic rhythms and thereby gives pertinence to discontinuities which would otherwise remain in a latent state as though drowned in duration. The other grid is cultural; it consists of the scale of musical sounds whose number and deviations vary according to cultures. This system of intervals supplies a first level of articulation to music, not by function of relative pitches—which result from the perceptible properties of each sound—, but by function of the hierarchical rapports which appear between the notes of the scale: whence their distinction into fundamental, tonic, dominant seventh, and dominant to express the rapports which polytonal and atonal systems enmesh without destroying.

The composer's mission is to adulterate this discontinuity without

---

[15] Lévi-Strauss, *Anthropologie structurale*, p. 234.

revoking its principle; at times, melodic invention hollows out momentary lacunae in the grid; at other times, but again only momentarily, it plugs up the holes or reduces their circumference. At times it perforates; at other times, it stops up a gap. What is true of melody is also true of rhythms since, by this second means, the times of the physiological grid which are theoretically constant are overlooked or accelerated, anticipated or overtaken by retardation.

Musical emotion stems precisely from the fact that the composer at each instant removes or adds more or less than the listener anticipated on the basis of his faith in a project which he believes he is incapable of penetrating genuinely because he is subject to a double periodicity: that of his thoracic cage, which stems from his individual nature, and that of his musical scale which is a function of his education. If the composer holds back even more, we experience a delightful impression of having fallen; we feel we have been torn away from the stable point of the sol-fa and thrown into the void, but only because the support which will be offered, did not come at the expected place. When the composer holds back less, the opposite happens: he forces us to more able gymnastics than we have been accustomed to. At times we are stirred; at times we are constrained to stir ourselves; but we always move beyond what on our own we would have thought ourselves capable of achieving. Esthetic pleasure is made up from this multiplicity of excitements and respites, expectations which are deceived only to be rewarded beyond expectation; these result from the challenge which the work delivers. They result, too, from the contradictory feeling music provides: the tests to which it submits us are insurmountable even at the moment when the work is preparing to offer us marvelously unforeseen means which will allow us to triumph over it. Though it is equivocal in the score which delivers it to us,

> . . . irradiant un sacre
> Mal tu par l'encre même en sanglots sibyllins,

the composer's design assumes reality, as does myth, through the listener and by him. In both cases, we are effectively observing the same inversion of the relationship between the sender and the receiver since, in the end, the receiver reveals himself as signified by the message of the sender. The music lives out its life in me; I listen to myself through the music. The myth and the musical work thus appear to be like orchestral conductors whose listeners are silent members of the orchestra.

If we ask where the real home of the work is, we find that no precise answer can be given. Music and mythology confront man with virtual objects whose shadow alone is real; they offer conscious approximations—a musical score and a myth can be nothing else—of ineluctably unconscious truths which are consecutive to them. In the case of myth, we conjecture as to the why of this paradoxical situation. It has to do with the irrational relationship which prevails between the circumstances of the creation, which are collective, and the individual nature of consumption. Myths have no author; from the moment when they are perceived as myths, and despite their real origin, they exist only as they are incarnated in a tradition. When a myth is recounted, individual listeners receive a message which in a very true sense comes from nowhere. It is for this reason that a supernatural origin has been assigned to it. It is therefore understandable that the unity of the myth should be projected on to a virtual home: beyond the conscious perception of the listener which it only traverses to a point where the energy it radiates will be consumed by the unconscious reorganization it has previously released. Music raises a much more difficult problem because we are thoroughly ignorant of the mental conditions behind musical creation. In other words, we do not know what the difference is between the small number of minds which secrete music and those, vastly more numerous, where no such phenomenon occurs even though such minds show musical sensitivity. The difference is so clear and manifests itself with such precocity that we suspect it implies properties of a special nature which are doubtless to be found at the deepest levels. But that music is a language by whose means messages are elaborated, that such messages can be understood by the many but sent out only by the few, and that it alone among all the languages unites the contradictory character of being at once intelligible and untranslatable—these facts make the creator of music a being like the gods and make music itself the supreme mystery of human knowledge. All other branches of knowledge stumble into it, it holds the key to their progress.

It would be wrong to invoke poetry in order to pretend that it causes a problem of the same order. Not everyone is a poet, but poetry utilizes a vehicle which is a common good: articulated language. It is satisfied with decreeing certain special constraints on the use of language. Music by contrast uses a vehicle which belongs properly to it and which otherwise does not lend itself to any general usage. By right if not by fact, any reasonably educated man could write poems, be they good or bad. Musical creation presupposes special aptitudes which cannot be brought to flower unless the seeds are already there.

Epilogue

IT was asserted in the Prologue that the study of mythology has been a quest for many different things at different times. Furthermore, it was contended that the concepts of myth adhered to by individual investigators at any given time are shaped by the prevailing theories, objectives, and methods of the disciplines to which these investigators are committed. These points were exemplified for the discipline of anthropology through the presentation of nine reading selections. The purpose of this essay is to consider in more detail the assumption which is implicit throughout this volume: that these nine writers are concerned with common subject matter and common problems for investigation. To accomplish this purpose, it will be necessary to deal with certain questions which are inherent in the studies themselves.

It is important initially to raise the question of terminology: Do all the writers represented in this volume actually utilize the term *myth;* and if so, with what consistency is it used among them? Four of the nine anthropologists—Rivers, Kluckhohn, Leach, and Lévi-Strauss—utilize the term *myth* exclusively to identify their data. Malinowski begins his discussion by employing terms native to the Trobriand Islanders; but later, he finds it convenient to substitute the word *myth* for the Trobriand *lili'u,* with which he is principally concerned. *Myth* and *legend* are used interchangeably by Boas and Radcliffe-Brown, although one can infer from linguistic contexts that both men made some slight, though unexplained, differentiation between the two words.[1] Benedict apparently considered *folktale*

---

[1] Radcliffe-Brown had very little to say about myth in any of his publications other than *The Andaman Islanders.* The only article that he ever wrote about myth, as far as I have been able to discover, is a diffusionistic study of an Australian myth about a rainbow serpent. (The reference is included in the Selected Bibliography.) Thus, I have been unable to determine just what differentiation he made between myth and legend.

Boas, on the other hand, probably devoted more time to the study of primitive folklore (including mythology) than any other modern anthropologist. Moreover, his great interest

222

and *myth* to be synonymous terms for her Zuni data, for she uses both and makes no stated distinction between them.[2] Firth prefers *traditional tale,* which, he notes, is a collective term for several kinds of data which are often referred to more specifically as *myth, legend,* and *history.*[3] The majority of the investigators, then, consider some form of the Greek word μῦθος "myth" to be an appropriate term, though not necessarily the only one, to identify their data. Firth alone consistently avoids using the word *myth,* but only because he feels that by utilizing it, he would have to use several other somewhat specific terms, among which he would then have to make quite arbitrary distinctions.

Terminology does not necessarily reveal anything significant, for lexical choice is, itself, quite arbitrary in many cases. But the terms utilized by these writers are instructive for a number of reasons. First, all of these terms *(myth, legend, folktale, traditional tale)* are native to the authors, not to the peoples with whom they are concerned. Malinowski alone attempts to describe his data from the viewpoint and with the terminology of the members of the society under discussion; but even he abandons this approach when he substitutes his own native words for those of the Trobriand Islanders. In addition, none of these terms is unique to anthropology; all have

---

in the subject was apparently instrumental in motivating many of his students and followers in American anthropology to collect and study folklore and to regard it as a potential source from which hypotheses about cultural processes might be generated. (For examples of such studies, see the items listed in the Selected Bibliography under the names of Boas, Dorothy Demetracopoulou, Clara Ehrlich, Melville Herskovits, Melville Jacobs, A. L. Kroeber, Robert Lowie, Paul Radin, Gladys Reichard, and Katherine Spencer.)

Boas and his followers in American anthropology tended to make a distinction between myths and folktales or tales. This was done largely on the basis of the time that the action in the narrative purportedly took place and the identity of the principal agents or actors. Thus, those stories which described actions from the remote past—usually before the world had established its present order—and which involved deistic or supernatural actors were usually called *myths,* while all others were referred to as *tales* or *folktales.* But *legend,* when it is used at all, is sometimes a synonym for *myth* and sometimes a term to identify a third type or category of oral narrative which is believed to be true, as myth is, but which is also believed to have occurred in the recent rather than the remote past.

[2] Benedict asserts that among the Zunis, "tales fall into no clearly distinguishable categories" (p. 122). She also notes that the divisions within her collection of Zuni tales and the terminology by which she identifies the data are employed arbitrarily and for convenience only. This explains why she uses the words *myth* and *folktale* interchangeably.

[3] Firth's decision to use *traditional tale* as a collective term for the more specific *myth, legend,* and *history* represents a change in practice, for in his earlier publications he actually does use the more specific terms which he here wishes to avoid. Thus, in his article "The Plasticity of Myth," listed in the Selected Bibliography, he calls the story about the origin of iron in Tikopia a *myth;* but in the selection reprinted in this volume, he refers to the same story (p. 171) as a *traditional tale.*

been used, in some linguistic form, by Western scholars in other fields of study (e.g., folkloristics, psychology, literature) to identify certain kinds of phenomena found in their own, as well as in other, societies. Finally, each of these terms has been employed in Western scholarship since before anthropology came into existence as a discipline, and all have been used somewhat arbitrarily and inconsistently throughout their history. There is no consensus among researchers— even among those in the same discipline—as to what the specific referents of these terms are or should be. There is a precedent, then, for utilizing the terms *myth, legend, folktale,* and *traditional tale;* but each term has always been used with a substantial range of referents, both within the investigators' own societies and within their common discipline.

These facts necessarily raise the question of meaning: What does the term *myth* (and the alternative or more inclusive terms *legend, folktale,* and *traditional tale* [4]) mean to these anthropologists, and to what extent is this meaning consistent among them? The studies provide no easy answers to this question. Only two of the writers— Rivers and Malinowski—offer definitions; the others provide nothing more than occasional hints. This is a significant point in itself, for it reflects a general tendency among twentieth-century anthropologists to avoid becoming involved in the kinds of semantic battles which preoccupied many of their nineteenth-century predecessors. Furthermore, their reluctance to present succinct definitions for phenomena which are obviously complex is understandable. The fact remains, however, that each investigator must have relied upon *some criteria initially* in order to isolate, for purposes of analysis, those data which he chooses to call by these terms.

Such criteria, which provide the very basis for scientific investigation, are always implicit in definitions. But when definitions are lacking, there is no direct or objective means of determining what these criteria were. To answer the question of meaning when the investigators themselves provide no answers, one is forced to ascertain through inference just what these criteria *might have been.* This procedure shifts the burden of proof from the investigator to his readers and increases the probability of misinterpretation, since the reader's own biases will undoubtedly contribute to the inferences which he makes. Nevertheless, it is necessary in this case, for it is the

---

[4] From this point on in the Epilogue, the word *myth* alone will be used to refer to "*myth* and the alternative or more inclusive terms *legend, folktale,* and *traditional tale.*"

only means of determining the extent to which common terminology indicates consistency in meaning for the nine writers.

It must be assumed, first of all, that each of the investigators discerned in his data certain formal characteristics which enabled him to differentiate these from other kinds of data. Thus, each of the writers must have noted initially that a myth constitutes, in one sense, a closed or self-contained system—i.e., that it is, to a large extent, complete in itself. Furthermore, he must have observed that each myth presents, through the interactions of human and/or humanlike agents in a given setting, an event or series of events during which a problem or series of problems is presented or arises. This problem/series of problems motivates one or more of the agents to act in order to attempt to alleviate the state of disequilibrium which results from the existence/creation of the problem(s). More specific formal characteristics might also have been noted by the investigators; but since the majority of them are silent about such matters (Benedict and Lévi-Strauss being the obvious exceptions), it is impossible to infer what these additional characteristics might have been for the nine anthropologists generally. It is sufficient to conclude that one of the criteria which might have enabled the writers to isolate and identify their data was their recognition of the fact that these data exhibit many of the same formal characteristics that can be found in narratives in general.

Another criterion which is implicit in the remarks made by the nine investigators is that these narratives are well known either among the members of the particular society/societies under discussion or of a specific group or groups within that society/those societies. This is suggested by such frequently used terms as "body of mythology," "mythic system," and "set of myths." It is also implied by such statements as Firth's comment that traditional tales "are part of the resources of the whole community, a sort of cultural furniture" (p. 168), and by Kluckhohn's assertion that myths are "part of the social heredity of a society" (p. 167). Furthermore, it is even implicit in the discussions of those six writers (Radcliffe-Brown, Benedict, Kluckhohn, Firth, Leach, and Lévi-Strauss) who assert that in the societies with which they are concerned, mythology is characterized by a plasticity which can be observed among different storytellers [5] and over a period of time. For while they note that many myths are unique to individual storytellers or storytellings, they also

---

[5] The terms *story* and *narrative* are used synonymously throughout the Epilogue.

observe that the society's myths, taken collectively, contain common content elements. These recurring content elements, as they are described, would appear to constitute, from the points of view of the investigators, the "raw materials" of which the society's myths are made. One must conclude, then, that even these common and familiar content elements, which apparently can and do frequently combine into new and meaningful sets, must have come from some common and familiar source. Unless these writers are concerned with a phenomenon which they consider to be universal—and none explicitly states that he is—this common and familiar source must be a "body of mythology" or "set of myths" unique to the society or group(s) in question. Thus, the notion of a basic corpus of myths which either circulate in a somewhat fixed form or serve as the basis for other (new) myths appears to have been a second criterion upon which these nine investigators relied to isolate and identify their data.

Besides suggesting that the data discussed in the nine reading selections (1) exhibit formal characteristics which are similar to those found in narratives in general and (2) appear to be well known to members of a particular society or a given group or groups within that society, it is impossible to draw any other defensible inferences concerning the common criteria which these investigators might have utilized to enable them to identify their data as *myths*. It can be inferred, in fact, that some of them relied upon these two criteria exclusively. This would appear to have been the case with Benedict and Lévi-Strauss. The majority of the writers, however, note or imply that additional criteria were involved; but those mentioned by one investigator are ignored and frequently are explicitly rejected by others.

In some instances, apparent disagreements between writers turn out to be nothing more than semantic differences. Kluckhohn, for instance, notes that it is the relative degree of "sacredness" of a narrative which serves as the basis for calling it a *myth*. But Leach asserts that in Kachin society, sacred tales cannot justifiably be differentiated from those (nonsacred?) tales which deal with recent past events, because both have the same function. One can infer, then, that Leach would prefer to use the term *myth* to refer to both sacred and profane stories (which Kluckhohn would appear to object to), or that he would prefer not to use the term *myth* at all. Closer examination, however, reveals that the source of the disagreement is really to be found in the meaning of the word *sacred* for each of the two writers. To Kluckhohn, *sacred* constitutes one extreme of a sacred-profane continuum; in other words, he uses the term in the sense that Émile Durkheim, the French sociologist, did.[6] On the other hand, Leach identifies "sacred tales" specifically as "tales about divine beings which are widely known" (p. 197). It is quite likely, then, that both Kluckhohn and Leach would call the same narratives *myths,* but not on the basis of the criterion of sacredness alone.

Other apparent disagreements stem from conceptual, rather than semantic, differences; and these are more significant. Malinowski, for example, notes that "myth possesses the normative power of fixing customs, of sanctioning modes of behaviour, of giving dignity and importance to an institution" (p. 99). But Firth contends that "*very often traditional tales are divisive, not unitive* for the society at large" (p. 175). In one sense, these are, indeed, irreconcilable positions; for Malinowski, like Radcliffe-Brown, finds that the analysis of the social functions of myth provides substantiation for the equilibrium model of society, which he believes to be valid. Firth, however, whose position appears to be similar to the one advanced by Leach, suggests through his statement that an equilibrium model is not adequate to describe the social function of traditional tales. Yet while the viewpoints expressed by both Firth and Leach constitute reactions against the models advanced by Radcliffe-Brown and Malinowski, both investigators also maintain a basic functionalist position. For Firth and Leach, like their predecessors Radcliffe-Brown and Malinowski, are still concerned with the social functions of the messages which are communicated by myths, not with the nature and functions of myths per se — i.e., myths as stories. In other words, Firth and Leach use the message content of the oral narratives collected in particular societies as a means of testing an hypothesis (the functionalist hypothesis) and a model (the equilibrium model of social structure) just as Radcliffe-Brown and Malinowski did. All four of these anthropologists, then, use their data to prove that the functionalist hypothesis is tenable. The equilibrium model is a different matter, however; for while Radcliffe-Brown and Malinowski use their analyses of the social functions of the messages of Andamanese and Trobriand myths to dem-

---

[6] It can only be *inferred* that Kluckhohn accepts Durkheim's distinction between the sacred and the profane as being valid, for he never commits himself in his essay. Moreover, Kluckhohn does not indicate from whose viewpoint the narrative is considered to be "sacred": from that of the investigator or from that of the members of the society. This is a major weakness in Kluckhohn's study, for he relies heavily upon the criterion of relative sacredness to identify myth, but he never explicitly states what he means by it.

onstrate the validity of the equilibrium model, Firth and Leach use their analyses of similar data (myths) from Tikopia and Highland Burma to prove that the equilibrium model is not adequate to describe the total social structure. The principal concern of these four investigators, then, is to corroborate and substantiate their theoretical positions concerning social structure; and myths merely provide the data for doing so.

This is such an important point that it needs to be discussed in greater detail, for it is applicable to all of the studies included in this volume and, in a more general way, to all studies of mythology. It is necessary, therefore, to return once again to many of the historical matters which were mentioned briefly in the Prologue and earlier in the Epilogue. The perspective will be different, however, for we will be concerned with the history of the *concept of myth* which serves as the foundation for the analyses rather than with the *concepts of myth* which emerge from the analyses themselves.

It was noted in the Prologue that the word *myth* entered the lexicons of Western societies by way of ancient Greek culture. The Greeks coined the term to identify certain stories, extant in their own society, which explained the origins of natural and social phenomena and the interrelationships among man, his deities, and his universe. It was also pointed out in the Prologue that the myths of classical antiquity became a subject of interest and source of speculation among investigators in such fields as philosophy, theology, and literature during and following the Renaissance. It was not until the nineteenth century, however, when stories with similar content and themes were discovered among nonliterate European peasants that oral narratives attracted the general attention of the scholarly world.

The publication of the *Kinder-und Hausmärchen* of the Grimm Brothers in 1812 provided an important stimulus for researchers in numerous fields to engage in comparative studies which might provide some insight into the nature, meaning, and significance of oral narratives. Systematic collecting of these story texts was undertaken by linguists and folklorists and by many lay antiquarians, while other investigators devoted their time to searching through ancient and medieval literary works for parallels and content and thematic similarities between the newly discovered oral tales and the long-cherished written narratives of Western civilization. Established literary terms, including the word *myth,* were used to distinguish among the various kinds of oral narratives which were coming to light in increasing numbers. Tentative hypotheses and speculative theories were advanced, often in direct opposition to each other, concerning the probable origins and symbolic significance of what tended generally to be referred to as the stories of the folk or *folktales.*[7]

Careful scrutiny of existing ethnographies soon revealed that folktales could also be found among non-Western and primitive peoples. This discovery provided the basis for speculation that folktales might even be universal. Many investigators accepted this speculation, a priori, as fact and used it as evidence both to develop and to substantiate theories about the origins and development of culture. The content and themes of oral narratives reported from non-Western and primitive societies were compared with those found in Western folktales; and on the basis of similarities discerned exclusively from the comparative study of oral narrative texts, it was concluded that myths, and perhaps other kinds of folktales as well, were universal phenomena which could, together with other types of universal phenomena, provide considerable insight into the history of culture and the nature of man.

The monistic and universal theories of the history of culture and the nature of man to which the comparative study of mythology contributed persisted for a relatively short time in anthropology, as was pointed out in the Prologue. Extensive testing of these theories in the field soon revealed that they were nothing more than premature and oversimplified speculations. Cultural universalism gave way to cultural relativism as the twentieth century began, and anthropologists commenced formulating new and different hypotheses based upon firsthand observation in primitive societies. The sociological analysis of the social structures of given societies and the sociopsychological analysis of culture traits of given cultures became the preoccupations of the new anthropologist *qua* social scientist. But not all was new, and not all that was old was rejected. Myth remained, and the concept of myth as a kind of oral narrative found among peoples everywhere persisted.

Some anthropologists, such as Rivers and Malinowski, attempted to redefine myth. But literal definitions consisted of nothing more than attempts to clarify what earlier ones had stated; and these

---

[7] Readers who are interested in knowing more about the internecine battles which raged among proponents of conflicting theories concerning the origins and symbolic significance of folktales can find brief discussions in Stith Thompson, *The Folktale* (New York, 1946), pp. 367-412; and Richard M. Dorson, "Theories of Myth and the Folklorist," in *Myth and Mythmaking,* ed. Henry A. Murray (New York, 1960), pp. 76-89.

definitions were no more consistent or generally accepted among anthropologists than previous ones had been among scholars in other fields of study. So myth retained its basic meaning as a narrative, well known among members of a particular society or of a group or groups within that society, which explained the origins of natural and social phenomena and the interrelationships among man, his deities, and his universe. Beyond this, the meaning of myth was an individual matter. But when it became a charter of belief, a storehouse of adjustive responses, a kind of cultural furniture, and a language of argument, then it was myth according to a given theory of culture or society.

The study of myth in twentieth-century anthropology, then, is largely the study of the same kind of data with which students of mythology from every discipline have always been concerned. And the questions which anthropologists have attempted to answer by analyzing myths are questions which constitute the principal preoccupations of their discipline. None of the nine writers represented in this volume can be called a cultural universalist, so none of them is concerned with universal problems as they relate to any kind of social or cultural phenomena, including myth. Boas and Rivers, who represent in this volume the first generation of anthropologists to break with the monistic theories of the nineteenth century, retain an interest in the kinds of cultural-historical problems which occupied their predecessors. But they are not interested in making universal statements, and they are careful not to make broad generalizations either. Both are concerned with how peoples whom they are considering got to be the way they are. Neither offers more than passing remarks (largely in vague psychological terms) as to the *ultimate* sources of culture traits or social phenomena, and both stress the fact that many phenomena which are observable in a given society came into existence as a result of culture contact. Boas is more interested in *how* cultural "borrowings" might have taken place and what presumably happened to these "borrowed" culture traits as they became the common property of a particular people. Rivers, on the other hand, is more concerned with *why* these phenomena arose *after* culture contact had taken place. The analyses of myth by Boas and Rivers, then, are typical of their analyses of other kinds of data as well. Moreover, the problems which they find it important to investigate reflect their transitional position in the history of anthropology. They remain committed to the cultural-historical approach of their predecessors, so they engage in diachronic studies. But they examine data gathered in individual societies through firsthand observation; and they analyze these data not as isolated phenomena, but rather within the broad social context of the culture(s) from which these data were collected.

Radcliffe-Brown, Malinowski, and Benedict represent the vanguard of twentieth-century anthropology, those who clarified and developed the ideas which were introduced into their discipline by the generation of which Boas and Rivers were part. They are interested in synchronic, not diachronic, analysis. None is directly concerned with how or why the peoples whom they study got to be the way they are; instead, they focus on the structures and patterns which can be discerned in these societies. Radcliffe-Brown and Malinowski are interested in *how* society operates. They describe social phenomena, including myth, as instruments of social control which unify the people, maintain societal beliefs and norms, and contribute to the equilibrium which they consider to be essential for a society to survive. Benedict, on the other hand, does not conceive of society as a well-balanced mechanism which operates with predictable precision. She conceives of cultural patterns as general frameworks within which individuals can make choices among alternatives. She is interested in discovering the range and types of choices which are available to individuals within their society, in ascertaining what choices these individuals make, and in explaining why they make the choices which they do. Thus, Benedict sees all cultural phenomena, including myths, as being plastic rather than rigidly fixed, and variable rather than stable because, in terms of her model of culture, man's actions are not merely determined by, but are also instrumental in determining, what his cultural pattern is. One can see, then, that Radcliffe-Brown, Malinowski, and Benedict are the heirs of the concepts of Boas' and Rivers' generation. Their clarification and development of many of these concepts provided the foundations upon which their successors could build further.

Kluckhohn, Firth, and Leach represent these successors. Their tasks have been to refine the concepts of their predecessors and test their hypotheses in the field. They push the concepts of social structure and cultural pattern to their ultimate limits; and by so doing, they find that these, too, have limitations. Firth and Leach find the equilibrium models of Radcliffe-Brown and Malinowski to be inadequate to account for variability and change in social phenomena of all kinds, including myth. This causes Firth to question the general applicability of the equilibrium model, but to Leach, it indicates the need for a more dynamic model of social structure which can accommodate unstable as well as highly predictable social phenomena. Kluckhohn, too, expresses dissatisfaction with existing models. He looks to psychology in general and psychoanalysis in particular for possible explanations of the behavior of individuals within society. Like Leach, Kluckhohn appears to be seeking a radically different model of society, but one which is based on behavioral rather than structural principles. His concept of cultural configuration is a step in this direction; but it is too reminiscent of the cultural pattern of Benedict to be sufficient. Thus, there is a feeling of dissatisfaction and uneasiness implicit in the selections by these three writers. They have learned well from their predecessors; but by refining and testing the prevailing concepts of culture and society, they have learned too much to be satisfied with what exists. They want something more.

Lévi-Strauss also wants something more, but he is more specific about what it is. He does not want a modified model of social structure or a more sophisticated concept of cultural pattern. He is seeking a unified theory of human behavior based upon logical constructs. Thus, his quest requires that he work with entirely different abstractions and methods. His model is one which is suggested not merely by earlier models in anthropology but by models in all the disciplines which are concerned with human behavior. Furthermore, it is not a completed model, but rather one which is in the process of evolving. Hence, it is not and cannot be superimposed upon the data, for it evolves, to a large extent, from the data themselves. The model, as it has developed up to the time of investigation, is applied to the data. If it reveals something new about the data, then Lévi-Strauss continues to use it to see what else it can reveal. But the data themselves can also reveal limitations in the model, in which case further modifications of the evolving model itself are made. This procedure makes Lévi-Strauss' discussions of myth seem as paradoxical as the binary oppositions which he discerns in his data. Because he is involved in the actual process of evolving a theory, his discussions make the nature of myth more comprehensible in some respects and more obscure in others. Lévi-Strauss' position, then, is somewhat similar to that of Boas and Rivers. It is a transitional position, but the direction is reversed. He begins with data collected firsthand in specific societies; but he works outwardly from these data toward something which is not culturally relative, but universal: the structure of human thought.

Whether Lévi-Strauss' efforts and those of his followers and successors will provide the basis for a new theory for the behavioral sciences generally or even for anthropology alone cannot be predicted. For as he himself admits, the task has just begun. Yet there are already indications that his view of myth, like the views of his predecessors and contemporaries, may be too narrow. For while he begins with the data—with myths as narratives—and examines and analyzes them as such by concentrating on their formal features, he seems to have overlooked an important fact: that the recorded texts with which he begins are only a partial record of something much larger and much more complex. For these stories are not communicated by linguistic codes alone; and recorded texts of these stories are nothing more than partial records of individual storytelling events. They provide us with the words which the storytellers used, but they give us no indication of how the words were spoken. Furthermore, texts provide no clues about the storyteller, his audience, and the interrelationships which existed between the two during the storytelling event itself. We do not know from texts what portion of the message of the storytelling event was communicated by nonlinguistic codes, and we cannot discern from texts what role feedback played in giving the story its final shape. Moreover, texts tell us nothing about the social forces which generate individual storytelling events, and they cannot help us understand what makes a storytelling event different from all other types of communicative events which occur in the continuum of communication. Lévi-Strauss' analysis of myths, then, is an analysis of oral narratives as one form of *literature.* But if we are to understand the nature and significance of oral narratives as orally communicated messages, then we can only do so by studying whole storytelling events as they occur in the continuum of communication. And recorded texts alone are inadequate for this task.

Throughout this volume, we have been concerned with a phenomenon which the ancient Greeks chose to call μῦθος. We have examined studies which have this phenomenon as their common subject matter. These studies reveal that the common subject matter is oral narrative or story. The studies also indicate that these oral narratives are well known among members of a particular society or of a given group or groups within that society. Furthermore, we have noted that from the analyses of these oral narratives, new concepts of the phenomenon which is μῦθος emerge. But these are always concepts of myth or traditional tale according to a given theory of culture or society. These theories of culture or society, moreover, tend to be super-imposed on the data rather than to have been generated by the data themselves. This explains why myth can be a charter of belief, a language of argument, a storehouse of adjustive responses, and a model of harmony. It also accounts for its being called a kind of history, an aspect of religion, a primitive science, an oral literature.

Yet the question of myth remains and the quest for myth continues. How can we best learn to understand it? Can one do so by analyzing it in terms of some model of society, or must one learn to comprehend it on its own terms as oral narrative? Perhaps we can more profitably study these oral narratives that are arbitrarily labeled *myth, legend, folktale,* and *traditional tale* if we remember that they are only one aspect of complex communicative events which are unique in the continuum of communication.

Notes on the Authors

Ruth Fulton Benedict (1887-1948)

Studied English literature at Vassar College, anthropology under Elsie Clews Parsons and Alexander Goldenweiser at the New School for Social Research and under Franz Boas at Columbia University, and received the Ph.D. degree in anthropology from Columbia in 1923; conducted fieldwork among the Serrano (1922), the Zunis (1924, 1925, 1927), the Apaches (1930), the Blackfoot Indians (1938); taught at Barnard College (1922-23), Columbia University (1924-48); major publications include *Patterns of Culture* (1934), *Zuni Mythology* (1935), *The Chrysanthemum and the Sword* (1946); source for additional information: Margaret Mead, *An Anthropologist at Work: Writings of Ruth Benedict* (1959).

Franz Boas (1858-1942)

Studied physics and geography at the Universities of Heidelberg, Bonn, and Kiel and received the Ph.D. degree from Kiel in 1881; conducted fieldwork among the Eskimos in Baffinland (1883-84), the Bella Coola (1886), the Indians of the North Pacific Coast (intermittently from 1901 to 1905), in Puerto Rico (1914); taught at the University of Berlin (1886), Clark University (1888-92), Columbia University (1899-1937); major publications include *The Mind of Primitive Man* (1911), *Ethnology of the Kwakiutl* (1921), *Primitive Art* (1935), *Race, Language and Culture* (a collection of previously published essays) (1940); sources for additional information: Melville J. Herskovits, *Franz Boas: The Science of Man in the Making* (1953), *The Anthropology of Franz Boas*, ed. Walter Goldschmidt (1959).

Raymond W. Firth (1901-   )

Studied history and economics in New Zealand, anthropology at the University of London and received the Ph.D. degree in anthro-

235

pology in 1927; has conducted fieldwork in New Zealand (1921-23), Tikopia (1928-29, 1951-52), Malaya (1939-40), West Africa (1945), the Solomon Islands (1928-29, 1951-52); has taught at the University of Sydney (1930-32), the University of London (1933-present) and served as visiting professor at the University of Chicago (1955); major publications include *We, the Tikopia* (1936), *Human Types* (1938), *Elements of Social Organization* (1951).

Clyde K. M. Kluckhohn (1905-1960)

Studied at the Universities of Wisconsin and Vienna and at Oxford and Harvard Universities and received the Ph.D. degree in anthropology from Harvard in 1936; conducted fieldwork among the Navaho Indians throughout his life; taught at the University of New Mexico (1932-34), Harvard University (1935-60); major publications include *Navaho Witchcraft* (1944), *The Navaho* (with Dorothea Leighton) (1946), *Mirror for Man* (1949), *Culture and Behavior* (a collection of previously published essays, ed. Richard Kluckhohn) (1962).

Edmund R. Leach (1910-   )

Studied mathematics and mechanical sciences at Cambridge University, anthropology at the University of London and received the Ph.D. degree in anthropology from London in 1947; has conducted fieldwork in Botel, Tobago, Formosa (1936), Kurdistan (1938), Burma (intermittently from 1939-45), Borneo (1947), Ceylon (1954, 1956); has taught at the University of London (1948-50), Cambridge University (1953-present) and has served as Provost of Kings College, Cambridge, since 1966; major publications include *Political Systems of Highland Burma* (1954), *Rethinking Anthropology* (1961).

Claude Lévi-Strauss (1908-   )

Studied philosophy and law at the University of Paris; has conducted fieldwork among the Indians of the Amazon region (intermittently from 1935-39); has taught at the University of São Paulo (1935-39), the New School for Social Research (1942-45), and has held the Chair of Social Anthropology at the Collège de France since January, 1960; major publications include *Anthropologie structurale* (1958), *La Pensée sauvage* (1962), *Le Totemisme aujourd'hui* (1962), *Le Cru et le Cuit* (1964).

Bronislaw K. Malinowski (1884-1942)

Studied mathematics and physical sciences at the University of Cracow and received the Ph.D. degree in 1908; engaged in post-doctoral studies at the University of Leipzig and the University of London and received the Doctor of Science Degree from London in 1916; conducted fieldwork in the Trobriand Islands (1915-16, 1917-18), among the Hopi Indians (1927), the Bemba and Chagga of East Africa (1934), the Zapotec of Mexico (1940-41); taught at the University of London (1922-39) and served as visiting professor at the University of California (1926), Cornell University (1933), Harvard University (1936), Yale University (1939-42); major publications include *Argonauts of the Western Pacific* (1922), *Myth in Primitive Psychology* (1926), *Sex and Repression in Savage Society* (1927), *Coral Gardens and Their Magic* (1935); source for additional information: *Man and Culture: An Evaluation of the Work of Bronislaw Malinowski*, ed. Raymond Firth (1957).

A. R. Radcliffe-Brown (1881-1955)

Studied psychology and moral sciences, later anthropology under W. H. R. Rivers at Cambridge University; conducted fieldwork in the Andaman Islands (1906-8), Australia (1910-11); taught at the University of London (1909-10), University of Cape Town (1920-26), University of Sydney (1926-30), University of Chicago (1931-37), Oxford University (1937-46), and served as visiting professor at Escola Livra de Sociologia in Brazil (1942-44) and, following his retirement from Oxford, at Farouk I University in Cairo and Rhodes University in Grahamstown, South Africa; major publications include *The Andaman Islanders* (1922), *Structure and Function in Primitive Society* (a collection of previously published essays) (1952).

W. H. R. Rivers (1864-1922)

Studied at Tonbridge and St. Bartholomew's Hospital, London, and received the M.D. degree; taught at Guy's Hospital and Cambridge University (1893-1922); conducted fieldwork in the Torres Straits area (1898-99), Melanesia (1908, 1914); major works include *The History of Melanesian Society* (1914), *Social Organization* (ed. W. J. Perry) (1924), *Psychology and Ethnology* (a collection of previously published essays, ed. G. Elliot Smith) (1926).

Selected Bibliography

THE selected bibliography which follows consists of three kinds of entries: (1) studies which exemplify the major anthropological approaches to primitive mythology, (2) theoretical works which have provided the foundations and directions for analyses of myths collected from primitive peoples, and (3) general studies of mythology which have drawn heavily upon anthropological research. Collections of myth texts per se have not been included. When more than one item by a single author appears, the entries have been arranged alphabetically by title. The following abbreviations are utilized throughout the bibliography: *AA, American Anthropologist; JAF, Journal of American Folklore; MAFS, Memoirs of the American Folklore Society;* and *SJA, Southwestern Journal of Anthropology.*

Barnouw, Victor. "A Psychological Interpretation of a Chippewa Origin Legend," *JAF,* Vol. 68 (1955), 73-85, 211-23, 341-55.

Bascom, William. "The Myth-Ritual Theory," *JAF,* Vol. 70 (1957), 103-14.

Bateson, Gregory. "An Old Temple and a New Myth," *Djawa,* Vol. 17 (1937), 291-307.

Benedict, Ruth. *Zuni Mythology.* Columbia University Contributions to Anthropology, XXI. New York: Columbia University Press, 1935. 2 vols.

Bidney, David. "The Concept of Myth and the Problem of Psychocultural Evolution," *AA,* Vol. 52 (1950), 16-26.

––––––. "Myth, Symbolism, and Truth," in *Myth: A Symposium,* ed. Thomas A. Sebeok. Bloomington, Ind.: Indiana University Press, 1958, pp. 1-14.

Boas, Franz. "The Growth of Indian Mythologies," *JAF,* Vol. 9 (1896), 1-11.

––––––. *Kwakiutl Culture as Reflected in Mythology. MAFS,* No. 28, 1935.

––––––. "The Mythologies of the Indians," *The International Quarterly,* Vol. 11 (1905), 327-42; Vol. 12 (1906), 157-73.

––––––. "Mythology and Folk-Tales of the North American Indians," *JAF,* Vol. 27 (1914), 374-410.

––––––. *Primitive Art.* New York: Dover Publications, Inc., 1957.

––––––. *Race, Language and Culture.* New York: Macmillan Co., 1940.

238

————. *Tsimshian Mythology.* 31st Annual Report, Bureau of American Ethnology, 1909-10. Washington, D.C., 1916.

Burridge, K. O. L. "Social Implications of Some Tangu Myths," *SJA,* Vol. 12 (1956), 415-31.

————. "Lévi-Strauss and Myth," in *The Structural Study of Myth and Totemism,* ed. Edmund Leach. London: Tavistock Publications, 1967, pp. 91-115.

Campbell, Joseph. *The Masks of God: Primitive Mythology.* New York: Viking Press, Inc., 1959.

Carpenter, Edmund. "The Timeless Present in the Mythology of the Aivilik Eskimos," *Anthropologica,* Vol. 3 (1956), 1-4.

Cassirer, Ernst. *Language and Myth,* trans. S. K. Langer. New York: Dover Publications, Inc., 1946.

Chase, Richard. *Quest for Myth.* Baton Rouge: Louisiana State University Press, 1949.

Cox, H. L. "The Place of Mythology in the Study of Culture," *American Imago,* Vol. 5 (1948), 83-94.

Demetracopoulou, Dorothy. "The Loon-Woman Myth: A Study in Synthesis," *JAF,* Vol. 46 (1933), 101-28.

————, and Cora DuBois. "A Study of Wintu Mythology," *JAF,* Vol. 45 (1932), 373-500.

Devereux, George. "Art and Mythology. Part I: A General Theory," in *Studying Personality Cross-Culturally,* ed. Bert Kaplan. New York: Harper & Row, Publishers, 1961, pp. 361-86.

Dorson, Richard M. "Theories of Myth and the Folklorist," in *Myth and Mythmaking,* ed. Henry A. Murray. New York: George Braziller, Inc., 1960, pp. 76-89.

Douglas, Mary. "The Meaning of Myth, With Special Reference to 'La Geste d'Asdiwal,'" in *The Structural Study of Myth and Totemism,* ed. Edmund Leach. London: Tavistock Publications, 1967, pp. 49-69.

Dundes, Alan. "Earth-Diver: Creation of the Mythopoeic Male," *AA,* Vol. 64 (1962), 1032-51.

————. *The Morphology of North American Indian Folktales.* Folklore Fellows Communications, No. 195. Helsinki, 1964.

————. "Structural Typology in North American Indian Folktales," *SJA,* Vol. 19 (1963), 121-30.

Durkheim, Émile. *The Elementary Forms of the Religious Life,* trans. Joseph W. Swain. New York: Free Press of Glencoe, Ill., 1965.

Eggan, Dorothy. "The Personal Use of Myth in Dreams," in *Myth: A Symposium,* ed. Thomas A. Sebeok. Bloomington, Ind.: Indiana University Press, 1958, pp. 67-75.

Ehrlich, Clara. "Tribal Culture in Crow Mythology," *JAF*, Vol. 50 (1937), 307-408.

Evans-Pritchard, E. E. *Witchcraft, Oracles and Magic Among the Azande*. Oxford: Clarendon Press, 1937.

Firth, Raymond. *History and Traditions of Tikopia*. The Polynesian Society, Memoir No. 33. Wellington, New Zealand, 1961.

―――. "The Plasticity of Myth," *Ethnologica*, n.s., Vol. 2 (1960), 181-88.

―――. *Tikopia Ritual and Belief*. London: George Allen & Unwin, Ltd., 1967.

Fischer, J. L. "The Sociopsychological Analysis of Folktales," *Current Anthropology*, Vol. 4 (1963), 235-73.

Fontenrose, Joseph. *The Ritual Theory of Myth*. University of California Folklore Studies, No. 18. Berkeley and Los Angeles, 1966.

Fortes, Meyer. *Oedipus and Job in West African Religion*. Cambridge: Cambridge University Press, 1959; reprinted in *Anthropology of Folk Religion*, ed. Charles Leslie. New York: Vintage Books, Inc., 1960, pp. 5-49.

Freud, Sigmund. *Totem and Taboo*, trans. James Strachey. New York: W. W. Norton & Co., Inc., 1950.

Gayton, Anna H. "The Orpheus Myth in North America," *JAF*, Vol. 48 (1935), 263-93.

Geddes, W. R. *Nine Dayak Nights*. London: Oxford University Press, 1961.

Goldfrank, Esther S. "The Impact of Situation and Personality on Four Hopi Emergence Myths," *SJA*, Vol. 4 (1948), 241-62.

―――. "Isleta Variants: A Study in Flexibility," *JAF*, Vol. 39 (1926), 70-78.

Gray, Louis H. (ed.). *Mythology of All Races*. New Boston, N.H.: Marshall Jones Co., 1916-32. 13 vols.

Grey, Sir George. *Polynesian Mythology and Ancient Traditional History of the Maori, as Told by Their Priests and Chiefs*, ed. W. W. Bird. Christchurch, New Zealand: Whitcombe & Tombs, 1956.

Hallowell, A. I. "Myth, Culture, and Personality," *AA*, Vol. 49 (1947), 544-56.

Hassan, Ihab H. "Towards a Method in Myth," *JAF*, Vol. 65 (1952), 205-15.

Herskovits, Melville J. "African Gods and Catholic Saints in New World Negro Belief," *AA*, Vol. 39 (1937), 635-43.

―――― and Frances S. *Dahomean Narrative*. Evanston, Ill.: Northwestern University Press, 1958.

―――. "Sibling Rivalry, the Oedipus Complex, and Myth," *JAF*, Vol. 71 (1958), 1-15.

Hocart, A. M. "The Common Sense of Myth," *AA*, Vol. 18 (1916), 307-18.

Jacobs, Melville. *The Content and Style of an Oral Literature: Clackamas Chinook Myths and Tales*. Chicago: University of Chicago Press, 1959.

Jensen, Adolf E. *Myth and Cult Among Primitive Peoples,* trans. Marianna Tax Choldin and Wolfgang Weissleder. Chicago: University of Chicago Press, 1963.

JAF, Vol. 79, No. 311 (1966). Special issue on "The Anthropologist Looks at Myth," ed. John Greenway and Melville Jacobs.

Jung, C. G., and C. Kerényi. *Essays on a Science of Mythology: The Myths of the Divine Child and the Divine Maiden,* trans. R. F. C. Hull. New York: Harper & Row, Publishers, 1963.

Kluckhohn, Clyde. "Myths and Rituals: A General Theory," *Harvard Theological Review,* Vol. 35 (1942), 45-79.

————. "Recurrent Themes in Myths and Mythmaking," in *Myth and Mythmaking,* ed. Henry A. Murray. New York: George Braziller, Inc., 1960, pp. 46-60.

————, and Dorothea Leighton. *The Navaho.* Garden City, N.Y.: Doubleday & Co., Inc., 1962.

Köngäs, Elli K. "The Earth-Diver (Th. A. 812)," *Ethnohistory,* Vol. 7 (1960), 151-80.

Kroeber, Alfred L. "Catchwords in American Mythology," *JAF,* Vol. 21 (1908), 222-27.

Lantis, Margaret. "Nunivak Eskimo Personality as Revealed in the Mythology," *Anthropological Papers of the University of Alaska,* Vol. 2 (1953), 109-74.

Leach, Edmund. "Lévi-Strauss in the Garden of Eden: An Examination of Some Recent Developments in the Analysis of Myth," *Transactions of the New York Academy of Sciences,* Series 2 (1961), pp. 386-96.

————. *Political Systems of Highland Burma.* London: G. Bell & Sons, Ltd., 1954.

———— (ed.). *The Structural Study of Myth and Totemism.* London: Tavistock Publications, 1967.

Leslie, Charles (ed.). *Anthropology of Folk Religion.* New York: Vintage Books, Inc., 1960.

Lévi-Strauss, Claude. *Le Cru et le Cuit.* Paris: Plon, 1964.

————. "Four Winnebago Myths," in *Culture in History: Essays in Honor of Paul Radin,* ed. Stanley Diamond. New York: Columbia University Press, 1960, pp. 351-62.

————. "La Geste d'Asdiwal," in *Ecole pratique des hautes études, Section des sciences religieuses, Extrait de l'annuaire 1958-1959.* Paris, 1958, pp. 3-43; reprinted as "The Story of Asdiwal," trans. Nicholas Mann, in *The Structural Study of Myth and Totemism,* ed. Edmund Leach. London: Tavistock Publications, 1967, pp. 1-47.

————. *The Savage Mind,* trans. George Weidenfeld and Nicholson, Ltd. Chicago: University of Chicago Press, 1966.

————. "The Structural Study of Myth," in *Myth: A Symposium*, ed. Thomas A. Sebeok. Bloomington, Ind.: Indiana University Press, 1958, pp. 50-66.

————. *A World on the Wane*, trans. John Russell. London: Hutchinson & Co., Ltd., 1961.

Lowie, Robert. "Myths and Traditions of the Crow Indians," *American Museum of Natural History, Anthropological Papers*, Vol. 25 (1918), 1-308.

————. "The Test-Theme in North American Mythology," *JAF*, Vol. 21 (1908), 97-148.

Luomala, Katharine. *Oceanic, American Indian, and African Myths of Snaring the Sun*. Bernice P. Bishop Museum, Bulletin 168. Honolulu, 1940.

Malinowski, Bronislaw. *Argonauts of the Western Pacific*. New York: E. P. Dutton & Co., Inc., 1961.

————. "Myth in Primitive Psychology," Psyche Miniatures, General Series No. 6. London: Kegan Paul, Trench, Trubner, & Co., 1926; reprinted in *Magic, Science and Religion and Other Essays*, ed. Robert Redfield. New York: Doubleday & Co., Inc., 1954, pp. 93-148.

————. *Sex, Culture, and Myth*. New York: Harcourt, Brace & World, Inc., 1962.

Middleton, John (ed.). *Myth and Cosmos: Readings in Mythology and Symbolism*. Garden City, N.Y.: Natural History Press, 1967.

The Monist, Vol. 50, No. 4 (1966). Special issue on "Symbol and Myth."

Murray, Henry A. (ed.). *Myth and Mythmaking*. New York: George Braziller, Inc., 1960.

 Opler, Morris E. "The Creative Role of Shamanism in Mescalero Apache Mythology," *JAF*, Vol. 59 (1946), 268-81.

Radcliffe-Brown, A. R. *The Andaman Islanders*. New York: Free Press of Glencoe, Ill., 1964.

————. "The Rainbow Serpent Myth of Australia," *Journal of the Royal Anthropological Institute*, Vol. 56 (1926), 19-25; also printed in *Oceania*, Vol. 1 (1930), 342-47.

————. *Structure and Function in Primitive Society*. New York: Free Press of Glencoe, Ill., 1965.

Radin, Paul. "Literary Aspects of Winnebago Mythology," *JAF*, Vol. 39 (1926), 18-52.

————. "The Literature of Primitive Peoples," *Diogenes*, Vol. 12 (1955), 1-28.

————. *The Trickster: A Study in American Indian Mythology*. London: Routledge & Kegan Paul, Ltd., 1956.

————. *The World of Primitive Man*. New York: Schuman, 1953.

Reichard, Gladys. *An Analysis of Coeur D'Alene Indian Myths*. MAFS, No. 41, 1947.

————. "Individualism and Mythological Style," *JAF*, Vol. 57 (1944), 16-25.

————. "Literary Types and Dissemination of Myths," *JAF*, Vol. 34 (1921), 269-307.

Rivers, W. H. R. *Psychology and Ethnology*, ed. G. Elliot Smith. New York: Harcourt, Brace & Co., Inc., 1926.

————. "The Sociological Significance of Myth," *Folk-Lore*, Vol. 23 (1912), 307-31.

Roheim, Géza. *The Eternal Ones of the Dream: A Psychoanalytic Interpretation of Australian Myths and Rituals.* New York: International Universities Press, Inc., 1945.

Rooth, A. B. "The Creation Myths of the North American Indians," *Anthropos*, Vol. 52 (1957), 497-508.

Sebeok, Thomas A. (ed.). *Myth: A Symposium.* Bloomington, Ind.: Indiana University Press, 1958.

Spencer, Katherine. *Mythology and Values: An Analysis of Navaho Chantway Myths. MAFS*, No. 48, 1957.

Spencer, Robert F. "Native Myth and Modern Religion Among the Klamath Indians," *JAF*, Vol. 65 (1952), 217-26.

Stern, Theodore. "Ideal and Expected Behavior as Seen in Klamath Mythology," *JAF*, Vol. 76 (1963), 21-30.

————. "Some Sources of Variability in Klamath Mythology," *JAF*, Vol. 64 (1956), 1-12, 135-46, 377-86.

Swanton, John R. "A Concordance of American Myths," *JAF*, Vol. 20 (1907), 220-22.

Thompson, Stith. "Myths and Folktales," in *Myth: A Symposium,* ed. Thomas A. Sebeok. Bloomington, Ind.: Indiana University Press, 1958, pp. 104-10.

Tylor, Edward B. *Primitive Culture.* London: John Murray, 1871. 2 vols.

Vansina, Jan. *Oral Tradition: A Study in Historical Methodology,* trans. H. M. Wright. London: Routledge & Kegan Paul, Ltd., 1965.

Warner, W. Lloyd. *A Black Civilization.* New York: Harper & Bros., 1958.

Waterman, T. T. "The Explanatory Element in the Folk-Tales of the North American Indians," *JAF*, Vol. 27 (1914), 1-54.

Weber, Max. *The Sociology of Religion,* trans. Ephraim Fischoff. Boston: Beacon Press, 1963.

Yalman, Nur. " 'The Raw: the Cooked : : Nature : Culture'—Observations on *Le Cru et le cuit,*" in *The Structural Study of Myth and Totemism,* ed. Edmund Leach. London: Tavistock Publications, 1967, pp. 71-89.

Index

Names of individuals, places, and cultures, and terms for concepts and topical matters are included in the Index only if they receive more than brief, passing mention in the volume. The symbol n. after an entry indicates that it is discussed or referred to in a footnote on the given page.

This book has been set 11 and 10 point Press Roman, leaded 2 points. Reading titles and reading authors are in 18 and 11 point Bulmer. The size of the type page is 27 x 45 picas.